THE SO
UNION

Politics, Economics and Society

From Lenin to Gorbachëv

Ronald J. Hill

SECOND EDITION

Pinter Publishers
London and New York

Second edition published in Great Britain in 1989 by
Pinter Publishers Limited
25 Floral Street, London WC2E 9DS

British Library Cataloguing in Publication Data
A CIP catalogue record for this book is available from the British Library.

Library of Congress Cataloging-in-Publication Data
Hill, Ronald J., 1943–
The Soviet Union: politics, economics, and society from Lenin to Gorbachëv / Ronald J. Hill.—2nd ed.
p. cm.—(Marxist regimes series)
Bibliography: p.
Includes index.
ISBN 0-86187-800-0—ISBN 0-86187-801-9 (pbk.)
1. Soviet Union—Politics and government—1917– 2. Soviet Union—Economic conditions—1918– 3. Soviet Union—Social conditions—1917– I. Title. II. Series.
JN6531.H44 1989
947.084—dc20 89-8621
CIP

First edition published in 1985.

Typeset by Joshua Associates Limited, Oxford
Printed in Great Britain by SRP Ltd, Exeter

Editor's Preface

Since the publication of its first edition in 1985, Professor Ronald J. Hill's contribution to the Marxist Regimes series has become a popular text analysing governmental-political and socio-economic features, the current problems and policy dilemmas of the Soviet Union. Several aspects of the first edition impressed reviewers in particular. Its comprehensive breadth and scholarship in a relatively slim volume were applauded: it surveyed 'the core elements of Soviet reality, interweaving a highly informed analysis of party-state institutions; the policy-making process; policy culture and socialization; the origin and effect of the dissident movement; policy outcomes and dilemmas in such areas as education, the economy, and ethnic relations; and even the determinants of Soviet foreign policy'. According to this reviewer, Hill showed 'a remarkable facility throughout the work to identify concisely the big picture and complexities inherent to each of these dimensions, an ability to ground his analysis in a historical perspective of continuity and change from the Russian imperial past, but also a sensitivity to similar realities of governance, working-class conflict, and inequalities between social classes and ethnic groups that confront advanced non-Marxist states'.[1]

Another reviewer praised the compact yet comprehensive assessment which provided 'a fine critical synthesis of most of the best contemporary sources, with a vast amount of empirical data and judicious analysis squeezed into a remarkably small bulk, yet elegantly presented and taking us through to the Gorbachëv accession'.[2] The Gorbachëv accession occurred as the first edition was about to be printed, which makes this second edition all the more necessary, though an effort has been made not to increase the number of pages greatly.

Another merit of the book emphasized by scholars was the absence of jargon—'A model of clarity, finding just the right balance between information and argument, it makes no attempt to minimize the controversial questions.'[3] Others pointed out that the book can be read at two levels: 'for the general reader there is a digestible narrative and explanation, backed, for the more specialist, by constant reference to the latest literature including many Soviet sources'.[4] It was said that Hill had demonstrated 'an impressive command of the literature in Soviet studies that he successfully [mined] from diverse and quite recent studies written by western Sovietologists, Soviet *émigrés*, and Soviet social scientists, as well as from Soviet primary data sources'.[5] He had presented 'both Soviet accomplishments and persistent failures in a balanced and fair-minded manner, judiciously [cited] alternative interpretations of the same phenomena raised by western analysts, and [allowed] for gray areas of uncertainty in Soviet political reality that preclude any definite generalizations'.[6]

This second edition includes revised lists of office holders, latest statistics, analysis of new policies resulting from *glasnost'* and *perestroika* (words among others that are added to the revised Glossary), the effects of the Party Conference in 1988 and the first results of the parliamentary elections in 1989. As the speed and pervasiveness of changes in the Soviet Union accelerate and become increasingly more complicated to understand and to follow, Professor Hill presents the reader with a new version of 'one of the most eloquently conceived and written introductory surveys of the Soviet Union for university classroom and informed western public opinion written over the past two decades'.[7]

For historical and methodological reasons the study of Marxist regimes has long been equated with the study of communist political systems. For many years it was not difficult to distinguish the eight regimes in Eastern Europe and four in Asia which resoundingly claimed adherence to the tenets of Marxism and more particularly to their Soviet interpretation—Marxism-Leninism. These regimes, variously called 'People's Republic', 'People's Democratic Republic', or 'Democratic Republic', claimed to have derived their inspiration from the Soviet Union to which, indeed, in the overwhelming number of cases they owed their establishment.

To many scholars and analysts these regimes represented a multiplication and geographical extension of the 'Soviet model' and consequently of the Soviet sphere of influence. Although there were clearly substantial similarities between the Soviet Union and the people's democracies, especially in the initial phases of their development, these were often overstressed at the expense of noticing the differences between these political systems. This makes the study of the Soviet Union a particularly important part of the exercise and this volume the linchpin of the Marxist Regimes Series.

It took a few years for scholars to realize that generalizing the particular, i.e. applying the Soviet experience to other states ruled by elites which claimed to be guided by 'scientific socialism', was not good enough. The relative simplicity of the assumption of a cohesive communist bloc was questioned after the expulsion of Yugoslavia from the Communist Information Bureau in 1948 and in particular after the workers' riots in Poznań in 1956 and the Hungarian revolution of the same year. By the mid-1960s, the totalitarian model of communist politics, which until then had been very much in force, began to crumble. As some of these regimes articulated demands for a distinctive path of socialist development, many specialists studying these systems began to notice that the cohesiveness of the communist bloc was less apparent than had been claimed before.

Also by the mid-1960s, in the newly independent African states 'democratic' multi-party states were turning into one-party states or military dictatorships, thus questioning the inherent superiority of liberal democracy, capitalism and the values that went with it. Scholars now began to ponder on the simple contrast between multi-party democracy and a one-party totalitarian rule that had satisfied an earlier generation.

More importantly, however, by the beginning of that decade Cuba had a revolution without Soviet help, a revolution which subsequently became to many political elites in the Third World not only an inspiration but a clear military, political and ideological example to follow. Apart from its romantic appeal, to many nationalist movements the Cuban revolution also demonstrated a novel way of conducting and winning a nationalist, anti-imperialist war and accepting Marxism as the state ideology without a vanguard communist party. The Cuban precedent was subsequently followed in one respect or another by scores of regimes in the Third World who used the adoption of 'scientific socialism' tied to the tradition of Marxist thought as a form of mobilization, legitimation or association with the prestigious symbols and powerful high-status regimes such as the Soviet Union, China, Cuba and Vietnam.

Despite all these changes the study of Marxist regimes remains in its infancy and continues to be hampered by constant and not always pertinent comparison with the Soviet Union, thus somewhat blurring the important underlying common theme—the 'scientific theory' of the laws of development of human society and human history. This doctrine is claimed by the leadership of these regimes to consist of the discovery of objective causal relationships; it is used to analyse the contradictions which arise between goals and actuality in the pursuit of a common destiny. Thus the political elites of these countries have been and continue to be influenced in both their ideology and their political practice by Marxism more than any other current of social thought and political practice.

The growth in the number and global significance, as well as the ideological political and economic impact, of Marxist regimes has presented scholars and students with an increasing challenge. In meeting this challenge, social scientists on both sides of the political divide have put forward a dazzling profusion of terms, models, programmes and varieties of interpretation. It is against the background of this profusion that the present comprehensive series on Marxist regimes is offered.

This collection of monographs is envisaged as a series of multidisciplinary textbooks on the governments, politics, economics and society of these countries. Each of the monographs was prepared by a specialist on the country concerned. Thus, over fifty scholars from all over the world have contributed monographs which were based on first-hand knowledge. The geographical diversity of the authors, combined with the fact that as a group they represent many disciplines of social science, gives their individual analyses and the series as a whole an additional dimension.

Each of the scholars who contributed to this series was asked to analyse such topics as the political culture, the governmental structure, the ruling party, other mass organizations, party-state relations, the policy process, the economy, domestic and foreign relations together with any features peculiar to the country under discussion.

This series does not aim at assigning authenticity or authority to any single one of the political systems included in it. It shows that depending on a variety of historical, cultural, ethnic and political factors, the pursuit of goals derived from the tenets of Marxism has produced different political forms at different times and in different places. It also illustrates the rich diversity among these societies, where attempts to achieve a synthesis between goals derived from Marxism on the one hand, and national realities on the other, have often meant distinctive approaches and solutions to the problems of social, political and economic development.

University College
Cardiff

Bogdan Szajkowski

Notes

1. Joel C. Moses, *Slavic Review* (Summer 1986), p. 338.
2. Alex Reid, *International Affairs* (Winter 1985–6), pp. 145–6.
3. Anthony Kemp-Welch, *Political Studies*, vol. 34, no. 3 (September 1986).
4. Dennis Kennedy, *The Irish Times*, 21 September 1985.
5. Moses, op. cit.
6. Moses, op. cit.
7. Moses, op. cit.

Contents

List of Illustrations and Tables

Map

Figure

Tables

Preface

The significance of the coming of the communists to power in the Russian Empire in October 1917 can be measured on several scales. In the first place, it represented the radical transformation of one of the most reactionary regimes and structurally backward societies in Europe. Secondly, this revolution took place in the largest territorial state in the world, with what has now become the third largest population (after China and India). Thirdly, it illustrated the validity of certain theories of social change and organizational arrangement that had been advanced in the previous generations by radical thinkers of the Marxist and similar hues: it thus provides a historical model for subsequent political movements. Related to this point, the significance of the revolution's occurrence in Russia (rather than, say, Germany or France) not only calls into question some of the original Marxist assumptions about the development of a capitalist industrial society towards socialist revolution, but also has had a profound impact on the subsequent development of the communist movement.

With the exception of Mongolia, where a Moscow-orientated communist regime came to power in 1924, the Soviet Union stood alone in the world as a successfully established Marxist regime from the early 1920s until the aftermath of the Second World War (see Szajkowski, 1982). During that period, following the adoption of the Stalin slogan of 'Socialism in One Country', and making use of such international organizations as the Communist International (Comintern), the Soviet Union established itself as the authentic model of a socialist society, and its approach to 'building socialism' as the only valid one. Soviet institutions and practices came to be adopted by many other countries that acquired Marxist governments in the ensuing years, whether or not the Soviet Union had a direct hand in placing those regimes in power. Still today, the Soviet leaders proclaim the universal validity of their experience for countries that are 'following the socialist path'. And yet, the 'model' of socialism and the means of achieving it might have looked very different if the first successful socialist 'revolution' had been achieved by a nation other than the Russians.

The transformation effected by the Stalinist form of socialism applied in the world's largest state has brought the inheritor of the Russian Empire to a position where it can challenge for supremacy the world's most powerful and economically dominant power, the United States of America. Out of this challenge the world has become dominated by ideological confrontation, as superpower rivalries tinged with ideological overtones are played out with frightening displays of military hardware in a struggle to project and protect global spheres of interest.

In twentieth-century history, the Soviet Union's rise has been a central theme. So it is important to examine and understand its origins, its make-up and its functioning, if we are to come to grips with the complex process of attaining and maintaining a *modus vivendi* among the nations of the world. It is the aim of this short study to provide the Western reader with basic information to assist that understanding.

Inevitably the preparation of a work such as this depends very heavily on the cumulative impression of the research and analysis of countless other scholars. It is invidious to identify individuals in the international academic community: those whose work has been specifically relevant are acknowledged in references in the text and bibliography, but the ideas of others may have lodged in my mind without my recollection of their source. Studying the Soviet Union is intellectually challenging and enjoyable, and I more than willingly concede my debt to academic colleagues, in both East and West, who have made their unwitting contribution to my thinking over many years. I naturally reserve for myself the responsibility for any errors of judgement or interpretation.

I should, however, like to record my grateful appreciation of the encouragement given by the series editor, my friend Bogdan Szajkowski, in a project that I have found rewarding, if at times exhausting. Peter Moulson, of Frances Pinter (Publishers), has been especially understanding about deadlines—and on that score I must also compliment the inventor of the word-processor.

Finally, it has long been my ambition to repay an enormous debt to Henry Treece, the late novelist, who as my English teacher some thirty years ago taught me what a sentence is. If my prose possesses any clarity and elegance, then much is due to his early guidance; and his lively and broad-ranging teaching style taught me that there is more to training a mind than bowing to the demands of an examination curriculum. With deep respect and gratitude, I dedicate this book to his memory.

Preface to the Second Edition

I am much gratified by the reception given to this book by professional colleagues and students, and regret a number of errors that may have left some readers misinformed. I have corrected such of these as have come to my attention, and I happily record my grateful thanks to colleagues and reviewers who kindly pointed them out. In preparing this revised edition, I have also updated statistics when new data have become available, and amended references to Soviet politicians, among whom there have been many changes of office under Mikhail Gorbachëv. New formulations in places reflect certain changes of emphasis in the light of further discussions with friends and colleagues in the Soviet Union and the West. However, the substantial re-writing that preparing this new edition has entailed reflects the sweeping changes in structures, practices and rhetoric that have become commonplace in the time since March 1985, as Gorbachëv pushes through what he refers to as a revolution, under the code words of *uskorenie* (acceleration), *perestroika* (restructuring) and *glasnost'* (openness). I am grateful to the University of Glasgow and the Netherlands Institute for Advanced Study for generously offering me Fellowships that have provided the time and facilities for completing this new edition. For any factual errors that still remain, I offer renewed apologies; for errors of judgement or interpretation, I obstinately retain full responsibility.

R.J.H.

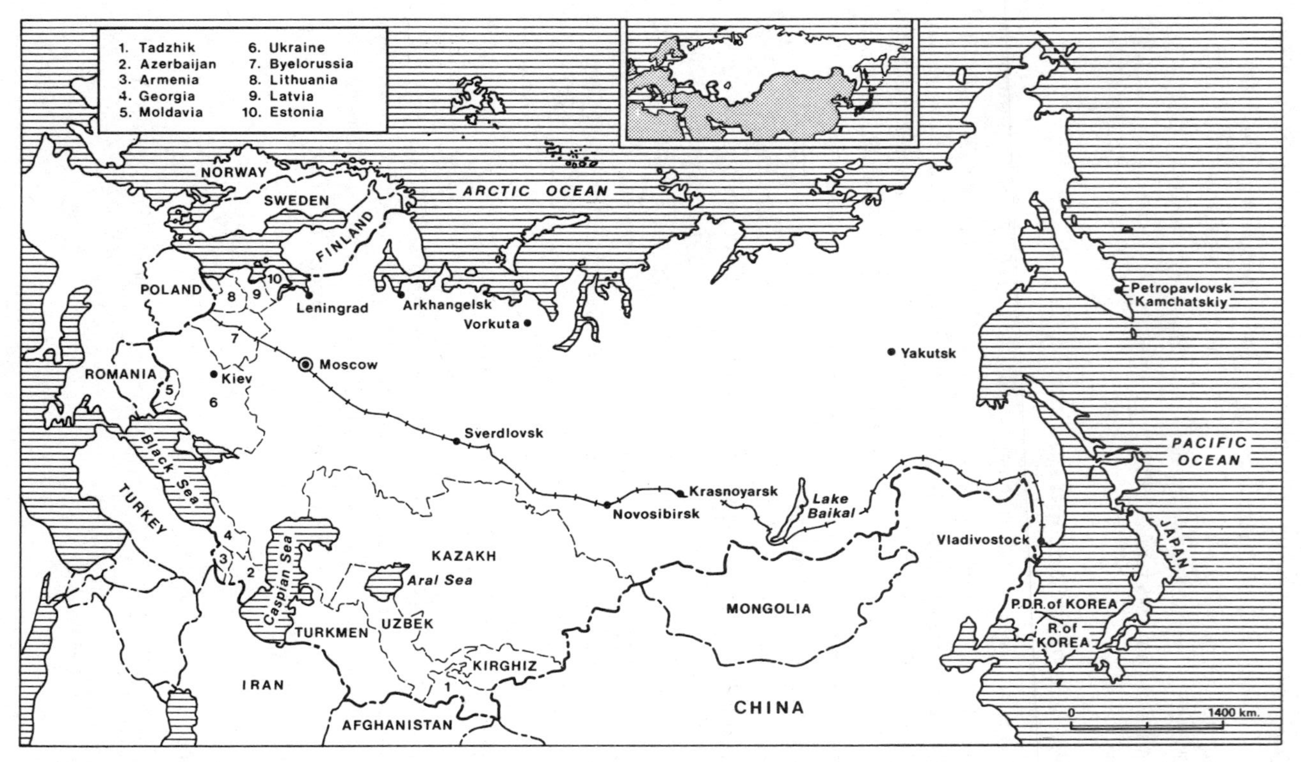
1. Tadzhik
2. Azerbaijan
3. Armenia
4. Georgia
5. Moldavia
6. Ukraine
7. Byelorussia
8. Lithuania
9. Latvia
10. Estonia
NORWAY
SWEDEN
FINLAND
ARCTIC OCEAN
POLAND
Leningrad
Arkhangelsk
Vorkuta
Moscow
Kiev
ROMANIA
Black Sea
TURKEY
Sverdlovsk
Novosibirsk
Krasnoyarsk
Lake Baikal
Yakutsk
Petropavlovsk Kamchatskiy
PACIFIC OCEAN
JAPAN
Vladivostock
P.D.R. of KOREA
R. of KOREA
KAZAKH
Aral Sea
Caspian Sea
TURKMEN
UZBEK
KIRGHIZ
IRAN
AFGHANISTAN
MONGOLIA
CHINA
0
1400 km.

Basic Data

Official name	Union of Soviet Socialist Republics (Soyuz Sovetskikh Sotsialisticheskikh Respublik)
Population	286.7 million (12 January 1989)
Population density	12.8 per sq. km.
Population growth (% p.a.)	0.77 (1988)
Urban population (%)	66.0 (1987)
Total labour force	131.7 million (1988)
Life expectancy	69.8 (1987)
Infant death rate (per 1,000)	25.4 (1987)
Ethnic groups	Russians 52.4%, Ukrainians 16.1%, Uzbeks 4.7%, Belorussians 3.6%, Kazakhs 2.5%, Tatars 2.4%, Azeris 2.1%, others 16.2%; over 100 nationalities in all (1979)
Capital	Moscow (Moskva)–8.8 million (1988)
Land area	22,402,200 sq. km., of which 10.7% arable, 8.5% swamp, 37.2% forest and scrub; 12% unutilized or unsuitable
Principal official language	Russian
Other significant languages	Ukrainian, Turkic group, Belorussian, Armenian, Georgian, Moldavian, Lithuanian, Latvian, Estonian
Administrative division	15 union republics; 20 autonomous republics; 8 autonomous provinces; 10 autonomous areas; 129 provinces
Membership of international organizations	UN since 1945; CMEA since 1949; Warsaw Treaty Organization since 1945
Foreign relations	Diplomatic and consular relations with 134 states; representatives of 120 countries residing in Moscow (1987)
Political structure	
Constitution	Adopted 7 October 1977; significant amendments 1 December 1988
Highest legislative bodies	USSR Congress of Deputies (2,250 deputies); USSR Supreme Soviet (542 deputies)

Highest executive body	USSR Council of Ministers
Prime Minister	Nikolai I. Ryzhkov (since July 1985)
President (Chairman of the USSR Supreme Soviet Presidium)*	Mikhail S. Gorbachëv (since October 1988)
Ruling party	Communist Party of the Soviet Union
General Secretary of CPSU	Mikhail S. Gorbachëv (since 11 March 1985)
Party membership	19,487,822 (1 January 1989)—9.7 per cent of adult population

Growth indicators (% p.a.)

	1970–80	1988
National income	6.8	4.4
Industry	8.4	3.9
Heavy	8.9	3.5
Consumer	7.1	5.0
Agriculture	1.0	0.7

Trade and balance of payments	
Exports	US$104,520 million (1988)
Imports	US$101,400 million (1988)
Exports as % of GNP	7.7
Main exports	Oil and energy products, gold, cars, clocks and watches, cameras, furs, iron ore, equipment
Main imports	Machinery and equipment, grain, meat, other agricultural produce
Destination of exports (% 1987)	Socialist countries 67.0, capitalist countries 21.8, Third World 11.2
Main trading partners	German Democratic Republic, Czechoslovakia, Poland, Bulgaria, Hungary, Cuba, Federal Republic of Germany, Finland
Foreign debt	US$24,000 million (1986, estimate)
Main natural resources	Oil and natural gas, peat, timber, coal, iron, manganese, platinum, gold, uranium,

* On 1 October 1988, Gorbachëv was elected to that office; constitutional amendments adopted on 1 December 1988 provided for the creation of a new post of Chairman of the USSR Supreme Soviet, which would enjoy many of the real powers of an executive president, compared with the essentially ceremonial functions of the Chairman of the Supreme Soviet Presidium.

	diamonds, lead, zinc, nickel, copper, mercury
Food self-sufficiency	Shortage of grain, especially for fodder, in drought years, but broad sufficiency is claimed; meat and dairy shortages reflect fodder shortage; imports of tropical products.
Armed Forces	Estimated 5.1 million (1988), including an army of 1.9 million (1.3 million conscripts); 458,000 in the navy (337,000 conscripts); total reserve (including males up to age 50)—approximately 55 million.
Education and health	
School system	11 years (6–17)
Primary school (millions 1987–8)	15.5
Secondary school	26.5
Higher education	5.0
Adult literacy (%)	100
Population per hospital bed	76.6 (1987)
Population per physician	231 (1987)
Economy	
GNP	US$1,350,960 million (1988)
GNP per capita	US$4,748
GDP by %	Industry 63.3; agriculture 20.4; services 16.2
State budget (expenditure)	US$414,420 million (1988)
Defence expenditure % of state budget	3 (official); 13–25 (estimates)
Monetary unit	Rouble (1 rouble = US$1.56 (1988))
Main crops	Wheat, maize, buckwheat, sugar beet, potatoes, cotton, sunflower seed, tea.
Land tenure	Collective and state farms, and up to 0.5 hectares usage rights for peasant family unit; experimental long-lease tenancy agreements being introduced.
Main religions	Russian Orthodox, Baptist, Roman Catholic, Uniate, other Christian churches (including Old Rite Orthodox), Islam, Judaism, Buddhism; sects of recent origin—Jehovah's Witnesses, Hare Krishna. Numbers uncertain.

Transport

Rail network	146,100 km. (1987), of which 51,700 electrified
Road network	1,609,900 km. (1987), of which 1,196,000 surfaced
Oil pipelines	70,000 km. (1988)
Gas pipelines	170,000 km. (1988)

Population Forecasting

The following data are projections produced by Poptran, University College Cardiff Population Centre, from United Nations Assessment Data published in 1980, and are reproduced here to provide some basis of comparison with other countries covered by the Marxist Regimes Series.

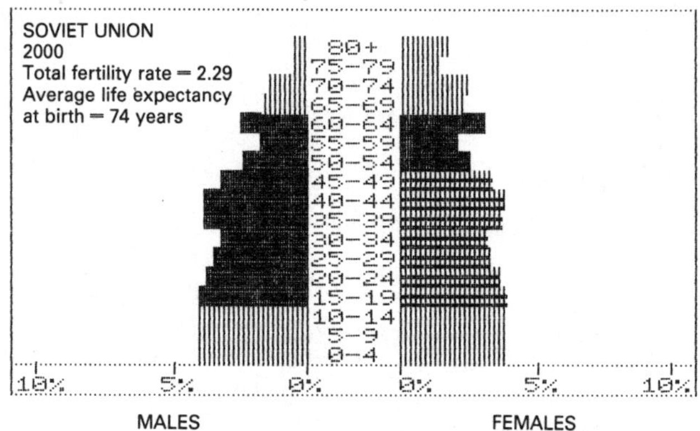

Projected Data for Soviet Union 2000

Total population ('000)	314,736
Males ('000)	151,957
Females ('000)	162,779
Total fertility rate	2.29
Life expectancy (male)	69.9 years
Life expectancy (female)	78.2 years
Crude birth rate	16.0
Crude death rate	8.7
Annual growth rate	0.73%
Under 15s	23.53%
Over 65s	11.85%
Population density	14 per sq. km.
Urban population	66.9%

Glossary and List of Abbreviations

agitpunkt	election campaign headquarters
CC	Central Committee (of CPSU)
Cheka	Extraordinary Commission, formed in December 1917, a forerunner of the KGB
CMEA	Council for Mutual Economic Assistance, Comecon
CPSU	Communist Party of the Soviet Union
dacha	country dwelling for vacation use
DOSAAF	Voluntary Society for Cooperation with the Army, Air Force and Navy
glasnost'	openness, publicity (a policy favoured by Gorbachëv; opposed to secrecy and heavy-handed censorship)
gorkom	city committee of CPSU
Gosplan	State Planning Committee
KGB	State Security Committee
khozraschet	cost accounting (by firms and organizations)
kolkhoz	collective farm
kolkhoznik	collective farm peasant
Komsomol (VLKSM)	All-Union Leninist League of Youth, Young Communist League
nakaz	electors' instruction to elected representative
NEP	New Economic Policy (1921)
nomenklatura	party control over appointments
obkom	provincial committee of CPSU
perestroika	restructuring
podmena	party interference
Politburo	Political Bureau (of CPSU Central Committee)
PPO	primary party organization
pravovoe gosudarstvo	law-based state; Rechtsstaat
raikom	district committee of CPSU
RSDWP	Russian Social-Democratic Workers' Party
RSFSR	Russian Soviet Federative Socialist Republic
samizdat	self-publishing
SMOT	Free Inter-professional Association of Workers (Russian initials)

sovkhoz	state farm
tolkach	illegal expediter in trade deals
uskorenie	acceleration (currently, of economic and social development)
USSR	Union of Soviet Socialist Republics, Soviet Union
VTsSPS	All-Union Central Council of Trade Unions

Dates: dates before 1918 are given 'old style' i.e. according to the Julian calendar in use in Imperial Russia, in the present century 13 days behind the Gregorian; the Bolshevik revolution took place on 25 October 1917 (o.s.) but is celebrated on 7 November.

1 History and Political Traditions

Geographical and Historical Setting

The Union of Soviet Socialist Republics is by far the largest territorial state in the world. Lying in the northern hemisphere and covering one-sixth of the land surface of the globe—as large as the face of the moon (von Laue, 1966, p. 38)—the country sprawls across Europe and Asia, from Poland to the Pacific and beyond: the sun takes eleven hours to cross its territory, a significant area of which lies east of Japan, 'the Land of the Rising Sun'. When Muscovites are rising in the morning, their fellow citizens in Vladivostok, on the Pacific coast, are already home after a day's work: moreover, when events of world significance are taking place in the United States, the Soviet press has already gone to bed along with the citizens who will scan *yesterday's* news *tomorrow* morning. From north to south, the country stretches from the Arctic wastes of the tundra (similarly inhospitable to northern Canada or Greenland) to the baking deserts of Central Asia, where summer temperatures compare with those of Colorado and Arizona. The climate is *continental*: hot summers, cold winters, extremes of heat and cold, with fickle, unreliable weather patterns in the more temperate parts of the country. In Yakutia, a vast territory in northern Siberia, average winter temperatures are around −50°C, and permanently frozen soil ('permafrost') creates severe difficulties for maintaining the population at an adequate standard of living, and indeed for the whole programme of economic exploitation and development of the region. In the Central Asian deserts, by contrast, with summer temperatures rising in places to over 40°C, the reverse conditions create a similar effect; the land is inhospitable, and effectively cannot be settled.

Between these two extremes—and the frozen conditions of Yakutia spread broadly across the north of the country and into the far north-east (indeed, close to Alaska, which shares these characteristics)—lie a broad forest belt with a relatively temperate climate, and, to the south of this, a band of rich Black Earth (*chernozem*) in a wedge from the Carpathians and the Central European Plain over past the Caspian and

Aral Seas to the foothills of the Pamir mountains. It is in the Black Earth and forest belts that the heartland of Russian civilization has lain, and where the bulk of the population of the Empire and now the Soviet Union has lived. These facts of geography and climate have their implications for the potential and problems faced by the society that inhabits the territory (see below).

The country's position on the globe also affects her relations with her neighbours. The modern Soviet Union has by far the longest borders of any state in the world: something in the region of 60,000 km. (37,000 miles), including land borders with a dozen states, not all of which are friendly towards Soviet interests. From the north-west they are Norway, Finland, Poland, Czechoslovakia, Hungary and Romania; Turkey, Iran, Afghanistan; China, Mongolia and finally Korea. Not far away from the western border are the ideologically hostile traditional rivals of Russia in Western Europe: Germany, France and Britain. Between them, sweeping across northern Europe, lies the plain over which invading armies from Napoleon to Hitler have marched three times in the last two centuries. The lessons of history seem to be that these powers and Russia cannot comfortably share the same continent. In Asia, too, a 4,000-mile border with China is a colossal liability, and although mountains serve as some protection for a portion of the extent, these two great peoples and cultures are separated only by navigable rivers for hundreds of miles.

In the south, Islamic cultures—which extend into Soviet territory—are likewise a form of pressure against which the modern Soviet Union needs to defend itself, in a part of the world, moreover, where the migratory way of life still exerts its influence and complicates the tasks of defending and developing a modern society. Seasonally migratory shepherding is still prevalent in the mountains of Soviet Turkmenia (Dienes, 1975).

Finally, in the late-twentieth century, the territory of the Soviet Union is vulnerable to missile attack from virtually any part of the globe, and specifically from over the North Pole: an inter-continental ballistic missile launched in North America can reach the Soviet Union within minutes, not to mention the potential effects of missiles launched from territory closer to the Soviet Union, or from submarines cruising in the seas and oceans that surround her: the Pacific, the Mediterranean, the Arctic, the Atlantic.

In part associated with the sheer vastness and diversity of the territory, the Soviet Union (and the Russian Empire before it) enjoys enormous wealth in valuable resources. The extent of this wealth is not known with certainty, since systematic exploration and prospecting were not undertaken until well into the present century, and new resources are constantly being discovered. Indeed, the number of higher educational students studying geology and related disciplines rose from 16,200 in 1950 to 38,000 in 1976, while those undergoing training in mining and working mineral deposits expanded over the same period from 20,900 to 55,900 (*Narkhoz 1977*, p. 585).

What is certain is that the resources of energy and valuable minerals are massive. Coal deposits, amounting to about half of the world's known reserves, would last centuries at present extraction rates; natural gas and oil are available in abundance—indeed, the Soviet Union possesses the world's greatest gas deposits, which occupy a central place in the country's economic strategy; almost two-thirds of the world's deposits of peat, millions of cubic metres of timber (forest covers half of the territory), plus a tremendous potential for hydro-electricity on the great rivers of Siberia: all these actual and potential energy sources combine to place the 'energy crisis' in some kind of perspective, and offer excellent prospects for medium- and long-term economic development, despite technical and other difficulties in the immediate future. Some Western estimates suggested that Soviet production of petroleum would peak in the early 1980s (see, for example, Bialer, 1980, pp. 289–9); even so, the long-term energy balance, if all actual and potential sources including solar, nuclear and tidal power are taken into account, looks more secure than that of other major industrial countries, most of which are extremely dependent on imported energy supplies (see Elliot, 1974).

In addition to basic energy resources, valuable minerals also exist in abundance. With some 40 per cent of the world's iron ore, the Soviet Union possesses more than the whole Western world; in addition, half of the world's potassium, almost 90 per cent of its manganese, gold (the Soviet Union is the second largest producer after South Africa), lead, silver, uranium, platinum and an array of other mineral stocks vital to the modern industrial economy give that country the prospect of sustained industrial development. Moreover, the wide-ranging climatic conditions and variations in topography and soil render the country potentially self-sufficient in agricultural products as well, to support an urban population and an industrial economy. As one distinguished observer commented, 'the richness and diversity [of resources] have been sufficient to give Soviet planners plentiful encouragement to contemplate a virtually closed economy and a high level of self-sufficiency' (Mellor, 1982, p. 102). This has indeed been the most obvious characteristic of Russia's development in the twentieth century, with the transformation of the essentially traditional agrarian economy and society into a modern urban and industrial complex.

The Russian Background and the Origins of Russian Marxism

The Soviet Union is the inheritor of an established political system of considerable antiquity, but one which was isolated from world developments throughout much of its existence. In the tenth century, a principality based on today's capital of the Ukraine, Kiev (Kyiv) flourished on the basis of trade via the water route down the Dnieper River and across the Black Sea to Byzantium. The Orthodox form of Christianity was adopted as the official religion of Kievan Rus (whence the modern name Russia) in the year 988 under Prince Vladimir, as a deliberate measure aimed at distinguishing the Slavonic-speaking peoples of the Kiev principality from surrounding tribes, notably the Roman Catholic Poles and Hungarians to the west and the Muslims to the south and east. This had the intended effect of setting Russia on a course different from that of Western Europe, particularly following the fall of Constantinople in 1453, after which Russia saw herself as the 'Third Rome', the repository and guardian of Orthodoxy. This helped to establish Orthodoxy as one characteristic of 'Russianness', and reinforced the distinctions of language and alphabet that separated the Russians from Western Europe.

Even more effective, however, was the invasion and domination by the Mongols, who had swept across from East Asia, capturing Kiev in

1240. Mongol rule in Russia—a cruel and harsh episode—lasted until the late-fifteenth century, causing the religious and intellectual upheavals and reawakening of the Renaissance and the Reformation in Western Europe to pass Russia by. During the two and a half centuries of Mongol rule (approximately 1240–1480), with the decline of Kiev and the rise to prominence of the princes of the more northerly city of Moscow, in the fifteenth century, a permanent shift in the centre of administrative and political power took place, and subsequent history has been based on the heartland of which Moscow is the centre.

Russia's history since that time can be seen as a repeating cycle: periods of stagnation followed by a discovery of the society's backwardness in comparison with its Western neighbours, leading to somewhat frenetic efforts to close the gap. Hence, in the sixteenth century, Ivan the Terrible (reigned 1533–84) associated with Western European countries, notably England, and attempted to modernize the governmental system of Russia by breaking the power of the boyars (the landed aristocracy). At the beginning of the eighteenth century, Peter the Great (reigned 1694–1725) embarked upon a sustained and largely successful attempt to raise Russia to the standard already reached by England, Holland and parts of Italy, by establishing textiles, paper, iron, shipbuilding and other industries, founding the country's first newspaper, creating a state service and making service on behalf of the state obligatory for all, taking a population census, reforming the taxation system, and bringing the Orthodox Church under the more direct control of the state (thereby reinforcing the Russianness of Russian Orthodoxy). By the time of his death, Russia had attained a level of administrative, industrial and military modernity equivalent to that occupied by the powers which she emulated, although the 'deep structures' of Russian intellectual and political life had not shared the transformation process (Orlovsky, in Rigby & Harasymiw, 1983, p. 183), and Russia slipped back steadily as the eighteenth century advanced. Towards the end of the century, Empress Catherine the Great (reigned 1762–96) again followed European trends by setting out to establish an empire comparable with those of the imperial powers, Spain, England, France and Holland, pushing back Russia's borders west and south, annexing the Crimea in 1783, and incorporating a segment of a partitioned Poland in 1795.

By then, Russia was engaging in much cultural and political contact with the countries of Western Europe. Catherine herself was German by birth, and French was the language of the Russian court; science was flourishing, after the founding of the Academy of Sciences in 1725 and the establishment of Moscow University by M. V. Lomonosov in 1755. The arts, particularly literature, were about to undergo a flowering hitherto unknown in Russia, with the prose writer Nikolai Gogol (1809–52) and the poet Alexander Pushkin (1799–1837) transforming—indeed, creating—Russian as a literary language.

Yet these modernizing trends left the social and political life of the Russian people singularly unaffected. The bulk of the population consisted of private or state-owned serfs, legally bound to the estate on which they were born, the property of the landlord, who could dispose of them at will, selling them, trading them, or even using them as gambling stakes. The country was ruled by an autocratic monarch who governed according to the Divine Right of Kings, separated from the common people by the hereditary nobility and by the gentry raised by the monarch himself in return for services rendered in the state service or on the battlefield. The Orthodox Church, from Peter the Great's time virtually a department of state, effectively functioned as a representative of temporal power in the countryside, and supported the autocracy by giving moral justification to the form of rule. The state service was ill trained and poorly paid, and as a result corrupt—witness the stories and plays of Gogol. There grew up over several centuries a tradition of *creating an image*, of reporting to the centre what it was believed the centre wished to hear: the so-called 'Potëmkin villages' (façades with no buildings behind them), erected to impress Catherine the Great as she cruised down the Dnieper, are but the most noteworthy historical example of a tradition in which the leader's lieutenants in the Soviet provinces in the twentieth century, up to our own day, have reported over-fulfilment of economic plans as a means of currying favour with their superiors.

The first stirrings of protest at Russia's primitive and poverty-striken condition came in the last decade of the eighteenth century when in 1790 Alexander Radishchev, a Russian aristocrat, educated in Leipzig, published an account of a *Journey from St Petersburg to Moscow* (that is, from Peter the Great's city to the traditional capital) in which he catalogued the miseries of Russian life as he saw them, bringing Russian realities face to face with liberal ideals. For his troubles, he was sentenced to death (later commuted to ten years' exile in Siberia), with removal of his noble status and other penalties—an indication that the suppression of dissident thought has a long history in that country.

From these beginnings to the October Revolution (and, according to one perspective, down to the present day), Russian radical thought passed through several distinct phases and encompassed a range of philosophies. In combination, they form a fascinating, at times exhilarating, and frequently tragic story that is of considerable interest in its own right.

In the first quarter of the nineteenth century, the stationing of Russian armies in France in the wake of the Napoleonic wars had at least two notable consequences. First, it introduced into the French language the word *bistro* (Russian *bystro*, 'quickly'—a demand for rapid service in a drinking establishment). More significantly, it introduced Russian officers to a different world, that of Western Europe, where they gained a forceful lesson in the gulf that existed between Russia and her near neighbours. Back in Russia, groups of these officers established secret societies aiming to overthrow the autocracy, and to replace it by a republic or at least a constitutional monarchy with severely curtailed powers. An attempt at revolution by the 'Decembrists', a conspiratorial group of army officers, on 14 December 1825, during a brief and confused interregnum between Alexander I and Nicholas I, provoked a severe reaction. The leading conspirators were executed and others exiled to Siberia, becoming revolutionary martyrs in the process, and a police state was instituted over the next few years, earning for the tsar the sobriquet of 'the Gendarme of Europe'. Severe censorship—intended to 'make printing harmless'—and extensive use of secret police had the long-term effect of further stimulating the radicals, who employed techniques of concealment that have become an established part of the political culture down to our own day, particularly the use of literature and literary criticism as a vehicle for radical social comment.

From the mid-1830s, an intellectual debate fomented that lasted until the middle of the century, and still finds echoes in the present, concerning the appropriate course of development for Russia. The gulf between Russia and Europe was widely recognized, but the prescriptions differed markedly. The 'Westernizers' concluded that Russia must adopt Western methods, beginning with the abolition of serfdom, and embarking on the path of industrial development urbanization and political reform. The Slavophiles, by contrast, bemoaned the evils of European society, particularly its destruction of traditional values, and suggested that Russia must avoid those errors at all costs. Her development should not copy the West, but rather should seek the positive virtues of her own (and more generally Slavic) society, and build a new society on their basis. The Orthodox Church, with its traditional values, was an obvious central distinguishing element, but so were such features of Russian society as the *obshchina* or village commune, though which the peasantry arranged its affairs. In the work of Alexander Herzen (1812–70), largely produced abroad, the Westernizing notion of socialism and the Slavophile stress on Russia's own traditions were combined in the idea of rural socialism based on the commune (see Malia, 1961, for a thorough study of the life and thought of Herzen).

Russia's disastrous showing against the British and French in the Crimean War (1854–6) demonstrated again that Russia was no match for those powers which she wished to emulate, and a radical restructuring of the society was the only way to achieve that goal above all by abolishing serfdom, an evil institution that was a blight on Russian society. The emancipation of the serfs was proclaimed in 1861 opening up the way to further reforms, and—more to the point—facilitating industrial development by freeing the rural population to move in search of jobs, and opening the prospects of rapid change in the country's social structure.

In the second half of the century, the dominant trend in radical thought was Populism (*narodnichestvo*), a movement that took on two distinct forms: an educative propaganda campaign, aimed at winning over the peasant masses to socialist ideals; and a terroristic approach aimed at forcing concessions from the regime. In 1881, after a number of lesser exploits, members of the latter tendency succeeded in taking the life of the supreme symbol of the system—the tsar himself. The reaction under his successor was profound, and led to the stifling of Populism.

Some circles in the radical movement went into emigration, as the only effective means of keeping Russian radicalism alive. Georgi Plekhanov, Vera Zasulich and Lev Deutsch went to Geneva, quickly became attracted to Marxism, and established the first Russian Marxist group, 'Emancipation of Labour', in 1883. From their vantage point among the lakes and mountains of central Europe, they looked at Russian realities with fresh eyes, their vision sharpened by both distance and the new ideological lenses.

This was not the first Russian contact with Marxism. Marx's views were becoming known in Russia in the 1840s and 1850s, although they had little influence on the radical movement there. Mikhail Bakunin, the Russian founder of modern anarchism, had frequent contacts with Marx in Paris from 1844 onwards, although their views differed sharply. Herzen was in London in the mid-1850s at the same time as Marx, and was without doubt aware of Marx's ideas. In the 1860s and 1870s, Russian Populists displayed a growing interest in Marxism, while for his part Marx learnt Russian and began to study Russian society. Bakunin made the first translation of *The Communist Manifesto* into Russian in 1862; Russian translations of *Das Kapital* appeared ten years later.

In the 1870s, radical Populists sought Marx's guidance over whether socialism could develop in Russia other than on a capitalist foundation. They hoped Marx and Engels could answer 'yes', since the alternative was cruel to contemplate: abandoning all hope of creating agrarian socialism, and encouraging the development of the capitalism, urbanization and industrialization which they abhorred. Marx and Engels, however, with their notorious scorn for 'the idiocy of rural life', wished to defend industrial socialism, and essentially hedged. In the preface to the Russian edition of the *Manifesto* (1882) they gave the following equivocal response: 'If the Russian Revolution becomes the signal for a proletarian revolution in the West, so that both complement each other, the present Russian common ownership of land may serve as the starting point for a communist development.' The Geneva 'Emancipation of the Labour Group' adopted the view that the future lay in proletarian socialism, and concluded that Russia suffered from both too much capitalism (since the exploitation of workers in industry had already become established, albeit on a small scale), and too little capitalism (since the proletariat was too weak to hope for an early revolution). Hence, the regrettable but necessary form of action for Russian Marxists must be to hasten the development of capitalism. In this way, Plekhanov in particular demonstrated the relevance of Marxism—a philosophical analysis based on the conditions of Western Europe—for backward Russia; but the political programme that followed from this conclusion was highly distasteful for Marxists. In adapting Marx's theories to Russian conditions, presenting these in a series of significant works, and sponsoring the translation of Marxist writings into Russian, Plekhanov gave a new direction to Russian socialism and wrought severe damage upon the Populist movement which never effectively recovered. (For an evaluation of Plekhanov's life and work, see Baron, 1963.)

The polemical debate with the Populists was joined most effectively by Vladimir Ul'yanov (Lenin, 1870–1924) in his works *Who the 'Friends of the People' Are, and How they Fight the Social-Democrats* (written in 1894) and *The Development of Capitalism in Russia* (published in 1899). He argued that, contrary to the Populists' assertions, capitalism was now inevitable in Russia; the question addressed to Marx and Engels in the 1870s was now irrelevant following the establishment of industry on the basis of a work-force of seasonally migrant peasants and of capital imported from the West. Time had rendered meaningless the Populists' aspirations to convert the traditional commune into rural socialism.

Social and economic development in the 1890s—an economic boom, leading to the expansion of the working class—prompted Lenin and other second-generation Russian Marxists to argue for an all-out struggle to bring about a socialist revolution along Marxist lines. Moreover, in a stunning analysis, *Imperialism: the Highest Stage of Capitalism* (written in 1916), derivative of the English economist J. A. Hobson, Lenin convinced sceptical colleagues of the validity of Marx's theories to economically and socially backward Russia. That country was seen to possess incipient capitalism, but it was not imperialist in the same sense as were, for example, Britain, Germany and France. Rather, Russia herself was subject to massive foreign investment, in mining and railways, for example, and to that extent was semi-colonial; her world position was that of the exploited proletariat, whose historic role was to destroy capitalism at its weakest link. Hence, Russia's very backwardness—as the 'proletariat' of the international economy—allowed her to lead the world to the socialist revolution.

This was a comforting doctrine for the adherents of a philosophy whose founding father only a generation earlier had held out little hope for Russia, other than either going through capitalist development and exploitation, or achieving socialism on the coat-tails of the industrial countries.

Lenin then set about creating an organization to bring about the longed-for revolution. First he established an organ for the movement: he set up clandestine presses to publish *Iskra* ('The Spark')—with the motto, 'From the spark shall burst forth the flame' of revolution. *Iskra* was printed mainly abroad and copies were smuggled into Russia, thereby circulating Marxist ideas among Russian radicals. More specifically, it circulated Leninist ideas, for Lenin was already making original contributions to the ideology now known as Marxism-Leninism.

Russia's first Marxist party, the Russian Social-Democratic Workers' Party (RSDWP), was founded in Minsk in 1898. Its leaders were arrested and exiled immediately after the founding congress, and the party existed more in the mind than in reality. Nevertheless, the fundamental move had been made, and in principle a Russian Marxist party existed. In the ensuing years, living mainly in London, Lenin developed his theory of the kind of party needed to bring about the revolution.

The great difficulty for the Russian Marxist movement was that there was no legitimate place for it inside Russia. The party was illegal; its leaders were in exile; it had few opportunities to propagate Marxist ideas among the workers, the very class on which it relied in carrying through the revolution. Serious debates took place within the *émigré* community over the appropriate strategy and tactics in such conditions. One school of thought held that the movement's main task was to spread Marxist ideas as broadly as possible among the Russian population. It would then not be so vulnerable to the kind of pre-emptive strike by the tsarist authorities that had removed the leadership following the party's foundation. Lenin argued otherwise. In his pamphlet *What is to be Done?* (1902) he urged that in the difficult conditions of tsarist Russia secrecy was the key to success, protecting the movement from the intrusions of the regime, by creating a small party of 'professional revolutionaries', dedicated to the cause and each other.

Both lines of argument were rational responses to the problem of how revolutionaries could function in a police state. The argument came to a head at the second congress, held in Brussels and London in 1903, in the key debate over a clause in the party rules defining membership. Lenin wished to stipulate that members should commit themselves to work 'in one of the party organizations', while Julius Martov suggested the wording 'under the guidance of one of the party organizations'—ostensibly a trivial distinction, but actually one of great importance. Martov's formulation would have permitted a much looser and probably far less disciplined mass membership; Lenin's would have required supreme dedication on the part of members. Moreover, Lenin added the principle of 'democratic centralism', as a means of imposing discipline upon the members. In its simplest form, it declared that debate within the party was to be free and open until the point when a decision was taken; after that, the decision became binding on all members, who forfeited the right to campaign for a reversal of policy.

From that congress, the party was effectively divided into two factions: the Bolsheviks, headed by Lenin, and the Mensheviks, led by Martov and others, to whose cause the veteran Russian Marxist Plekhanov was to adhere. Subsequently attempts were made to unite the two factions, notably at the 1906 Stockholm congress, but effectively they remained separate entities, bitterly divided over strategy and tactics, and separated by personal animosities.

By then Russia had already experienced revolution. Dismay at Russia's dismal performance in war with Japan during 1904—a 'short victorious war' had been hoped for by the authorities, to deflect popular attention from revolution—led to demonstrations in St Petersburg on 'Bloody Sunday' (9 January 1905), which were fired on by loyal troops, provoking spontaneous street violence and revolutionary activity in the capital and other cities. Events were quickly brought under control, although sporadic outbursts continued into 1906 in rural areas. Moreover, the authorities made concessions, the most significant being the creation of a State Duma (Council) with consultative functions and the tsar retaining a veto.

More important over the longer term was the experience that the events of 1905 gave to the working class of Russia in managing a revolution: Lenin later referred to this as the 'dress rehearsal' for the socialist revolution. Most significantly, the working class in revolution created the Soviets of Workers' Deputies: committees comprising delegates elected from individual factories and plants. They functioned essentially as strike committees, co-ordinating the workers' revolutionary activity; and, as creations of the working class itself, they became imbued with particular significance in the political mythology of the movement, and ultimately were made the basis of the socialist state.

Formation of the Present Regime

Following the 1905 revolution, the tsarist government introduced a number of reforms, particularly land reform. In terms of constitutional development, however, the Duma proved largely ineffectual, and fresh elections on a gradually more restricted franchise led to increasing bias in favour of the existing regime (see Hosking, 1973).

Russia's entry into the First World War provoked a surge of patriotism comparable with that which engulfed the other European belligerent nations—to the despair of Lenin who, living in Swiss exile, called for the working masses of all countries to turn the imperialist war into an international civil war of proletarians against bourgeoisie. Alas for him, this call went largely unheeded, as socialist parties in the parliaments of Europe voted the resources needed by their governments to fight the war. By 1916, however, the sheer incompetence of military organization on the part of the Russian royal family led to a gross undermining of confidence in the tsar's leadership. Bread riots in St Petersburg (since 1914 renamed Petrograd) on 23 February 1917 quickly spread to the working-class districts, and within three days the city was in riot, a Provisional Committee had been elected by the Duma and a new Soviet of Workers' Deputies had been formed. On 2 March the tsar abdicated; his brother Mikhail refused the crown; the Romanov dynasty came to an end, and Russia was ruled by a

Provisional Government under Prince L'vov (replaced in July by the socialist Alexander Kerensky).

At the same time—on 2 March—the Petrograd Soviet issued its Order Number One, which effectively instructed army units to obey their officers only if their orders did not contradict those of the Soviet. The Provisional Government—provisional pending the election of a Constituent Assembly to devise a constitution for post-imperial Russia—was in effect forced to share power with the Petrograd Soviet, which enjoyed the confidence of the working class that had created it. A system of 'dual power' was in operation, which confirmed the weakness of the bourgeoisie in Russia. At a time of revolution—the more so in the middle of a catastrophic war—firm leadership is required, something the leaders of the Provisional Government proved incapable of supplying.

Lenin returned to Russia from Switzerland in April 1917, a journey facilitated by Germany in a so-called 'sealed train'. In his first speech, at the Finland Station in Petrograd, he endorsed the Soviets as genuinely revolutionary bodies, urged the party (i.e. the Bolshevik wing of the RSDWP) to win control of them, and proclaimed the forthcoming socialist revolution.

To his more orthodox colleagues this was preposterous: their reading of Marx (and certainly that of the Mensheviks) had taught that the bourgeois revolution must be followed by a lengthy phase of economic development. After all, *The Communist Manifesto* had clearly described the ideal situation for a successful socialist revolution: society would be industrialized, with a developed network of communications; the proletariat would constitute the bulk of the population; bourgeois freedoms (of speech, assembly and the press) would have been long established; and society at large would have grown used to them and the political culture would have developed. These conditions were lacking in Russia, yet Lenin insisted on going ahead with a revolution to usher in socialism (and ultimately communism): in the light of this the revolution has been called 'premature', and Soviet society—an amalgam of feudal, capitalist and socialist relationships—a 'syncretic society' (Casals, 1980). However, as Isaac Deutscher (1967, p. 9) pointed out, the revolutionaries who pushed forward to revolution in Russia in 1917 'acted as they did because they could not act otherwise'. A revolutionary is no revolutionary who does not seize whatever opportunities arise for attaining power; Lenin occupies a leading place in world history in the twentieth century because he saw an opportunity and worked insistently to bring it to fruition.

The events of the revolutionary year 1917 have been widely reported, both by participants (e.g. Trotsky, 1932–3) and by historians with many intellectual concerns and of a variety of political persuasions. Pivotal moments are the 'July Days', when the Provisional Government—by then under Kerensky—ordered what turned out to be a disastrous military offensive in Galicia and the Bolsheviks supposedly made a premature attempt to provoke an uprising against the Provisional Government; and the events of August, when the Provisional Government, having apparently invited a monarchist armed force under General L. G. Kornilov to stage a show of strength against the Soviet and its supporters, apparently lost confidence, and thereby surrendered its credibility.

From September, the Bolsheviks enjoyed majorities on the Soviets in Petrograd and Moscow, the former chaired by Leon Trotsky, who formed a Military Revolutionary Committee to carry through a revolutionary seizure of power, timed to coincide with the Second All-Russian Congress of Soviets, due to convene on 25 October. On the previous night, the cruiser *Aurora* moved up-river, and the start of an almost bloodless coup was signalled by her searchlights and a blank shot over the Winter Palace, where the members of the Provisional Government were in emergency session. By the following morning, Lenin and his comrades were in control. In a single night they had 'seized the state power of Russia', to quote the American eyewitness John Reed (1966, p. 9), and on the following day, at the Congress of Soviets, they 'placed it in the hands of the Soviets'.

This brief survey of the historical background to the Soviet regime is instructive on several counts, for—to repeat an important truism—'no revolution creates *ex nihilo*: every revolution works in the social environment that has produced it and on the materials it finds in that environment' (Deutscher, 1967, p. 11). The Bolsheviks were themselves the product of Russian society, although heavily overlain with a coating of European cosmopolitanism, in common with previous generations of Russian radicals. Russia's ambiguous and ambivalent relationship with the West has been an enduring theme of her historical experience, and it is reflected in the problem of identity that still faces the Soviet Union today.

In material terms, the Soviet Union has succeeded in attaining a level of development comparable with that of the country's traditional rivals. By devising an original political and economic system, which owed something to the pre-revolutionary traditions of harshly imposed discipline and state sponsorship of economic development, the Soviet Union was able to withstand the onslaught of the Second World War. Through these means, Stalin performed a feat that the tsars had ultimately failed to do: that is, to win acceptance by those powers against whom Russia had traditionally measured her own performance. Russia, transformed into the Union of Soviet Socialist Republics, had won what she regarded as her rightful place in the world, alongside the most powerful, those who set the pace. Since the Second World War, the Soviet Union has no longer been seeking simply to 'catch up' with the West, but in significant areas—space exploration, sports achievements, military advances—has set the pace herself. In such terms, therefore, the Soviet Union has 'made the grade'.

However, the political backwardness that characterized the Russia of the tsars has not been eliminated. The complexities of the Soviet system will be examined in later chapters. For the moment suffice it to note that there has never been a tradition of personal liberty in that country, and that the values of collective rights over individual rights—partly associated with Russia's avoidance of the impact of the Enlightenment—have been one form of continuity between the *ancien régime* and the socialist present. The parallels between the autocracy of the tsars and the dictatorship of Stalin are too numerous to mention here: but the impact of the continuity of traditional attitudes, patterns of thought, institutional practices and the like cannot be overlooked. Indeed, this area of study has been given increasing attention by scholars in recent years (see White, 1979; Orlovsky, in Rigby & Harasymiw, 1983).

The Soviet Union represents the culmination of many centuries of historical development, reflecting a broad range of influences and experiences, but purposely accelerated in a process of induced change in the last sixty years. In the ensuing chapters its various forms will be explored in greater detail.

History of the Present Regime

In its history of over seventy years, the Soviet Union has passed through a number of distinct periods (for a succinct recent account, see Hosking, 1985). The initial task was to secure peace and take Russia out of the war: indeed, the Bolsheviks' very first decree was the 'Decree on Peace', and shortly thereafter a team of negotiators met German imperial representatives at Brest-Litovsk. Negotiations were stretched out into 1918, and the Treaty of Brest-Litovsk ('the forgotten peace': Wheeler-Bennett, 1966) led to severe losses of both territory and population. Trotsky, the chief Bolshevik negotiator, refused to accept the terms, and demagogically declared a state of 'neither war nor peace'. But urged by Lenin's authority, the new regime accepted the terms, allowing time to consolidate (see Debo, 1979).

Virtually immediately, however, a bitter Civil War broke out that raged until mid-1920, and was complicated by the intervention of Russia's former allies against Germany: France, Britain, the United States, and also Japan and a garrison of Czech deserters, caught in Russia and anxious to leave (via the Pacific coast) and return to Europe to fight against Germany (for a recent account of the Civil War, see Mawdsley, 1987). In this fraught period, when not only the Bolshevik regime but also (as that regime saw itself) the only socialist regime in the world was fighting for survival, severe measures were introduced as the only way of keeping the country together. Known collectively as 'War Communism', they included the gradual nationalization of most of industry, banking, foreign trade and other 'commanding heights' of the economy; the elimination of other political parties (including the Mensheviks and the Socialist Revolutionaries, with the left wing of which the Bolsheviks initially shared government); the institution of the purge and the terror under the Cheka (forerunner of the KGB, or State Security Committee); and the use of forced methods to secure food supplies to the cities, including the deployment of armed detachments of workers into the countryside. The regime's relationship with the Russian peasantry has been a perpetual source of political difficulty.

The next phase was that of the New Economic Policy, adopted by the party on Lenin's insistence at the Tenth Party Congress in March 1921. This was aimed at revitalizing the shattered economy, by encouraging the peasants to grow surplus produce and selling it at the market price in the towns. The risk of encouraging 'capitalistic' tendencies among the peasants was explicitly recognized at the time; but the need to get trade established again was deemed vital, and basic food supplies were secured by a tax in kind. Industry, by contrast, remained firmly in state hands, so that there could be no full-scale reversion to capitalism in those areas that Marxists deemed of greatest political-economic significance.

In May 1922, Lenin, Chairman of the Council of People's Commissars (i.e. prime minister), the master-mind and driving force of the revolution, suffered the first of three strokes, which removed him from the day-to-day direction of government at a critical time. The fact that he periodically returned to his desk (and, indeed, even from his sickbed attempted to hold the reins of government) led to the postponement of decisions about the development of the revolutionary regime that really needed to be taken. To be sure, Soviet Russia did not stand still: but it was not clear that a reversion to capitalism had been permanently avoided; by 1923–4 the New Economic Policy was under strain, as the peasants discovered there were no goods on which to spend the profits from their trade. The *smychka*, or alliance, between workers and peasants, which had been a cornerstone of Lenin's political and economic strategy, appeared threatened, at a time when its architect was incapacitated and unable to maintain his direction of the project. By 1927 NEP was effectively abandoned.

Lenin died in January 1924, at the age of 53. There ensued a power struggle among his survivors, many of them highly gifted men, but all possessing human personality failings. Lenin himself had pointed to some of these in his so-called 'political testament': Trotsky's intellectual brilliance was praised, but his excessive self-assurance and his inclination to become too much enthralled by the detail of administration counted against him. Stalin's rudeness particularly offended Lenin. Other members of the leading circle feared the 'Bonapartist' tendency of Trotsky, while Stalin's position as party General Secretary, running the central offices as a superior clerk, appeared to pose no threat. In the event, it was Stalin's political acumen, coupled with skilful exploitation of the powers to select and elevate party officials to posts of influence, that led to his emergence as supreme leader.

Quickly moving to edge out his rivals, Stalin allied himself first with Bukharin, on the right, against Trotsky, Zinov'ev and Kamenev (the 'left'), and then from the left attacked his former rightist colleagues, Bukharin, Rykov and Tomsky. By such manoeuvrings, he secured a compliant party.

In his rise to power, Stalin had proposed the concept or slogan of 'socialism in one country', as opposed to Trotsky's notion of 'permanent revolution'. By the time of Lenin's death, it was imperative that a firm policy should be adopted to point the way forward. The Bolsheviks had seized power on the assumption that revolution in Russia would be greeted by workers' uprisings in the advanced capitalist countries. This did not happen on the scale or with the success expected and required, and more or less by the time of the ending of the civil war the Bolshevik regime stood alone in the world. Moreover, following the ending of the First World War in 1918, the capitalist world quickly recovered, and some of its leaders (such as Winston Churchill) called for an anti-Bolshevik crusade. Something had to be done.

Trotsky held that the Russian revolution could not survive alone. It was therefore vital to take steps to avert the swamping of socialism by the bourgeoisie, if necessary by provoking supporting revolutions abroad; only in that way could the revolution be made permanent. Such an analysis acknowledged the infant Soviet Union's fundamental dependency on factors beyond its direct control. Moreover, such a policy, if adopted by the Soviet Union and applied with vigour through subversion in the capitalist states, might well provoke intervention that could lead to the regime's downfall, such was its economic and military weakness.

Against such an argument, Stalin proposed to build on Russia's own resources, and make a start on creating the basis for socialism. The country was itself vast; it had a large population and enormous resources; it need not rely on a foreign proletariat that had already shown itself unable to overthrow capitalism, even when capitalism was weakened by war. 'Socialism in One Country' proved an attractive slogan to a country and a party in need of a boost to its self-confidence, and by the mid-1920s it was adopted as the Bolsheviks' policy.

This was in many ways the most profound decision ever reached in the history of the regime, taking advantage of earlier milestone decisions adopted under Lenin's guidance, but now setting the country on a path that was to transform it, economically and socially, within a generation, and establishing a political mould that has proved itself serviceable in certain circumstances, but intractably difficult to break away from as circumstances changed in later years. From the late 1920s and through the 1930s, the basic features of what was deemed to be an (indeed, *the*) authentic model of socialism became established in the Soviet Union under Stalin.

In 1928, with the introduction of the first Five-Year Plan for economic development, based on massive investment and subsequent reinvestment in heavy basic industries (mining, iron and steel, railways), the Soviet economy began one of the most spectacular periods of expansion ever known. A crude but effective planning system, in which specific targets—very often deliberately unrealistic—were set for different industries and even specific plants, ensured that the priority sectors expanded at a rapid pace. The state's propaganda backed up these politically motivated goals, with the aim of both encouraging their attainment and convincing the Soviet people that they were building 'socialism in one country', and doing so by the only way possible. The results were impressive, in terms of tons of coal mined, tons of iron and steel smelted, numbers of new dams, railways and canals built, and new engineering and machine-building plants established (see Nove, 1972, pp. 191–5, for a balanced account).

At the beginning of the 1930s, in order to bring under political control a peasantry whose recalcitrance had been demonstrated several times in the previous decade, and in the process to guarantee the supply of food to the expanding cities (and also to regulate the supply of labour migrating from rural to urban areas), a course of forced collectivization of the peasant farms was embarked upon (see Lewin, 1968). This was done under the slogan 'Eliminate the kulaks [rich peasants] as a class', and applied with such ferocity that Stalin in March

1930 felt obliged to write a notorious article in *Pravda*, accusing of 'dizziness with success' those engaged in enforcement, and urging them to slow down the pace. The peasants responded to the pressure, for the last time, by fighting back: slaughtering their livestock and devouring their seed corn, causing widespread famine in 1932–3. The consequence, however, was that, by 1935, 83.2 per cent of peasant households were in collective farms (Nove, 1972, p. 174).

The enforcement agencies were also extended to the industrial sector: after all, if planning is a serious effort then steps have to be taken to apply its provisions. Living standards were kept low, and pressure was applied against virtually the whole population, to ensure their compliance with the goals of the plan. 'Slackers' were accused of being saboteurs and wreckers, inspired by the international bourgeoisie or by the world-wide 'Trotskyite clique', and given ferocious sentences as a means of showing Stalin meant business. Hundreds of thousands—millions, indeed: precise figures are impossible to establish, and this question, a matter of great controversy among Western scholars, has been taken up by Soviet historians in the 1980s—were taken to forced labour camps in the far north and the far east. There they were made to work on prestigious construction projects, such as the White Sea Canal, in conditions superbly described by Alexander Solzhenitsyn in his novel, *One Day in the Life of Ivan Denisovich*, and more extensively depicted in his massive work, *The Gulag Archipelago*. Many never returned.

From December 1934, with the murder of the Leningrad party secretary Sergei Kirov, Stalin increased the pressure, in a series of purges that in waves destroyed whole categories of Soviet citizens: political opponents, Old Bolsheviks (members of the party since before the revolution), bourgeois specialists employed under Lenin for their expertise, army officers, and a range of other categories who might have been suspected of potential disloyalty to the system, or to Stalin personally. In the years 1937–8, in the Great Purge, virtually the whole of the political establishment was destroyed, many of the General Secretary's long-standing comrades perishing after show trials on trumped-up charges in the period known as the *yezhovshchina*, after N. I. Yezhov, secret police chief at the time. Again, verifiably accurate figures for the politically inspired carnage are impossible to find, not least because they most likely do not exist. However, in 1956 Nikita Khrushchev gave the following figures for the fate of individuals associated with the 1934 congress: 70 per cent (98 out of 139) central committee members and candidate members were arrested and shot, mainly in 1937–8; 1,108 out of the 1,966 delegates to that congress were arrested, charged with anti-revolutionary crimes (from text of Secret Speech to Twentieth Party Congress, in Christman, 1969, p. 175).

In a supreme irony, in the midst of all this 'infringement of socialist legality' (a euphemism used after Stalin's death), on 5 December 1936, to the strains of the fourth movement of Beethoven's choral symphony (his setting of Schiller's 'Ode to Joy'), a new constitution was introduced, declaring the Soviet Union to be 'a socialist state of workers and peasants'. This constitution 'guaranteed' all basic human rights, including inviolability of the person and of the home, privacy of correspondence, and so forth, together with a range of political rights that might put some liberal democracies in the shade. Certain well-known and widely respected socialists from the bourgeois world travelled and marvelled in the country that was building socialism: Sidney and Beatrice Webb (1944, pp. 333–40 and *passim*), interpreting the Soviet Union in the light of liberal principles of legality, concluded that Stalin was no dictator and Soviet communism was 'a new civilisation'.

There were more 'positive' sides to Stalin's socialism, most especially the extension of educational and health-care facilities to ever wider sections of the population: this kind of welfare provision, while obviously of value from the economic viewpoint alone, did benefit many millions of Soviet citizens, whose education permitted them to take advantage of the opportunities for social and geographical mobility that industrial expansion offered. The same economic development also enabled the state to claim that by 1930 unemployment in the state sector had been eliminated. That said nothing, of course, about the continuing rural unemployment and underemployment, but it was a very valuable propaganda point when the capitalist world was suffering profound economic depression.

The menace of Hitler was something only slowly recognized by Stalin, and by the summer of 1939 the Soviet armed forces were so unprepared for war (not least because its best officers had been killed in the purges) that Stalin concluded a non-aggression treaty, the so-called Molotov-Ribbentrop pact, with Nazi Germany. Nevertheless, the Soviet Union moved to place its economy on a war footing, so that when the German invasion came, on 22 June 1941, the country was slightly better prepared than it had been two years previously. Even so, the German armies were able to advance rapidly eastwards, laying siege to Leningrad in September 1941, and threatening Moscow a month later. Moscow was successfully defended by troops under the able command of Georgi Zhukov (assisted by the severity of the winter), but the people of Leningrad were to suffer siege for nine hundred days—it was finally lifted on 27 January 1944. Stalingrad, the city on the lower Volga whose very name made it a highly symbolic prize, was fought over street by street, house by house, before fresh Soviet armies, coming from the north and attacking in a pincer movement, in January 1943 destroyed the German armies under General Paulus. The battle of Stalingrad is seen as the turning-point of the war in the east, and possibly of the whole war, yet there was no sudden collapse. At Kursk, in western Russia, 'the greatest tank battle in history' (Clark, 1966, ch. 17) was won by the Soviet Union in the summer of 1943. From then on, the German armies were in retreat, and the Red Army pushed steadily westwards, liberating capital cities and countries of eastern and central Europe: Bucharest, Warsaw, Budapest, Vienna, Prague and finally—in May 1945—Berlin.

The Soviet Union emerged from the war—'the Great Patriotic War'—a devastated victor: its own dead numbered twenty million; its economy was in ruins; its citizens' homes were destroyed, and many lived in dug-outs and survived on grass soup in the summer of 1945. But victory brought control of most of Eastern Europe, where Stalin established communist regimes (which were joined by communist regimes that won power unaided in Albania and Yugoslavia). By the end of the decade, 'socialism in one country' had become 'socialism in one zone'. The Second World War and the events that followed also established the Soviet Union as a great power. When Stalin met Roosevelt and Churchill at Tehran in November 1943 and acted as host at the Yalta conference of February 1945, he met the allied leaders as an equal, at least in political terms, and there appears to have been every expectation on the Western side that wartime collaboration with the Soviet Union would continue in peacetime. Stalin's actions in setting up pro-Soviet governments in Eastern Europe, and more particularly his ten-month blockade of Berlin in 1948, quickly undermined confidence in such expectations: but they served to underline the fact that the Soviet Union was now a power to be reckoned with in the world. Soviet emulation of the United States in acquiring an atom bomb in August 1949 underlined that fact.

The years between the end of the Second World War and Stalin's death, on 5 March 1953, were a time of reconstruction, involving a continuation of the harsh discipline of the 1930s uninterrupted during the war. There is evidence that on the eve of his death Stalin was preparing a further round of purges, signalled by the arrest in January of nine Kremlin doctors, six of them Jews, on poisoning charges that were denounced as false immediately following the dictator's demise. An era came to an end, and tears of genuine grief were shed by millions of Soviet citizens, accustomed to being ruled by the 'Red Tsar' with the genial face and smiling eyes. Under his stern leadership, the country had suffered immense deprivation, as personal living standards had been sacrificed for the sake of general growth; it had been torn apart and atomized so that no real political life was possible; but it had acquired an industrial economy and a rapidly urbanizing society, with new industries and vibrant new cities in the Urals and the east; it had passed the stern test of world war, and had emerged as a superpower on the world stage. Stalin claimed the credit for this, and no one could contradict him.

Change was swift. Georgi Malenkov, Stalin's designated heir, was made to opt for the post of prime minister and to relinquish that of party secretary. Lavrentii Beriya, Stalin's fellow-Georgian secret police chief, was arrested at gunpoint in the presence of his Politburo colleages (according to a participant, Nikita Khrushchev, 1971, pp. 335–8) and executed. Modest relaxation in domestic policy led people to believe that there would be no repetition of the horrors of the 1930s. In addition, the Soviet Union began to play a more positive role in world affairs, with its leaders—notably Khrushchev, accompanied by others—travelling abroad on what must have been highly educative tours.

In 1956, at the Twentieth Party Congress, Khrushchev and his colleagues launched an anti-Stalin campaign, attacking their late colleague and leader for his ruthless treatment of the party, quoting statistics that revealed something of the devastation caused to party ranks, and generally undermining the 'cult of the personality of Stalin'. In the next few years, hundreds of thousands of those who had languished in the camps were rehabilitated and allowed to return to their families; many more thousands were rehabilitated posthumously. The anti-Stalin campaign culminated in 1961, when, during the Twenty-Second Congress, Stalin's embalmed body was removed from the mausoleum on Red Square, which reverted to being simply the Mausoleum of V. I. Lenin.

That was the heyday of Nikita Khrushchev's period of rule. Khrushchev, whose working life began in the mining town of Yuzovka, became party boss in the Ukraine in the 1930s and was brought to Moscow to supervise the construction of the underground railway system. A peasant in his outlook and manner (and in his earthy language), as a lieutenant of Stalin he had much blood on his hands. But the mood of the Politburo members after Stalin's death (presumably in total harmony with the mood of the people) was a desire to remove the uncertainty of arbitrary terror, which affected the leaders as much as those under them. After all, Khrushchev himself in his memoirs (1971, p. 614) quoted Bulganin to the effect that a Politburo member was unsure when invited to the Kremlin where he would be sent next: to his home or to gaol.

The de-Stalinization campaign was a political slogan used by Khrushchev, accompanied by a call to 'return to Leninist norms' in the party, including a restoration of the party's central role in the political system. Stalin had undermined that role, ruling instead through the state's administrative apparatus. Khrushchev, as party secretary, competed for power against Malenkov, head of the government, whom he accused, along with his supporters, of being 'anti-party'. Malenkov would have been on equally strong ground in arguing that governing through the state was a Leninist principle, since Lenin, as chairman of the Council of People's Commissars, held no formal party post. But policy issues also divided the two rivals: Malenkov proposed to shift the balance of investment to favour the production of more consumer goods, while Khrushchev argued for a programme of investment in agriculture, bringing virgin lands in the east and in Kazakhstan under the plough. In these terms, the power struggle played itself out.

Malenkov was forced to resign as prime minister in February 1955, but the crisis of the 'anti-party group' came to a head in June 1957, over Khrushchev's plans to destroy the power of the state apparatus by abolishing most of the central ministries. The issue was resolved in Khrushchev's favour by an appeal, quite within the letter and the spirit of the party rules, to the Central Committee. Malenkov and his supporters were expelled from the party organs, and indeed from the party itself. However, in a clear demonstration that times had changed, they were not executed, but were sent off to serve the Soviet state as ambassadors to unimportant countries, to manage power stations or perform similar useful but politically insubstantial functions.

Under Khrushchev, there was a good deal of relaxation, both internally and in foreign relations, although the path was not smooth in both areas.

Domestically, the renunciation of the worst of Stalin's terroristic methods did lead to a freer society, in which citizens were no longer afraid to step out of line: indeed, the point is that the 'line' encompassed a much broader range of *legitimate* activity than it had previously. The publication of *One Day in the Life of Ivan Denisovich* was symptomatic of this. So was the opening up of the Soviet Union to foreign influences, including the establishment of artistic and scholarly exchange programmes that sent Soviet workers in the cultural, scientific and artistic fields abroad and brought some of their Western counterparts to the Soviet Union, with a beneficial educative effect. However, on the negative side, Khrushchev refused to permit the poet and novelist Boris Pasternak to publish his Nobel prize-winning novel *Doctor Zhivago*, and he vilified experimental artists in public. He conducted a campaign of severe repression against the churches, in which thousands of church buildings were closed and worshippers were harassed and persecuted. He also waged war against 'economic crimes', in a campaign with anti-Semitic overtones. While boosting the country's prestige by success in space research (the first sputnik in October 1957; Yuri Gagarin's manned space flight in April 1961), implying significant technological advance in industry, he failed to solve the country's mounting crisis in agriculture and food supply, despite a number of moves to reform the system. And he surrounded himself with a 'personality cult' which, while by no means comparable with Stalin's, nevertheless led to accusations of wilfulness and interference in the processes of government.

In the international arena, the Soviet Union under Khrushchev began to play an increasingly active role. As party secretary and prime minister, he travelled to the West on a number of occasions, including a notorious summit conference in Paris in May 1960, effectively torpedoed by the shooting down of an American U-2 spy plane over Soviet territory and the capture of its pilot, Francis Gary Powers. In November 1956, he had authorized the use of Soviet tanks to crush an anti-Stalinist and anti-Soviet popular revolution in Hungary, itself a response to his own anti-Stalin 'secret speech' of earlier that year. Berlin remained a contentious issue, and with Khrushchev's support the wall between the Soviet sector and the three Western sectors was built in August 1961. A meeting with President Eisenhower in September 1959 led to the 'Spirit of Camp David' in American-Soviet relations. But in the autumn of 1962, the world appeared to be on the brink of nuclear war following the introduction of Soviet missiles into Cuba and the subsequent imposition of a 'quarantine' by the United States: in that crisis, Khrushchev was forced to back down ignominiously.

His period in rule was brought to an abrupt end on 13 October 1964, when his Politburo colleagues confronted him with an ultimatum, and forced him to resign on grounds of 'old age and deteriorating health'. Appeals to the Central Committee on this occasion were useless, and he retired on a state pension to a country house, occasionally appeared in public (for the benefit of Western newsmen), dictated his memoirs, which were smuggled abroad and published illegally, and died on 11 September 1971, a political nonentity by then, but one who in his time had contrived to make his country rather more attractive and humane than he found it.

Khrushchev's post as party first secretary was taken by Leonid Brezhnev, then aged 57, and the post of prime minister by Aleksei Kosygin. Anastas Mikoyan became president, to be replaced in December 1965 by Nikolai Podgorny. The country appeared to be run by a genuinely collective leadership, which embarked on a programme of economic reform, under Kosygin's guidance. However, resistance to the reform on the part of managers and workers in the administrative apparatus led to its virtual abandonment, and subsequently to the eclipse of Kosygin by Brezhnev, whose title reverted at the Twenty-Third Party Congress (1966) to general secretary, the title by which Stalin had been known. Indeed, in this essentially conservative leadership—dubbed by Zbigniew Brzezinski (1966, p. 7) as 'the regime of the clerks'—there were several signs of a reversion to the approach, if not directly the methods, of the Stalin era. Most characteristic, and the event that caused most consternation abroad, including communist circles in the West, was the trial in 1966 of the witers Andrei Sinyavskii and Yuli Daniel, found guilty of publishing works abroad without permission, and sentenced to long prison terms. Two years later, when Soviet-led Warsaw Pact troops invaded the reformist Czechoslovakia of Alexander Dubcek, the prestige of the Soviet Union and its ideology plummeted as it had after the similar intervention in the affairs of another ally twelve years earlier.

By the early 1970s, Leonid Brezhnev was clearly the dominant leader, and he launched a powerful diplomatic drive for a relaxation of tension with the West, popularly known as *détente*. This involved the expansion of East–West trade, particularly in grain to overcome the Soviet Union's repeated harvest failures and in advanced technology to help exploit the country's wealth in Siberia, increased contacts through tourism and cultural exchanges, regular visits by Soviet and Western leading figures to each other's countries, and the projection of an image of statesmanship and responsibility around the world. Diplomatically, the peak of this policy came in the summer of 1975, when representatives of thirty-five European and North American countries met in Helsinki to sign the Final Act of the Conference on Security and Co-operation in Europe. This Final Act, at least in some interpretations, appeared to commit the Soviet Union and her allies to wide-ranging relaxation, not only in dealings with the outside world, but also in their treatment of their own citizens.

Clearly the Soviet Union did not see *détente* in this light, and insisted on pursuing the world-wide aims of the socialist revolution. Indeed, in the late 1970s, the Soviet Union began to play the global role that

Russia had perhaps always coveted, deploying new, modern and powerful naval forces far from Soviet shores, and becoming heavily involved, both directly and in support of Cuba, in the Horn of Africa and in the south of that continent. So, when Leonid Brezhnev's health deteriorated seriously in the late 1970s, the country continued to expand its world role, while near stagnation in policy matched the drift to economic stagnation at home.

The promulgation of a new concept, 'developed socialism' or 'mature socialism', said to be a new stage on the road towards communism, opened the possibility of political changes and reforms; but these were largely not forthcoming. The early 1980s were characterized by inertia and drift. A drive to introduce greater rationality into the process of government was undermined by the retention of long-serving, unimaginative officials in the apparatus. Cynicism and corruption came to characterize the system (see Simis, 1982), and despite frequent calls to recruit a different type of administrator, the country ground along, largely under its own momentum. The system created by Stalin to accomplish the task of basic industrialization was proving less and less capable of running the product of that transformation: a relatively wealthy superpower, peopled by a new generation of well-educated citizens, who had enjoyed steadily rising living standards and who now presented to the system the demands generated by rising expectations.

The death of the general secretary, on 10 November 1982, brought the Brezhnev 'era' to an abrupt if long-expected close. He was succeeded by Yuri Andropov, who until May 1982 had been chairman of the KGB, the security police which under his guidance had skilfully and persistently rooted out dissidence, thereby causing considerable consternation among liberal circles in the West. He took over at a time when East–West relations were at their worst for over a decade. The notion of *détente* had been finally abandoned by Western governments following Soviet military intervention in Afghanistan in December 1979, and relations rapidly deteriorated to cold war with the election of conservative Republican Ronald Reagan as US president in November 1980, and the development of a severe political and economic crisis in Poland that began in the summer of 1980 and was to culminate in the imposition of martial law in December 1981.

Domestically, Andropov initiated a thorough shake-up of the apparatus, cutting out dead wood (including some at the top: the Minister of Internal Affairs, Nikolai Shchëlokov, was removed from office in December 1982 and subsequently expelled from the Central Committee), and emphasizing the need for discipline at all levels. Time-wasting, work-dodging and other widespread hindrances to efficiency were condemned, and the militia were given authority to enforce labour discipline in an effort to take up the slack that clearly existed. However, Andropov suffered a kidney failure in February 1983, barely three months after taking office. In May he assumed the presidency, left vacant since Brezhnev's death, and continued to appear in public occasionally until August. But his political control was in doubt, and his death on 9 February 1984 was not unexpected.

There was considerable surprise in the choice of his successor: Konstantin Chernenko, at 72 already older than Andropov, and also not in the best of health. Surrounded by septuagenarians such as foreign minister Andrei Gromyko, defence minister Dmitri Ustinov (died 20 December 1984), prime minister Nikolai Tikhonov, party secretary Boris Ponomarëv and Russian republic prime minister Mikhail Solomentsev, his was clearly a transitional administration, which ended with his death on 10 March 1985.

The generation that rose to political prominence in the Stalin era then at last handed over power to its successor. Members of the post-Stalin generation had already been brought into high positions of authority, and they were poised to assume supreme responsibility for the fate of their country, perhaps also of socialism and the world. They included Chernenko's successor, Mikhail Gorbachëv, born in 1931 (the year in which Brezhnev and many others joined the party), and hence only in his early twenties when Stalin died. A capable and well-educated leader, he rose through Komsomol (Young Communist League) and party posts to a regional party secretaryship at the age of thirty-nine, was brought to Moscow in 1978 as a Central Committee secretary in charge of agriculture, entered the Politburo as a non-voting candidate member the following year and attained full membership in 1980. His range of responsibilities was extended under Andropov, so he gained added experience; he also travelled abroad, including a fence-mending visit to London in December 1984. While not the most experienced Kremlin politician, Gorbachëv had enjoyed a meteoric career, and acquired valuable experience with which to lead the country out of the rut into which it had drifted; his legal training (at Moscow University) and his evident intelligence, self-confidence and urbanity distinguished him from those around him and qualified him for the confidence that Andrei Gromyko expressed in his nominating speech.

Gorbachëv's accession to the most powerful post in the Soviet political system—General Secretary of the Communist Party Central Committee—was hailed with great expectations of a more sustained dynamic approach to the country's problems than had been possible for a decade. The country faced an adaptation to 'the politics of stringency' (Bialer, 1980, ch. 15). There was a desperate need for reform of the economic mechanism; the depletion of resources in the west imposed an obligation to overcome the enormous technical difficulties and exploit the wealth of Siberia; a falling birth-rate in the European Soviet Union, coupled with a population explosion in the Muslim areas of Central Asia, posed a demographic crisis with ethnic, economic and perhaps political implications that demanded urgent attention. In addition, the growing sophistication and experience of the population made political reform objectively more feasible, subjectively more desirable, and perhaps politically more necessary than at any time previously in Soviet history.

It was in response to a perception of these problems that Gorbachëv—while deftly moving to secure his own political position by removing rivals, promoting supporters and generally cutting out the dead wood in the political apparatus (see Hill & Frank, 1986b; Gustafson & Mann, 1986, 1987)—introduced new concepts as code words for his approach. His initial slogan of *uskorenie* (acceleration) quickly gave way to *perestroika* (restructuring), a word that has swiftly gained currency in foreign languages, particularly when Gorbachëv himself wrote a book, published in many countries, explaining his approach to his country and the world (Gorbachëv, 1987).

In the time since he became General Secretary—to which he added the presidency in October 1988—Gorbachëv has displayed tremendous energy in attempting to redirect the course of his country's history. He appears to be seeking a new form of socialism, which is fundamentally different from the Stalinist heritage that came to be known as 'real socialism' under Brezhnev, and he has moved on all fronts in order to convince his own people and the world that things can be done differently in a society that claims to be socialist. His principal weapon is *information*: under the policy of *glasnost'* (openness, or publicity), the criminal and corrupt are being exposed, dismissed and brought to trial, including individuals close to the late Leonid Brezhnev; closed pages in Soviet history are being re-opened (indeed, history examinations were cancelled in 1988 since the available textbooks were so economical with the truth compared with what had by now been admitted about the 1930s); old towns and streets are shedding their recently acquired names of now-dead leaders; the economy is being opened up to private and foreign enterprise, with the prospect of a market supplementing the planning system, if not replacing it completely; the political structures are being re-designed, and the party is being induced to modify its overbearing, interfering supervisory role *vis-à-vis* other institutions.

Already the Soviet Union appears superficially very different from the way it looked half a decade ago, and certainly far different from what anyone in the West would have predicted when Gorbachëv came to power. The freedom given to the mass media to report diverse facts and express virtually heretical opinions has captured the imagination of Soviet citizens and the rest of the world. This process reached a peak at the end of June 1988, when a party conference—the nineteenth, and the first to be held since 1941—met to discuss the democratization of the Soviet system. Political argument came out into the open, with delegates attacking and defending ideas, and indeed one another, raising points from the body of the hall, and even criticizing the General Secretary and calling for the retirement of elderly members of the leadership. All of this was fully covered in the press and on radio and television, which made this the most exciting political event for more than half a century.

Quite clearly, the Soviet Union is in a state of transition. It is possible to gain a reasonable picture of what it is moving from—although even there, new evidence is appearing in abundance to supplement with detail the general outlines as they have been perceived in the past. What is not yet clear is what the ultimate goal is—or whether such a goal has been clearly identified by Gorbachëv and his colleagues. Talk of 'democratization', of 'socialist pluralism of opinions', and of the creation of a 'socialist *Rechtsstaat*' (state based on law: *pravovoe gosudarstvo* in Russian) needs to be filled with content before we can make reliable judgements about the nature of the post-Brezhnevite Soviet Union.

There is certainly a good deal of movement, and still more rhetoric, some of it remarkably eloquent. Yet the tasks that face Gorbachëv, his colleagues in the leadership, and indeed the whole country, are substantial—some would say formidable—and their resolution is already proving more difficult than some imagined when the new leadership took over. In the remainder of this book, some of the dimensions of the task will be elaborated.

2 Social Structure

The Social Structure: an Overview

In this century, the Soviet Union has undergone a transformation of its social structure on an unseen scale and at an unprecedented pace. The Russian Empire, with its mainly agrarian economy augmented by a small amount of state-sponsored industry in a few cities, has been transformed into one of the world's industrial states—technically lagging behind the advanced capitalist countries of North America and Western Europe, but in world terms one of the richest, its wealth based on industrial production.

The political turmoil that accompanied and stimulated the economic development is well known, and has already been outlined. There is much scope for legitimate argument as to whether the political regime of 'Stalinism' was necessary for the economic turn-round (see Nove, 1964). What is indisputable is that a social upheaval of equally devastating impact was an integral part of this economic development. For whereas economic growth, even at a rapid pace, can be accomplished in a variety of *political* circumstances (witness the cases of Japan or West Germany in the post-Second World War period, compared with the Soviet experience), similar economic development is unthinkable without radical *social* change. The broad social structure of the Soviet Union has been almost completely reversed in the period since the industrialization drive began, with the decline of the peasantry, and the rise of the industrial working class and the administrative-managerial-professional groups in society. The traditional rural community has declined and been replaced by a fundamentally urban society.

As a backdrop to these changes in social structure there have been demographic developments.

Population Trends

The Soviet Union has exhibited a complex and dynamic population development, reflecting both the benefits of welfare improvements made possible by socio-economic progress and also some of the calamitous political events that the country has endured. The first and the clearest trend has been one of population *expansion*, partly associated with the incorporation of new territories, but mainly resulting from improved sanitation, living conditions and health care. In 1913 the population of the Russian Empire stood at 159.2 million; in 1939, the Soviet Union (which then excluded the three Baltic states of Lithuania, Latvia and Estonia, plus Moldavia and the Western Ukraine) had a population of 190.7 million; by 1959, inside the country's present borders there resided 208,826,650 persons; and by the time of the population census of 17 January 1979, this had grown to 262,463,227; the latest available figure, which relates to 12 January 1989, is 286.7 million (figures from *Chislennost' i sostav*, 1984, p. 6; and, for 1989, *Pravda*, 23 April 1989).

However, this expansionary trend has not been steady. Famine in 1921 led to some 5 million deaths, and millions more died in the widespread famine of twelve years later; the Second World War is officially estimated to have cost 20 million Soviet lives; and Stalin's harsh regime not only directly eliminated unknown millions, but also so disrupted social life that the reproduction rate fell markedly. Kerblay (1983, p. 26) notes a population shortfall of some 16.7 million in January 1937 compared with the projection made only five years earlier. Moreover, these various blows at the population fell unevenly. In particular, the Second World War hit young men especially severely, causing an 'inverted bulge' in the birth-rate in the late 1940s which has had a long-term impact on the population structure; that war, and the effects of the purges of the 1930s (which hit men harder than women), have led to an excess of females over males that has had a marked social impact in the past half-century.

A further characteristic feature of Soviet demographic trends is a decline in the rate of population expansion in the past quarter-century. As the figures given above indicate, the Soviet population continues to grow; but the rate of growth is much lower than a generation ago.

Women are having fewer children, particularly in the urbanizec western areas. There the nuclear family of parents plus one or, at most two children has become the norm, replacing the traditional extendec family. Newly-weds, especially in towns, nowadays prefer to set u their own home, and tolerate living with their parents only as temporary measure (Solov'ev, 1981, pp. 11–12). A Soviet scholar severa years ago identified 79.2 per cent of urban and 79.9 per cent of rura families as being of the nuclear type (Dzarasova, in Valentei, 1979 pp. 40–1), a slightly unexpected balance that reflects the urban housin shortage. The various pressures created—lack of space, competin demands on limited income resources, the absence of an availabl child-minder in the form of a grandparent—have led to a marke decline in the average family size. This stood at 4.1 persons (parents an children) in 1939, fell to 3.7 in the 1959 and 1970 censuses, and furthe declined to 3.5 by 1979; the equivalent figures for the urban populatio were 3.6, 3.5 and 3.3, while for their rural counterparts they were 4.3 3.9 and 3.8, indicating a similar trend in both urban and rural area According to the 1970 census figures, 35.4 per cent of familie contained one child, 26.4 had two, 17 per cent had three or mor children, and 21.2 per cent were childless (census figures quoted i Solov'ev, 1981, p. 11).

This is not the whole story, since there are sharp region variations, bearing an ethnic and cultural dimension, and posin serious difficulties for the government's economic and soci planners, and perhaps implying political consequences in the ne century. In brief, the steep decline in the birth-rate that directl influences the long-term population growth has occurred mainly i the *urbanized, European* parts of the country—specifically wester Russia, the Ukraine, Belorussia and the Baltic region. In those area the birth-rate stands at some 14–16 per thousand which, with death-rate now more or less stabilized, leads to a rate of populatio increase little above zero, with actual decline forecast for some par unless the trend is reversed. By contrast, the largely rural areas Central Asia and the Caucasus, populated in large measure by peopl of Muslim stock, ethnically, linguistically and culturally unrelated t the Russians and other Europeans, have been experiencing wh amounts to a population explosion, with birth-rates of over 30 p thousand in Tadzhikistan, Turkmenia and Uzbekistan (see Feshbach, 1982, p. 17, Table 4).

This change in fertility is reflected in trends in family size in the different republics. At the extremes, we find that in Belorussia, an average family size of 3.7 members in 1959 reduced to 3.6 in 1970 and 3.3 in 1979; in Russia the respective figures were 3.6, 3.6 and 3.3; in Lithuania 3.5, 3.4 and 3.3; and in Modavia 3.8, 3.8 and 3.4—a very sharp decrease in the 1970s; in the Central Asian republics, by contrast, the trend was the opposite: Uzbekistan registered an increase from 4.6 persons in 1959 to 5.3 in 1970 and 5.5 in 1979; Turkmenia showed an increase from 4.5 to 5.2 and 5.5; and Tadzhikistan, with an average family size of 4.7 in 1959, had boosted this to 5.4 by 1970 and 5.7—the largest of all—by the end of the decade. In Estonia, the most urbanized and industrialized republic, the average family size had already stabilized by 1959 at 3.1 persons—below the replacement fertility rate (figures from Golod, 1984, p. 12, Table 1).

Possible explanations for these patterns include the lingering influence of Islamic values, particularly in matters of the social position of women and relations between the sexes, the lower educational standards and even the lesser availability of birth control information and materials, since those are relatively underdeveloped societies, that still have much in common with neighbouring states rather than with the more modernized and 'sophisticated' parts of the USSR.

However, the observed trend may also be associated with industrialization and its accompanying changes in social roles, psychology, educational experiences and private and public values. Thus, Rein Taagepera (1969) argued that the sheer fact of urbanization accounted in large measure for the changing fertility pattern as it spread across Western Europe from France to Scandinavia and into the Baltic states (now the Baltic republics of the USSR) before the Second World War, reaching parts of Eastern Europe in the late 1950s, and extending into Russia in the 1960s.

Taagepera observed a creeping tendency towards a decrease in family size, as couples took advantage of both changing mores and greater awareness and availability of birth control techniques (including abortion on a wide scale, when this was legally available) to restrict the number of children in favour of consumer goods, an enriched cultural life or other perceived benefits of the urban environment. In the traditional rural way of life, children were regarded as necessary for the maintenance and preservation of the family unit; in urban society, by contrast, work is centred outside the home and a variety of other pursuits and interests (including the acquisition of goods) beckon the educated citizen bent on self-extension and personal fulfilment, and children are seen as competing for both the time and the limited resources of the family. This change in opportunities and values has not yet reached the more 'backward' areas of Central Asia. However, an early benefit of the modernization process, and one particularly in tune with the official ethic of the Soviet Union, is the improved social welfare provision, in the shape of clean water, better nutrition, improved health care and safety legislation. This has the social impact of dramatically reducing the death-rate—notably among infants—and extending life expectancy, so that more citizens live into old age, and more young people grow up to have children. Soviet Central Asia reached this stage of development in the 1950s and 1960s; it has not yet absorbed the change in values—the preference for consumption, in a variety of forms, over the traditional value placed on children as indicators of fertility and wealth, or as the guarantee of comfort in old age.

Whatever the explanations of these disparate trends, the effect is to face the planners with complex tasks in matching the regime's aspirations to the population (see below). Moreover, no matter how this complex task is to be resolved, current trends imply a significant shift in the population distribution, in favour of the warm south and to the detriment of the old heartlands of Russia, away from Europe to Asia. This is a present reality. For a Soviet government that is, after all, the inheritor of the Russian Empire, and is still run largely by (if not for) Russians and their Slavic brethren, the Ukrainians and the Belorussians, the prospects must be fraught with anguish. It is clearly a problem of a profound and long-term nature that the new generation of Soviet leaders has inherited from its predecessors.

The Historical Inheritance

The Bolsheviks inherited from tsarist Russia a peasant society. The bulk of the population consisted of peasant families, living in villages, raising their crops and livestock mainly for their own consumption, and producing small surpluses to satisfy their modest needs or the products of industry—clothing, perhaps, and candles, kerosene, galvanized buckets or enamel bowls; to hire the services of specialists—the miller, the wheelwright, the farrier or the shoemaker; or to pay their tax obligations to the state in cash or kind.

The family was the basic economic and social unit, its way of life largely unchanged for generations. Life was hard and poor. As a unit, the family possessed all the skills needed in running the domestic economy, passed on down the generations. All members of the family unit were involved in production, with the division of labour traditionally established according to age and sex, the work pattern determined by the needs of the farm, the rhythm of life imposed by the seasons and the weather, to some extent by inclination and to a greater degree by habit. A primitive, fatalistic attitude towards life accompanied near-universal illiteracy, compensated for by wiliness and the accumulated wisdom of generations past. Social intercourse was limited, and the notion of the family's self-reliance hindered the development of class consciousness. Marx's contemptuous, dismissive words about the French peasants as forming a class 'much as potatoes in a sack form a sack of potatoes', and as 'the class that represents barbarism within civilisation' could well be applied to Russia (quoted from Shanin, 1971, pp. 229–31).

Towns were essentially administrative and market centres, rather than the location for industrial production. The rural market town bore little resemblance to the industrial city familiar in the late-nineteenth and twentieth centuries (or earlier in those countries that had previously experienced the industrial revolution). The merchant, the state administrator, the baker, the doctor, the lawyer: these were familiar figures in the Russian city, who occasionally made sallies into the rural hinterland but who otherwise scarcely came into contact with the mass of the people. The peasants would travel to the towns for fairs, and occasionally to engage in business with the professional groups. But in general, town and the country remained separate worlds.

The Church, as an institution, to some extent bridged the gap, its priests serving in country villages and town alike, representatives of both religious authority and temporal power, since the Orthodox Church had been subject to state control since the time of Peter the Great.

Finally, there were the aristocracy and the court, marginal to society in numerical terms, but wielding enormous power as landowners and political figures, as patrons, as military officers—and as oppressors of the masses. From the late-eighteenth century, increasingly cultured and educated in West European traditions, they had spawned the Russian intelligentsia, characterized by a dedication to ideas, but often devoid of the capacity for effective action.

In pre-revolutionary Russia, therefore, the village community was substantially isolated, its contact with the towns interrupted by snow in winter, and by rain and floods from the thawing snow in autumn and spring, when the dirt-track became axle-deep in mud and impassable. Fairs brought rare opportunities for the peasants to trade their surplus produce, and to sell the fruits of their long winter indoors: carved and painted wooden spoons and bowls, woven willow baskets and carpet-beaters, and home-fermented wine and illicitly distilled spirit. The village had been accustomed to the occasional visit by state inspectors (witness the plays of Gogol, notably *Revizor*, or 'The Inspector-General'), but for long periods it was cut off—remote both physically and politically from the centres of authority, trade, commerce, education and culture, and largely unaffected by their influence.

This was what the Bolsheviks hoped to fashion into a model communist society—and less promising material could scarcely be imagined. It was almost totally lacking in the skills and attitudes modern industrial society requires.

Almost—but not quite. In the last two decades of the nineteenth century an interesting phenomenon of Russian society had been the migrant worker: the peasant who, freed from his legal tie to the land by the 1861 Act of Emancipation, chose to travel to the growing industrial towns, there earning handsome wages in the winter, and returning to the village in time for the spring sowing season. Along with the high earnings to be got in the cities, these migrants also picked up some of the values, skills and attitudes of the urban dwellers alongside whom they worked, and transmitted these to the rural areas. This had stimulated a wave of permanent migrants to the cities in the boom period of the 1890s and there were still after the First World War many rural dwellers who had personal contacts with the members of the new urban population. This ambivalent status had its impact on the working class; but it meant that significant numbers of peasants had acquired at least some contact with the urban way of life, and might be induced to adopt it permanently.

Until the Emancipation in 1861, industrial development had been severely hampered by the lack of surplus labour for recruitment into the towns. The serfs were legally tied to the estates on which they were born, except when released by the landowner. The conversion of the serfs into a free peasantry made possible their hiring for industrial jobs. Inevitably some became permanent migrants, swelling an urban population of about 3.4 million in the mid-nineteenth century to triple that number by 1914 (Bater, 1980, pp. 15–16). These formed the core of the Russian working class, on which the Bolsheviks and other Marxists placed their hopes of revolution at the beginning of this century.

In the first decade the flow of peasants decreased, and this working class consolidated its position and began to acquire the attributes of a proletariat, distinct from the displaced peasantry it had been in the previous period. This consolidation, and with it a growing class consciousness, was facilitated by certain features of industrial organization in pre-revolutionary Russia. First, the bulk of Russian industrial capacity was located in a relatively small number of centres, notably St Petersburg (the capital), Moscow, Odessa, Nizhnii Novgorod (now Gorky), Kiev and Lodz (in Poland, at that time incorporated into the Russian Empire). Secondly, partly a function of the scope of state sponsorship and partly to do with the involvement of foreign capital, investment was often in large plants employing hundreds or even thousands of workers (compared with the pioneer countries in the industrial revolution, where scores of small, family-owned factories were the norm). These factors both tended to concentate the workforce, a feature enhanced by the worker estates of barrack-like housing, typical of the Russian industrial urban scene. These conditions helped the party's 'professional revolutionaries' in educating and organizing large numbers of workers relatively easily, whether through political Sunday schools in the main centres, or through planting party 'cells' in places of work.

Even so, on the eve of the First World War the industrial working class comprised no more than 11 million workers and their families, amounting to a mere 7 per cent of the total population of the Empire. Moreover, following the revolution, many thousands of the newest recruits deserted their adopted milieu and returned to the villages to take advantage of the fresh legislation that appeared to give the peasants the right to the land, thereby dramatically revealing where their hearts and their class consciousness lay. Under the New Economic Policy introduced in 1921, the peasantry re-established its dominant position, quickly displaying the qualities of economic independence and entrepreneurial initiative that the more successful among them—dubbed the *kulaks*—had manifested following the Emancipation. Lenin's political faith in *smychka* or alliance between worker and peasant, between town and village, between industry and agriculture, quickly dissolved, and the social structure of the infant Soviet Union showed little sign of movement in the desired direction. It was in these conditions that Stalin launched his 'revolution from above' in the late 1920s, attempting to force the rate of socio-economic change.

Table 2.1 Class structure of Soviet society, 1928–82 (per cent)

	1928	1939	1959	1970	1979	1982
Workers	12.4	33.7	50.2	57.4	60.0	60.9
Intelligentsia and office workers	5.2	16.5	18.1	22.1	25.1	25.8
Collective farmers and artisans	2.9	47.2	31.4	20.5	14.9	13.3
Individual peasants and artisans	74.9	2.6	0.3	—	—	—
Merchants and rich peasants	4.6	—	—	—	—	—

Source: A. Amvrosov, *The Social Structure of Soviet Society*, p. 29; *The USSR in Figures for 1982* p. 15.

The scale and pace of change brought about as a result of these continuing policies can be seen in the statistics for the class structure of

Soviet society at various dates, shown in Table 2.1. Although there are a number of definitional problems with the class categories employed in the official analysis (particularly the inclusion of state farm workers in the working class), these figures do show the broad shift that has taken place in the socio-economic structure. By 1987 the workers' share had risen to 61.8 per cent, and that of the peasants had fallen to 12.0 per cent (*Naselenie SSSR 1987*, p. 107).

The industrialization drive required a radical extension of the range and level of skills available in society: a raising of the general educational level, plus training in specific skills. An industrial society needs *skilled* workers, specialists, as well as mere muscle power, and the higher the technological level of the economy, the greater the demand for mental rather than manual skills. In addition, modern industrial production requires the presence of a further type of specialist: individuals with administrative or managerial skills, for whom mental training is vital. Intermediate skills—such as those of office secretaries or (increasingly) data-processing equipment operators—also become of greater relevance as the administration expands and adopts modern techniques. The development of Soviet society has involved the training of a new working class, with the manual skills appropriate for that, and a new intelligentsia, comprising managers, administrators and educators, scientists and engineers. These groups were created by refashioning the existing society, so there has taken place a drastic reduction of the peasantry, and the transformation of its remnants into a different social entity.

The Peasantry

The peasantry, the backbone of imperial Russian society, was a cause of great anguish for the Bolsheviks. In the mid-nineteenth century Herzen, and later the Populists, had envisaged developing agrarian socialism based on the peasants' village commune, the *obshchina* or *mir*. Even Marx and Engels, when directly asked about the prospects for this (in the light of their preference for industrial socialism), were somewhat non-commital, and did not rule it out in certain circumstances. After all, on several historic occasions, the Russian peasantry had demonstrated a capacity for rebellion, as under the leadership of

Stenka Razin in the seventeenth century and Pugachëv in the eighteenth. However, by the end of the nineteenth century the prospects for this had evaporated: capitalism, industrialization and urbanization had already developed too far, and Russia was suffering the booms and slumps of the business cycle. So Lenin and his colleagues could with equanimity push for a proletarian revolution, although duly recognizing the social, economic and potentially political importance of the peasants.

But ideology could not alter the facts of Russia's social structure. As a distinguished observer expressed it, 'It is natural to think of the Russian as a peasant' (Maynard, 1962, p. 31); and, indeed, even some of the most typically Russian names bore peasant connotations (Gerhart, 1974, pp. 28–9). They constituted some three-quarters of the population, and were characterized by poverty, illiteracy, social and cultural backwardness, a primitive way of life, superstition and religious beliefs, political inexperience and other features unattractive to a group that hoped to build a society based on Marx's ideas. They were, moreover, divided into groups along virtual class lines, the more successful (often merely because they possessed better land) growing wealthy at the expense of the less fortunate, who in significant numbers were obliged to work for their more prosperous neighbours. An intermediate group—the 'middle peasants'—scraped by comfortably (although comfort was and is a relative term). The period of the New Economic Policy, from 1921 on, exacerbated these differences, with the so-called *nepmen* able and willing to exploit the revived opportunities for profit-making. These became the kulaks against whom Stalin waged an offensive a decade later, with the slogan, 'Eliminate the kulaks as a class'. They were, in a real sense, the mainstay of Soviet agriculture, the successful farmers on whom the country needed to rely for its food supply, but whose entrepreneurial proclivities conflicted with the regime's ideological goals.

By the early 1930s, the privately farming peasantry had indeed been 'destroyed as a class', and the vast majority were enrolled as collective farmers (*kolkhozniki*). They were deemed now to be in a different social class, differing from other classes not only by their occupation in farming (a social role shared with *state farm workers*), but also by their distinct property relations. In law, ownership of the means and products of the production process—seeds, equipment, farm buildings, the produce of their labour (although not the land, which is state-owned)—was no longer private, in the name of the individual peasant household, but collective through the collective farm or *kolkhoz*. This is still the official position. This element in the definition has been enhanced since 1958, when under Khrushchev the state-run Machine-Tractor Stations (MTS), hitherto responsible for holding heavy agricultural implements—combine-harvesters, balers, heavy tractors and ploughs and the like—and providing services to the collective farms, were abolished and the kolkhozy themselves were given the right to own such equipment. This distinction is, of course, essentially legal, rather than sociological, although the collective pattern in ownership and production has undoubtedly brought about significant changes to rural society.

The peasant of the traditional Russian countryside, so romanticized by Leo Tolstoy and other nineteenth-century writers, has all but disappeared in economic and social terms (see I. Hill, 1975). Even so, it does not seem fanciful to suggest that the peasant mentality and 'culture' are still alive, and may be witnessed in the collective farmers' markets in any sizeable town and city. There, the men, unshaven for half a week and dressed in shiny, baggy suits and enormous caps (or, in winter, fur-lined hats with ear-flaps, quilted jackets and knee-length boots, perhaps the old felt *valenki*), and the women in heavy shawls or headscarves and gaudy flower-print dresses, appear to have changed very little over the decades of Soviet power. Indeed, as they sell their produce at over-the-odds prices compared with the state food stores, they are engaging in the quintessentially peasant form of trade. In fact, there is much evidence of a continuing attachment to the land, in the form of the small plot on which the collective farmers may produce for their own use or for sale (see Kerblay, 1983, pp. 104–5). And it is the peasantry, and particularly the women, that still most strongly adheres to the Russian Orthodox Church, flocking regularly to church services, and displaying religious icons on the walls of their cottages.

Socially and economically, however, the collective farm peasant is a world apart from his true peasant ancestors. The peasantry proper is a pre-industrial social entity, and in the Soviet Union, as elsewhere, it has both dwindled in numbers and adapted in quality as the nature of society shifted from agrarian to industrial. The peasantry represented a *mode of production* now superseded following the advent of superior technology, industrially produced but applied to revolutionize agriculture; it also represented a *way of life* that cannot be accommodated with the new technology, whose operation requires skills and disciplines that cannot be adequately gained within the peasant family unit. Modern agriculture relies on machines and equipment, uses chemicals in pest control and as fertilizers, applies scientific breeding and processing techniques, and—most significantly—produces for sale to an external (i.e. urban) population rather than for direct consumption by the producers: it is far removed from the traditional lifestyle of the peasantry. Hence, Soviet commentators are quite correct to point out that the 'collective farm peasantry' differs from the traditional peasantry, and also from the private farmers in other countries.

According to official statistics, private peasants still constituted 2.6 per cent of the population in 1939; this had reduced to 0.3 per cent by the time of the 1959 population census, and had been eliminated by 1970. As the figures in Table 2.1 show, the collective farm peasantry has also been in clear decline, in both share of the population and absolute numbers. Calculations based on official figures reveal that there were some 92 million peasants in 1939 and only about 36 million in 1982. This decline is absolutely clear, and is a necessary concomitant of industrialization.

In Soviet eyes, this has been more than compensated for by qualitative changes. It was claimed that rural illiteracy had been reduced from over three-quarters in 1897 to just 16 per cent at the end of the 1930s (see figures in *Naselenie SSSR*, 1980, p. 18). Education at primary and secondary level has likewise been expanded into the rural areas, and some collective farmers have been given special skills as animal workers, machine operators or agronomists, and others have acquired expertise in modern management methods—accountancy and bookkeeping, for example. There remain those with a very low general educational standard—the unskilled fieldhands close to the bottom of the occupational prestige hierarchy (see below).

Other important factors lead to social distinctions within the peasantry, notably those that affect their economic success. As well as proving vitally important in the general performance of Soviet agriculture, the private plot remains a significant source of supplementary income for all peasant households, and it is frequently made the wife's domain, while the regular work on the collective fields is performed by the males. However, the successful exploitation of this asset is not evenly distributed. Some peasants are more energetic or efficient than others in producing crops that command high market prices; the vagaries of climate and soil conditions likewise affect yields and the profitability of the enterprise. Possibly even more significant, the proximity of an accessible town, in which to sell the produce for cash, to spend on the goods and services provided there, can markedly affect the consequent return on such private effort (see Matthews, 1972, pp. 164–7).

In his proposals to reform the economy, Mikhail Gorbachëv intends to encourage family-based leasehold farming, following the approach adopted under NEP almost seven decades ago, in order to capitalize on the peasant's essentially emotional relationship with the land and his way of life. The expectation is that this will encourage diligence and, presumably, therefore foster greater output. If successfully applied on a wide scale, it would bring about a change in the class structure, with a revival of the category of individual farmer. It will also probably lead to greater social distinctions within the rural population.

For twenty years or more, it has been officially recognized that rural living standards, measured by the provision and accumulation of goods and services, lagged significantly behind those of most urban dwellers. Indeed, the 'elimination of the essential differences between town and country' was posited as a major social policy goal. Khrushchev attempted to solve the problem by creating *agrogoroda* (agro-cities), in which farmers would enjoy an essentially urban life-style. That idea was stillborn, but from 1965 massive investments in the agricultural sphere included money for better housing, improved health and education establishments, road connections with towns, more and better-stocked shops, services such as travelling hairdressers, cleaners and repair facilities for household goods, libraries, cinemas and other leisure amenities. The intention was in part to encourage the better-trained young to remain in their villages as collective farmers, raising the quality of the rural workforce and indirectly stimulating village cultural standards.

The results have been patchy, and there remains a massive gulf between the typical collective farmer's living standard and that of his urban counterpart, the industrial worker.

The Working Class

In contrast to the peasantry, the rapidly expanding working class has enjoyed tremendous prestige as the class that was supposedly leading towards the communist future, and on whose behalf the system is supposed to have been created. As one distinguished scholar expressed it, 'the [Soviet] political regime has based its claims to legitimacy for more than 50 years on the declaration that it represents the aspirations and interests of the working class' (Arcadius Kahan, in Kahan and Ruble, 1979, p. ix). The working class's 'leading position in the system of socialist social relations', according to one popular account, 'is determined by its revolutionary spirit, good discipline and organization and its sense of collectivism. *The leading role of the working class shapes the course of history* . . .' (Amvrosov, 1978, p. 71; original emphasis).

The Soviet working class has grown enormously in the process of economic development, and its share of the work-force continues to expand (see Table 2.1). By the early 1980s, it stood at some 165 million, or 60.9 per cent of the population (figure derived from *SSSR v tsifrakh*, 1983, pp. 7, 15).

In fact, the general pattern of social change in this century has been such that the peasants' loss has been the workers' gain, since the peasantry formed the pool from which the expanding industrial working class was recruited, and substantially still is. In this the Soviet Union is not unique. Western Europe experienced that pattern in the eighteenth and nineteenth centuries, when displaced peasants and agricultural labourers left for the towns and became the first proletarians; as noted above, in pre-revolutionary Russia this was an express aim of the Emancipation of 1861.

According to the 1979 census, there were 157,122,843 members of the working class in the Soviet Union, or 60.0 per cent of the population; somewhat over 106 million of these lived in towns and cities, and they made up 65.3 per cent of the urban population. These figures include dependants (spouses, children), since there were slightly fewer than 81 million workers among the employed population (60.0 per cent), or 56.9 million employed urban workers (63.7 per cent) (figures from *Vestnik statistiki*, 1981, no. 1, pp. 66–7).

It should be repeated here that Soviet accounts use the concept of 'working class' to include *state farm workers*, who stand in the same relationship to the means of production as industrial workers: they are all employees of the state, which owns the means of production and pays them a wage in return for their labour power. Official figures report 9,780,000 'workers' employed in agriculture in 1982 (*SSSR v tsifrakh*, 1983, pp. 164–5). Moreover, their numbers are increasing (they stood at under 8 million in 1965), partly the result of administrative measures, as collective farms are reorganized as state farms. Their whole lifestyle and occupation are fundamentally different from those of the industrial proletariat, with whom they share less than with the collective farm peasantry. The following discussion will concentrate on the *industrial* working class, which has come to be dominant in the numerical sense: at the time of the 1979 census, it stood at approximately 134 million, or 51.3 per cent of the population—by far the largest class category in the official analysis (figures in *Vestnik statistiki*, 1981, no. 1, pp. 66–7).

They provide the labour for the mines, the industrial plants, the factories, the transport system, the power-generating installations, the construction enterprises, the distribution network and everything else on which twentieth-century material wealth depends. Moreover, since Soviet industry lags behind the advanced capitalist countries in its technical level, that country still depends rather more on the energy of human beings performing largely traditional tasks: the age of the industrial robot and the silicon chip has barely dawned in Soviet industry. Hence, there are still many millions of Soviet workers engaged in activity recognizable as *industrial labour* even to the founding fathers of Marxism-Leninism: miners, construction workers, loaders, train crews and others, all of whom, although perhaps working with rather more sophisticated equipment and materials, are still primarily adding muscle power to the machine. Around half of the industrial work-force was expected to be engaged in manual tasks as late as 1980 (Kahan & Ruble, 1979, p. 8).

As observers have persistently pointed out, the decline in population growth in the country's industrialized areas seriously threatens further industrial growth by the traditional extensive methods. The rate of expansion of industrial employment declined precipitously from the mid-1960s (Feshbach, in Kahan & Ruble, 1979, p. 7), and the long-term prospects are forcing the Soviet authorities themselves to stress the intensive rather than extensive method for further economic advance: raising productivity, rather than increasing the work-force. It is already clear that, in the Soviet Union as elsewhere, the relatively unskilled segment of the working class is declining as a proportion of the workforce, and even as a proportion of the working class itself. Available figures suggest that in the first quarter-century of the industrialization drive (from 1925 to 1950) the number of skilled and highly skilled workers increased by 268.1 per cent, and that of low-skilled by 116 per cent (Foteeva, 1984, p. 84, Table 14). A more recent estimate suggests a rise of the category of 'highly skilled' from 67.9 per cent of industrial workers in 1959 to 75.2 per cent in 1975, with a commensurate decline in the low-skilled from 12.6 per cent to 10.8 per cent, and in the unskilled from 19.5 to 14.8 per cent (cited in Foteeva, 1984, p. 86, Table 15).

Moreover, the very nature of a 'highly skilled' worker's training and skill profile is changing as well. The high priority accorded to machine-building, metal-working and other defence-releated sectors (Kahan & Ruble, 1979, p. 7)—areas characterized by rapid technological advance and the application of new scientific discoveries—means there is less demand for the worker with lower skills, and the number of jobs for those possessing practically no skills is declining rapidly, although not yet eliminated. Individuals trained for the trades of fitter, turner, welder and so forth are still required in heavy industrial production, as are blast-furnace operators, train drivers and coal miners. However, today, in order to slot individual workers into the modern industrial economy, there is an increasing demand for *mental* skills: understanding of theoretical principles, the ability to make judgements on the basis of an overall view of a process. A mechanic maintaining a sophisticated assembly-line needs to possess diagnostic techniques that may involve an understanding of electronics as well as of mechanical processes. Hence, an important development affecting the internal structure of the working class is a rise in skill levels, backed up by a broader and deeper general education—reflected in the tendency to increase the period of formal schooling, now standing at eleven years (increased from ten in an educational reform in 1984 with precisely this goal in mind).

A further trend within the working class stems from the rational application of scientific management techniques to production. There is indeed a perceptible need for more highly skilled technicians (or for workers to become more like technicians); but there is also a tendency for production design to be so rationalized that rather *less* skill is required on the part of the operatives. An excellent example is the electronics assembly-line, where individual workers equipped with a soldering iron perform highly routinized tasks that require little initiative or even attention, and certainly practically no education to speak of. The rapid expansion of these industries in Third World Asian countries in the past twenty years demonstrates the point; but a similar tendency can be observed elsewhere, including the Soviet Union.

Hence, different trends can be identified. On the one hand, the general educational and specific skill levels are rising, in response to the needs of an industrial establishment experiencing the 'scientific and technological revolution'. Individuals are acquiring a much broader general education than hitherto, which has the effect of enriching their potential for enjoying the benefits of cultural life, and perhaps also for more effective *political* involvement. On the other hand, the same 'scientific and technological revolution' is so rationalizing production processes—at its ultimate, by mechanizing and automating functions traditionally performed by workers—that skills are largely redundant. The psychological implications of this trend, with potentially damaging social consequences, are beyond the scope of this book (but, it should be noted, have not escaped the notice of far-sighted Soviet observers). A consequence of interest to social scientists—and equally to the Kremlin's ideologists—is the change being wrought in the Soviet working class itself.

These fragmentary tendencies led Alex Pravda (1982) to ask whether it is now appropriate to speak of a Soviet 'working class' at all, except as an important political myth that 'must be kept separate from the working class as social reality' (p. 1; see also Kahan & Ruble, 1979,

p. 316). It is not simply Western critics bent on undermining confidence in the Soviet ideology who have been making these points, he notes, but Soviet social scientists, themselves loyal Communist Party members as well as scholars of integrity. The picture that has emerged, says Pravda, is one 'in which stratifications by skills, education, income, and cultural attributes within and across class divisions assume greater salience than class distinctions themselves' (p. 2).

On the basis of a thorough examination of Soviet writings on the topic (some of them also surveyed by Yanowitch, 1977, and edited in English translation by Yanowitch & Fisher, 1973), Pravda identifies distinctions between the working class and other social groups, and also within the working class, according to skill levels, levels of income and various other forms of remuneration (housing provision, cafeterias, health care, etc.), consumption patterns, educational levels, prestige rankings and finally class and group identification. Pravda concludes that the 'old' or traditional working class, relatively poor and disadvantaged in terms of education and status, still exists alongside the 'new' working class, whose skill, education and status levels bring them closer to the technicians ('engineering-technical workers', or ITRs, in the Soviet jargon), but whose greater awareness makes them less satisfied with their (rather better) lot, and therefore alienates them from the official version of 'the working class'. The 'new' working class uses the technical, managerial and professional groups as its reference point, rather than its 'old' working-class brothers, thereby weakening working-class solidarity while simultaneously challenging the social and economic status quo.

More generally, the Soviet working class shows signs of internal development at odds with the official mythology. This states that there are no objective reasons for disaffection leading to industrial or other protest, since the property relations in Soviet society have eliminated antagonistic interests. In fact, in addition to the growing disparities between workers with different skill levels, some groups of workers have displayed dissatisfaction with the managerial and administrative group. Labour disputes have been occurring for many years, and their incidence seems to have increased of late (see below). So far, the pressures have been contained; but it seems unlikely that the government can resist indefinitely the implications of the long-term trend towards a better educated, industrially (and, increasingly, politically) experienced working class, with rising self-confidence and growing expectations, born in part of the regime's own rhetoric.

The Soviet working class today is already very different from the 'horny-handed sons of toil' whom Marx, Engels and Lenin had in mind as they developed their theories, and the trend must continue, with possibly serious consequences if the regime does not adjust and amend its own rhetoric and political practices. The British Labour Party's problems in finding an appropriate identity in the 1980s are identical to those likely to be faced by the Soviet leadership by the end of the century.

Such a feature of modern working-class life has obvious implications for the notion of class consciousness, a question about which little is known for certain, since it is essentially out of bounds for investigation by Soviet scholars. It is possible, however, to speculate, and Walter D. Connor (in Kahan & Ruble, 1979, pp. 313–32) has produced a very plausible conjecture. He points to the continuous dilution of the ranks of workers by peasant migration, on the one hand, and by the creaming-off of the most advanced workers through promotion to supervisory, managerial or bureaucratic positions, on the other. In addition, the regime dissuaded the development of institutions that would foster class solidarity, creating instead a class-transcendent loyalty to the system (symbolized by Stalin in the 1930s and 1940s). The values of loyalty to a system that provides order, security, welfare and a standard of living that until very recently was steadily and perceptibly rising are shared among practically all sectors of Soviet society, and are not the prerogative of the working class alone; nor is the 'apolitical' political culture. Furthermore, the legitimation by the regime of the desire to rise out of the working class must have done much to undermine class-consciousness and pride (p. 322). Patterns of delinquency and deviance may suggest that the working class does not mentally associate itself with those who control the system—and may also indicate a reciprocal suspicion on the part of the 'leaders' (pp. 324–6; see also Connor, 1972, for a fuller examination of this question). Yet these are slender pieces of evidence of working-class consciousness, and Connor saw little likelihood that this would change, either through a process of politicization led by the intelligentsia, or through disenchantment with the country's economic performance.

That may have changed, however, under Gorbachëv, under the policy of *glasnost'*, which involves giving publicity to negative features of the system and permitting groups of citizens to express their dissatisfactions. The frustrations at continuing shortages of food and manufactured goods surfaced in speeches to the party conference in the summer of 1988, and have been addressed to Gorbachëv in person on his visits to different parts of the country. Moreover, with the establishment of individual and co-operative economic and business enterprises since the early summer of 1987, there is a growing division within the working class, with a revival of the attitudes of the 'nepmen' of the 1920s: a tendency to exploit shortages by profiteering, causing widespread resentment among their customers and clients. This is the latest form of divergence of interest within the working class, augmenting those caused by developing stratification which already affect individuals' social and political attitudes.

This is a development not foreseen by the official ideologists, for whom it poses certain difficulties. The myth of the working class remains an important element in the regime's ideological underpinnings, even though the practice that has evolved over the years of Soviet power, and the distribution of power and privilege that has grown up with it, has diverged from what certainly many in the West—including especially socialists—see as appropriate in a socialist society. How these trends are perceived and interpreted, as positive or negative, depends to some extent on the view adopted of the non-working-class, non-peasant element in society, known in Russian as the *intelligentsia.*

The Intelligentsia

The concept of intelligentsia originated in nineteenth-century Russia, and referred to those critical thinkers who lived by their brain power, often after education in Western Europe. Not quite congruent with the English idea of 'intellectuals', they at least shared the broad intellectual horizons, the curiosity about ideas in a wide field of mental endeavour, that are the best quality of informed thinking persons. They are clearly not peasants or workers, who earn their livelihood from *physical* labour; nor are they aristocratic landowners or bourgeois bankers or merchants, living on the basis of trade, rent or interest. In

Soviet usage, the concept has been broadened to include practically all who primarily use the mind rather than the muscles. Hence, the term still embraces genuine intellectuals, but extends into many areas of modern society to encompass engineers, designers, managers and other administrators (including even government and party officials)—practically anyone, indeed, who cannot be neatly fitted into one or other of the two recognized classes, the collective farm peasantry and the working class.

In fact, there is considerable argument about the boundaries of this group, and this sociological question carries certain ideologically embarrassing dimensions. On a broad definition—say, including all with specialized secondary education—the intelligentsia will be identified as very large, bearing testimony to the opportunities under Soviet socialism for social advancement by the formerly oppressed classes: one recent account put the figure at 28.6 million in 1980 (Senyavskii, 1982, p. 189). However, that has the effect of reducing the size of the working class, central to the ideology and the 'leading force' in building communism. The difficulty is further exacerbated by the regime's ambivalent attitude towards intellectuals, also reflected linguistically in the existence of two Russian adjectives: *intelligentnyi*—intelligent, possessing the qualities of critical thinking of the nineteenth-century radicals; and *intelligentskii*—indecisive, weak-willed, given to fine rhetoric but incapable of action (as depicted in the character of Rudin in Turgenev's novel of that name).

The Soviet intelligentsia is said to be something different, and indeed it is a charge of latter-day Russian nationalists that the Soviet regime has, as it were, appropriated the intelligentsia and destroyed it in the process, the critical faculties that typified it in the past having been replaced by unthinking loyalty to the ideals and policies of the Communist Party of the Soviet Union.

In an attempt at an 'objective definition in the Marxist tradition', Churchward (1973) adopted the view that the intelligentsia could most properly be seen as consisting of those with higher education, those undergoing higher educational training (i.e. students in third-level institutions), and those in occupations that normally required higher educational qualifications; the category therefore included retired and non-working graduates. On that basis, Churchward computed an intelligentsia of some 10.7 million individuals in 1967, distributed as follows:

(i)	gainfully employed professionals	5,565,000
(ii)	third-level students	4,311,000
(iii)	unemployed graduates (Churchward's guess)	500,000
(iv)	military specialists (Churchward's guess)	200,000
(v)	others (Churchward's guess)	100,000

In that year, this represented some 4.55 per cent of the total population. At the present time, there are well over 20 million members of the intelligentsia on a similar definition, such has been the rate of third-level training in recent decades. In 1987, 24.3 million persons had at least partial higher education, presumably including current students (see *Naselenie SSSR 1987*, 1988, p.57).

Churchward's breakdown demonstrates the breadth of the concept, although there are limits. It is rarely, if ever, used quite so loosely as indicated by Nove (1975, p. 617), who includes 'teachers, librarians, bookkeepers, hospital nurses, shop assistants, as well as senior officials': he calls it a 'remarkably wide and socially meaningless definition'. In fact, the category to which Nove is probably referring is that of 'employees'—*sluzhashchie* in Russian—which is indeed as vague as he indicates. This point is explicitly made in a recent Soviet account (Senyavskii, 1982, pp. 186–7).

The members of the intelligentsia are not considered to constitute a class. They are recruited from the two classes that are acknowledged to exist, the peasantry and the working class, and they stand in no independent relation to the means of production: some, like workers, are employed in state enterprises (engineers, doctors, teachers); some are members of collective farms (veterinary surgeons, agronomists, etc.); others depend on royalty and fee income, and may also teach in state institutions (writers, composers). It may be inferred that education is the key to this form of social mobility in Soviet society. In fact, this has been a further characteristic feature of Soviet social history, for, alongside the rapid expansion of the working class, the process of economic development has equally entailed the expansion of the intelligentsia, particularly with the training of industrial managerial staff and administrative officers for the burgeoning state service. Churchward (1973,

p. 9) identified this as 'the most rapidly growing sector of Soviet society', and historically that expansion benefited the workers, whose upward mobility simultaneously deprived the working *class* of many of its best-skilled and politically aware members. Indeed, as Connor (in Kahan & Ruble, 1979, p. 332) expressed it, 'Communism, for all its collectivist emphasis, has legitimated individual striving', which has been expressed in the aspiration for social mobility into the intelligentsia, either within a single career or at least from one generation to the next. Socio-economic development has made this possible on an extensive scale, although it should be added that the requirement of 'redness' (ideological rectitude) as well as technical expertise has been an additional factor affecting individual cases.

A number of characteristics of the modern Soviet intelligentsia can be identified. The first is, indeed, the pace of its expansion. Compared with 1.2 million in 1939, by 1987 there were 20.8 million persons with completed higher education (*Naselenie SSSR 1987*, p. 97); in the academic year 1940–1 there were 812,000 higher education students, a figure that stood at 5,026,000 by the 1987–8 academic year (figures from *Narkhoz 1987*, p. 476).

The intelligentsia, like the working class, is also largely *urban-based*, although not exclusively so, since there has been a drive to raise the scientific level of agricultural operations and improve the cultural level in the villages. Census figures illustrate this point: in 1970, of an urban adult population (i.e. persons over 16 years old) of slightly under 100 million, 7.1 per cent had higher education, compared with 1.7 per cent of a rural adult population of somewhat over 67 million; further calculations reveal that some 86.2 per cent of those with third-level qualifications lived in towns (figures from *1970 Census*, vol. III, p. 30; percentages calculated); a similar picture emerges from the 1979 Census results. The same figures reveal that the proportion of the adult population with higher educational qualifications is a little over 5 per cent—a tiny fraction of the total population, indicating that this group's social and economic importance clearly outweighs its numerical strength.

The intelligentsia today is also a *post-revolutionary* phenomenon. More than seventy years after the revolution, it is Soviet-bred and trained; it has been brought up imbued with the values, aspirations and expectations fostered by the regime, and it owes its privileged position in society to the system of which it is a part. With the notable exception of a particular segment—the so-called 'dissident intellectuals' (see below)—the Soviet intelligentsia is a very reliable and even conformist group, whose loyalty has been courted by Gorbachëv by opening up the mass media and the arts to greater freedom of self-expression than has been available for over sixty years. Its members have much to lose in terms of social status and privilege (although not necessarily income) by rejecting the system: as a group they are an incorporated segment of society, who collectively help to shape society's further development. They—not the workers—determine the pattern of economic development, design the products and the factories in which they are made, establish the work patterns, produce cultural and intellectual artefacts to inform and entertain the masses. In this sense, perhaps, they might be seen as a ruling class—although, like the workers among whom there are disparate segments, there are clear divisions among them which may preclude applying the term 'class'.

Soviet sociologists distinguish a number of groups within the intelligentsia, which probably lack a sense of shared values, lifestyles and expectations. First is the *creative intelligentsia*, the group closest to genuine intellectuals: writers, poets, musicians, painters, philosophers, artists and the like. These have always posed a problem for the regime, since critical thinking is essential to their identity: their function is to have ideas and to present them in a challenging and perhaps entertaining way, so as to evoke a response in their audience. The lack of a tradition of intellectual freedom places this group in a politically vulnerable position, although it is the group that has gained most from Gorbachëv's policy of *glasnost'*, which has permitted a degree of liberty of expression that they have not been slow to exploit: indeed, they have been accused by more conservative politicians of using their freedom as *licence* to challenge the values of the system.

Less under threat, because it deals less in abstract ideas and more in practical matters directly relevant to economic development, is the *scientific and technical intelligentsia*, which includes engineers and technologists, together with those engaged in more basic scientific endeavour, plus industrial engineers, senior medical staff and others who might belong to the professions in a Western society. This is the fastest growing segment: there are over 12.5 million engineers and some 1.4 million scientific workers in the Soviet Union today (see Senyavskii, 1982, p. 189, for 1980 figures and comparative figures for earlier years). Even here, though, certain branches of scientific research were and are subjected to the influence of pseudo-Marxist dogma: Stalin imposed his own views on the discipline of linguistics, for example; relativity theory was long subject to an official ban; genetics was destroyed as a science under the influence of the charlatan Trofim Lysenko (to the long-term detriment of Soviet agriculture); and the social sciences in general have always been subjected to close supervision (although the latitude enjoyed by social scientists in presenting unorthodox interpretations and views fluctuates).

There is also the *administrative intelligentsia*, including administrators from Politburo members down to (perhaps) the manager of a housing list in a provincial town, as well as hospital directors, industrial managers, economic planners and persons in scores of other professions and jobs requiring higher education and conferring responsibility and a relatively high status on their occupants. The fact that these individuals are largely appointed to their positions through the mechanism of the party *nomenklatura*, with all that implies about their established status in the system, leads Nove (1975) to identify them as constituting the closest thing to a ruling class in Soviet society, a position also adopted by Voslensky (1984), but rejected by other scholars (e.g. Hirszowicz, 1976).

This group has been accused of 'bureaucratism' and identified by Gorbachëv as one of the principal social opponents of his policy of *perestroika* (restructuring the system). Under Leonid Brezhnev, it exploited its commanding position to expand its privileges and perquisites, and to cover up its crude anti-social activities, including favouritism, dishonest reporting, corruption and involvement in organized criminal activity, particularly in certain parts of the country: the Central Asian republics, Moldavia, and the city of Moscow under Viktor Grishin. Much of the political rhetoric in the late 1980s has concerned the need for administration without bureaucratism, or administrators rather than bureaucrats: in a sense, this call represents the intellectual segment of the intelligentsia attempting to define the appropriate values and ethic of the administrative segment.

In view of their advanced mental training and the social and economic positions they occupy, the members of the intelligentsia also possess far greater political influence than other social groups. Whether or not they are directly engaged in political or administrative activity, or are active as citizens in the party or other sectors of public life, as a group they are in a far stronger position to influence political outcomes than are the workers or peasants. They may not have the potential political muscle that sheer numbers give to the workers (such as the Polish working class has demonstrated on more than one occasion); but their sensitive positioning throughout Soviet society gives them more subtle ways of having their voice heard than resorting to overt pressure.

Moreover, there are clear signs that the rate of recruitment of new members of this stratum has slowed down substantially. In the light of intense competition for university places, there are now fewer opportunities for children from disadvantaged backgrounds to gain access at least to the better establishments (see Matthews, 1978, pp. 47–9; 1982, pp. 158–61). Increasingly, those who succeed academically come from intellectual families, where a supportive home environment, the ability and willingness of parents to pay for private coaching, and possibly even the ability to pull strings, can help a child outshine a less fortunate working-class or peasant competitor, who will be consigned to an inferior institution or to a course for which there is less competition. The intelligentsia, in other words, is showing signs of crystallizing out as a class, membership of which is hereditary: upward social mobility has decreased; downward social mobility is scarcely known (see Lane, 1982, ch. 4).

Under Gorbachëv, as implied above, the privileged status enjoyed by some segments of the intelligentsia has been undermined, while the position of other segments has been enhanced. The regime's relationship with the intelligentsia therefore remains a complex and ambiguous one. There is little evidence of any links between the intelligentsia and other social categories that could have serious political consequences.

Education Trends

The modernization of Soviet society obviously required the extension of educational facilities, both elementary—to give the whole population basic literacy and numeracy—and advanced, up to and including research and higher learning. The results, as revealed in official statistics, show the success attained: in 1987, 20.8 million citizens had higher education and a further 3.5 million incomplete higher (a figure that appears not to include current students), 30.9 million had specialized and 65.6 per cent general secondary education, and a further 43.6 million had acquired education beyond the primary level (*USSR '88*, p. 230); differently expressed, 125 in every 1,000 employed citizens had higher education and 764 had some degree of secondary education in the same year (*Naselenie SSSR 1987*, p. 97). By any standards this is no mean achievement in a country as backward as the Russian Empire was at the turn of the century, despite genuine doubts about the quality of the training (see, for example, Kahan & Ruble, 1979, p. 10; on Soviet education, see also Avis, 1987).

This success is a natural source of pride, and statistics are regularly published showing the improvements in the Soviet population's educational level. There is a continuing general rise in educational standards among all workers; however, particularly noteworthy is an increase in more highly educated manual workers, related to the training of more technicians, coupled with a sharp decline in the non-manual workers with incomplete secondary education: this implies also a better-trained force of office and other administrative workers.

The trend may betoken a rise in the level of sophistication and social awareness of Soviet citizens, which would have marked implications for the kinds of demands placed upon the economic and political systems: this has been recognized by Gorbachëv. However, that is not necessarily the case: there is evidence that a better educated and richer population with more leisure time makes use of its new opportunities to pursue anti-social goals. The image of a spoilt young generation, impressing its friends not by its own talents and achievements but by expensive consumer items bought at parents' expense, has been presented by leading politicians (e.g. Chernenko, speaking in June 1983). Such an image has a familiar ring to it in the light of experience in Western countries, where rising educational levels have not been accompanied by the elimination of philistinism, delinquency or similar manifestations of dissatisfaction, alienation or anomie. In the different circumstances of the Soviet Union, the appearance of drunkenness, political indifference, high labour turnover, acquisitiveness and other deplored social phenomena was in clear evidence in the mid-1970s (see, for example, G.N. Manov, writing in Tikhomirov, 1975, pp. 277–8). In recent years, along with the implementation of a severe drive against alcoholism, the Soviet press has discussed the existence of a serious problem of drug abuse, and the emergence of street gangs in Soviet cities has been given publicity (for example, Shchekochikhin, 1988; see also Riordan, 1986). This all suggests that the Soviet effort at public enlightenment has not entirely succeeded in instilling more positive and desirable attitudes, however impressive its performance in raising the level of mental and manual skills in society.

Role Differentiation

A concomitant of economic development is the changing role profile in society. By the time of the Bolshevik Revolution, there had already been some erosion of the traditional social structure. Following the Emancipation the peasantry had become increasingly polarized into rich and poor, partly reflecting their individual talents and drive, but also related to their endowment of soil and climate. The kulaks (the well-to-do peasants) took increasingly to hiring the labour of their less fortunate neighbours, who themselves bore the characteristics of a rural proletariat. These were the seasonal migrants, becoming part-worker and part-peasant, or eventually joining the permanent urban industrial labour force. They increasingly acquired industrially relevant training including elementary education—reading and writing—and lost the broad spectrum of manual skills typical of the peasantry.

The greatest impact on the social structure was naturally brought about by the vigorous and sustained industrialization drive begun in the late 1920s, involving all the forms of change typical of socio-economic development: urbanization, industrialization, migration from rural communities to old and new urban centres, decline of the peasantry, rise of the working class and the new managerial intelligentsia, rising educational levels and expansion of the professions, improving health and consequent greater longevity and reduction in infant mortality.

However, in addition to the marked change in the total social balance—from some 75 per cent of the population consisting of peasants in 1928 to 13.3 per cent in 1982; from 12.4 to 60.9 per cent workers over the same period; and from 5.2 to 25.8 per cent white-collar (see Table 2.1)—a particularly significant form of social change has been the increasing diversity in the population's occupational profile. Some social categories have virtually disappeared: there is no longer a gentry, and the Orthodox clergy are now an insignificant group, numerically and, in particular, socially and politically. But economic development has meant a proliferation of occupations and roles; specialization characterizes the Soviet form of socialist industrial society as it does advanced industrial capitalism. The utopian notions, entertained by Marx and Lenin, of multi-role citizens who would perhaps engage in an industrial occupation in the morning, work in the fields in the afternoon, and involve themselves in the administration of society at weekends, shows no sign of coming to pass. Indeed, any such development would have flown in the face of world-wide economic and social trends in the twentieth century, following in the wake of advances in science and technology that have led, almost inevitably, to a highly developed division of labour. Modern productive processes impose demands that can be met most effectively and readily by giving groups of workers highly specialist training. In addition, as each occupational group develops its particular *esprit de corps*, perhaps fostered by a trade union or professional organization (although less effectively so in the Soviet Union than in capitalist countries), so the various basic classes themselves become highly fragmented and *stratified.* The special skills required by one profession become less and less transferable to other occupations—a teacher cannot easily become a nurse; a computer specialist would have difficulty in retraining as a civil engineer; a diesel locomotive driver's skills would have to be replaced in a transfer to a modern factory job. Individuals become locked into careers according to their initial training and experience; and in an era of rapid technical change, the demanding new jobs are taken by fresh recruits to the work-force, recently trained in the latest techniques.

To repeat: these tendencies are not peculiar to the Soviet Union, but are part and parcel of a global process of technology-led industrial development that is engulfing the whole world. In this respect, as in others, the USSR is increasingly exhibiting the characteristics of an advanced industrial and urban society.

Nevertheless, the long-term goal of the leadership is to promote the development of a *socially homogeneous* society, in which social differences have been essentially eliminated (see Kerimov, 1980, pp. 53–4), and specifically in which *classes* will no longer exist, since 'classlessness' is part of the definition of communism. The question of the further development of society in such a direction continues to attract the attention of Soviet writers. The point is made that under socialism, despite the elimination of inequalities stemming from property relations, other forms of inequality continue to exist, based on differences in working and living conditions, location, sources and levels of income, and the presence or absence of facilities for personal development, all of which are associated with adherence to particular social groups (Rogovin, 1984, pp. 28–9). Indeed, the same author notes (p. 30) that differences according to the character, content and conditions of work are coming to replace class differences as a basic form of social differentiation in Soviet society. Hence, he observes (p. 31), a 'classless society' and a 'socially homogeneous society' are not identical, for even when the class differences between workers and peasants have disappeared, other forms of social differentiation—such as that between physical and mental work—will continue to exist until all differences in type of work have been eliminated. This, he concludes, 'will require significantly longer historical time-periods than the liquidation of differences between classes'.

Stratification

This increased social differentiation and diversity has led to an increasingly sophisticated system of occupational and social stratification. In the traditional hierarchy, the court and the aristocracy occupied the 'top', while the peasants—referred to contemptuously as *chërnye lyudi*, 'the black people', with all the connotations of dirt, ignorance and superstition implied by the term—were at the bottom of the social pile. The removal of the aristocratic elements from Soviet society, through civil war, execution, exile or social relocation, immediately modified the stratification of society, and the official rhetoric repudiates any notion of hierarchy in the modern Soviet Union. There is certainly social *differentiation*: a range of classes and other social groups are acknowledged to exist, as are social distinctions based on nationality and other non-occupational features. However, all social groups are said to stand equal: officially, no superiority attaches to a particular kind of occupation or to membership of specific racial or national groupings. The lines of social differentiation are said to be drawn vertically, not horizontally, so that equality of social status persists despite manifest distinctions in this complex social structure. At the same time, political rhetoric continues to give pride of place to the industrial working class, the 'builders of communism', the revolutionary class on whose behalf the whole enterprise was undertaken.

In practice, however, Soviet society is stratified hierarchically, and a lot of evidence from a variety of sources inside and outside the Soviet Union supports this assertion. Considerable attention has been paid to this question in recent years by David Lane, who challenges the notion that the attainment of 'socialism' has in any way led to 'the end of inequality' (1971, 1978, 1982). Other writers too, notably Yanowitch (1977) and A. McAuley (1979), have demonstrated the same point, and their evidence has been augmented by a major study of recent émigrés (Millar, 1987, chs 6, 9). Differences of income, prestige, working conditions and other aspects of specific occupations combine with a general social aspiration for 'improvement' within the lifetime of individuals and from one generation to the next, and this combination renders some jobs more desirable—in Orwellian terms, 'more equal'—than others. As Lane (1982, p. 152) observes, the Bolshevik Revolution successfully changed power and property relations, but 'it has not subsequently created a society ensuring the equality of men, one in which social stratification . . . is absent'.

As a general principle, occupations that demand higher skill qualifications enjoy the greater prestige. Unskilled field workers on farms are perhaps at the bottom of the social hierarchy, and those in this group aspire to become mechanized workers (say, tractor drivers or combine-harvester operators). Skilled mechanics, trained to handle, operate and service complex farm machinery, form a kind of rural working aristocracy, distinguished in a variety of ways from their class-fellows: by earnings, prestige, consumption patterns, cultural life, perhaps even social networks, and so forth. In general, however, agricultural occupations enjoy low prestige (see Lane, 1982, p. 69), and many peasants aspire to an industrial job. The unskilled industrial worker in turn hopes to acquire skills that will improve both earnings and social status, either within the working class, or in a white-collar job, or at the margins as a technician. Among the white-collar occupations, the medical profession enjoys high prestige but modest earnings, while factory managers and genuine intellectuals (professors, rather than teachers) enjoy relatively high earnings and high prestige. As Mervyn Matthews (1978, pp. 38–43) has pointed out, however, it is not so much earnings or even responsibility that make a particular job desirable, but rather a combination of these with privileged access to goods and services in short supply. From that perspective a political career, with the network of valuable social contacts that builds up around it, is attractive; but that of course requires the individual's devotion to the system, and it also bears with it a high level of risk (see Lane, 1978, pp. 404–11): there is no 'second career' for a failed politician. The earnings of a district party committee worker are between a fifth and a quarter those of a coal-miner, for example (*Pravda*, 30 June 1988, p. 2), and those who are deemed to have exploited their position for personal gain are shown little mercy when the political climate changes with the political leader.

Soviet scholars, too, have begun to examine the question of stratification, prudently quoting Lenin's formulations in support of their positions. Thus, Rogovin (1984, pp. 29–30) points out that the classes and other groups of Soviet society are internally differentiated according to such factors as the complexity of an occupation and qualification levels, the type of function performed, or the extent to which the work is physically demanding or harmful to the worker's health: these 'objective social characteristics of work' are reflected in the public evaluation of it, through the level of remuneration given.

Other forms of differentiation in Soviet society relate to lifestyle, and include cultural level, leisure pursuits and so forth. Such distinctions are frequently associated with other important differences: for instance, those between town and country, between small towns and large cities, between different economic regions—all of which can affect the opportunities for and access to education, medical assistance, cultural facilities, modern housing, restaurants, places of entertainment, and so on, enjoyed by individuals, whose life chances are thereby affected (A. McAuley, 1979, is the most thorough examination of these questions). Even different climatic conditions can affect the distribution and consumption of wealth—say, in the availability of fresh food. Cultural distinctions of a national or religious nature can also have an impact on life chances, if only indirectly through the influence of fertility on family size, and hence on the share of available resources an individual receives. In principle, these differences can be moderated and their impact reduced, if not completely banished: but that requires a complex programme of measures (not simply levelling out differences in earnings, for example), and will require sustained attention over a very long period (Rogovin, 1984, pp. 33–8).

The Nationalities

In addition to social classes and strata, Soviet society is characterized by a multiplicity of racial, ethnic or national groups. Indeed, such is the scale of ethnic diversity that no other modern state possesses the linguistic and cultural richness that this implies, nor faces the actual or potential problems and difficulties. There is a wealth of scholarly literature on this subject, which has become topical in the light of the ethnically related demographic imbalances examined above, and, more especially, in the light of the newly-extended right to express dissatisfaction. This right has been exercised by various nationalities from the Kazakhs protesting at the appointment of a Russian as party first secretary, to the Estonians and Lithuanians in the Baltic region, anxious to win some economic and political autonomy from Moscow, to the Armenians in conflict with the people of Azerbaidzhan.

A leading Western commentator, Zbigniew Brzezinski, in the late 1960s conjectured that the nationality issue in the Soviet Union might become politically more important than the racial issue had been in the

United States (in a Foreword to Chornovil, 1968, p. vii). A more recent scholarly study of Russian nationalism and inter-nation relations in the Soviet Union observed, 'The nationalities question will represent a morass for whoever rules the USSR' (Dunlop, 1984, p. 165). Another recent study, which became a best-seller in France, analysed the nationality question and concluded that the Soviet Union is an empire in decline (Carrère d'Encausse, 1979).

There are, moreover, signs that Soviet commentators and even politicians have grown alarmed at the implications and possible consequences of the present shift in the national balance. One somewhat notorious Soviet study projected growth rates of the major nationalities between 1970 and 2000, and displayed them in what can only be described as an alarmist graphic presentation. This showed the Estonians and Latvians declining in numbers, the Russians, Belorussians and Ukrainians comfortably holding their own, and the Georgians, Armenians and Moldavians showing moderate increases, while spectacular growth was projected for the Muslim peoples of Soviet Central Asia: the Kirgiz, Turkmenians, Uzbeks and Tadzhiks, whose populations were expected to more than triple over the three decades (Bondarskaya, 1977, p. 93). Alarming (if not actually alarmist) though they may be, these projections correlate with trends in family size discussed above.

The official concern over a number of years was revealed in statements by leading political figures. The official line for a long time was that, thanks to the party's Leninist policy, the 'national question' had been solved, and all the various nationalities lived together in 'a fraternal family of nations' (Groshev, 1967). Leonid Brezhnev proudly proclaimed in 1972, on the fiftieth anniversary of the establishment of the Union, that 'a new historic community' had been created—the Soviet people (*Pravda*, 22 December 1972); yet Brezhnev's successors indicated that, nevertheless, the question had not been entirely removed from the agenda (Chernenko, in *Pravda*, 15 June 1983). Under Gorbachëv's policy of *glasnost'*, the nationalities have more than once demonstrated their dissatisfaction with their situation on cultural, economic or political grounds, and in certain cases have posed issues that challenge the USSR Constitution: the Armenians in the Spring of 1988 calling for the return of the enclave of Nagorno-

Karabakh from Azerbaidzhani to Armenian control, and the Estonians in November that year proclaiming the right to 'veto' legislation emanating from Moscow.

This is an extremely complex and delicate matter, and it may ultimately prove insoluble. It is distinguished by many dimensions, some of which come into conflict in the elaboration of an equitable and non-discriminatory policy. The complexity stems from several factors. The first is the sheer number of national and ethnic groups: official recognition is accorded to over 100 nationalities—far more than in most other modern nations. This in itself poses policy problems associated with the preservation of the identity of many of them, particularly the smaller nations who might easily become submerged among their more populous neighbours. The second point, therefore, is the inequality seen both in the numerical size of the different national populations and in their level of economic, cultural and political development (see Table 2.2). The Russians are by far the largest group, accounting for some 52.4 per cent of the total population at the time of the 1979 census, followed by the Ukrainians, far behind—although still a big population in comparison with other European nations—at over 42 million (16.2 per cent), then the Uzbeks (almost 12.5 million, 4.7 per cent), and the Belorussians (slightly under 9.5 million, 3.6 per cent). The range extends to small tribes, with as few as 146,631 Kalmyks, 16,033 Shorians, and a mere 1,370 Itelmens and 1,198 Orochi, 835 Yukagirs, 546 Aleuts and 504 Nehidalsy, with scores of intermediate groups (figures from *Chislennost' i sostav*, 1984, pp. 71–3; percentages calculated).

Many national groups have always lived on territory that now forms the Soviet Union, and were incorporated into the Russian Empire during its expansion in the previous two centuries. This has been their homeland for generations, and they are not sufficiently numerous to exist as independent nations: they are destined always to exist in close contact with another, larger group—which in practice must lead to cultural if not political domination. A number of the larger nations have been officially recognized by the establishment of a form of statehood—the union republic, autonomous republic, autonomous oblast (province) or autonomous region. Examples are the Ukrainians, Moldavians, Estonians, Georgians, Kazakhs and Tadzhiks, who enjoy

Table 2.2 Major nationalities of the Soviet Union, 1979 Census

Nationality	Number	%
Russians	137,397,089	52.4
Ukrainians	42,347,387	16.2
Uzbeks	12,455,978	4.7
Belorussians	9,462,715	3.6
Kazakhs	6,556,442	2.5
Tatars	6,317,468	2.4
Azeris	5,477,330	2.1
Armenians	4,151,241	1.6
Georgians	3,570,504	1.4
Moldavians	2,968,224	1.1
Tadzhiks	2,897,697	1.1
Lithuanians	2,850,905	1.1
Turkmenians	2,027,913	0.8
Germans	1,936,214	0.7
Kirgiz	1,906,271	0.7
Jews	1,810,876	0.7
Chuvash	1,751,366	0.6
Peoples of Dagestan*	1,656,676	0.6
Latvians	1,439,037	0.5
Bashkirs	1,371,452	0.5
Mordvinians	1,191,765	0.4
Poles	1,150,991	0.4
Estonians	1,019,851	0.4

Source: *Chislennost' i sostav naseleniya SSSR*, 1984, p. 71; percentages calculated.

* This category includes ten national groups, ranging in number from 482,844 Avars to 12,078 Aguls.

the benefits of union republic status within the Soviet Union and all the trappings of statehood: flag, national anthem, coat of arms, government and even communist party organization (with the exception of the largest republic, the Russian Soviet Federative Socialist Republic—RSFSR). The Karelians, Abkhazians, Mordvins, Buryats and others have been granted autonomous republics within the union republics. Indeed, nationality is the basis of the Soviet federal structure. Yet it has not satisfied even the major nationalities: during 1988, for example, the Lithuanians and Estonians fought for (and gained) the right to use their pre-Soviet national flags and anthems, and more radical demands for distinctiveness and autonomy have been aired, with the support of republican communist party leaders.

Among the nationalities granted their own autonomous province are the Jews, for whom Stalin established Birobidzhan, in the east, as an alternative national homeland. The fact that very few Soviet Jews have volunteered to live there (10,166 at the time of the 1979 census, against over 170,000 Russians and Ukrainians, and over 1,800,000 Jews who lived elsewhere in the country: *Chislennost' i sostav*, 1984, pp. 71 and 84) and in increasing numbers have grown to think of Israel as their natural home, illustrates a further complicating element in the Soviet nationality picture: namely, that a number of nationalities have their nation-state outside the Soviet Union. These range from the almost two million Germans (descendants of the Volga German farming community established by Catherine the Great: many of these have left for West Germany in recent years) and over one million Poles to 389,000 Koreans and 361,000 Bulgarians, 344,000 Greeks, 171,000 Hungarians, 129,000 Romanians, 77,000 Finns and smaller contingents of other groups incorporated into India, Pakistan, Iran and other modern states. In addition, there are groups such as the Moldavians whose separate identity is a cause of dispute between the Soviet Union and Romania, and the Gagauz, concentrated mainly in Soviet Moldavia but also living outside the Soviet Union, with no state of their own. There are also some 209,000 gypsies, related to the Romany people who live across Europe. The existence of significant overseas communities of native Soviet national groups—Ukrainians, Lithuanians and Armenians, for example—in the Soviet Union's principal ideological and political rivals adds yet a further complicating element to an already complex political problem. So, too, does the fact that they are not concentrated in neat parcels such as could be given self-government. As elsewhere in the world, boundaries are in many cases arbitrary. Populations have migrated and inter-married over many generations, and in the Soviet period there has been a deliberate policy of encouraging migration of workers in the interests of economic development, quite apart from the deportation of whole nationalities by Stalin thousands of miles from their traditional homelands.

The different cultural levels attained by these various peoples are a further form of differentiation among them. The Russians have made impressive contributions to world cultural developments, particularly in the nineteenth century in the fields of music, literature and science; they have played a prominent part in European and world history, comparable in both its positive and negative facets with that performed by other great historical civilizations. The Ukrainians, too, proudly recall that the first Russian civilization was based on their capital city, Kiev, long before the rise of Moscow. The Armenians and Georgians and the Muslim peoples of Uzbekistan likewise have centuries of cultural development behind them, and many exquisite relics survive to demonstrate the point. The inhabitants of the three Baltic republics—Lithuania, Latvia and Estonia—recall their existence as independent states between the two World Wars. Many of the smaller and more remote national groups and tribes, by contrast, until the twentieth century lived pastoral and in some cases nomadic lives, with no settled existence (hence, no adminstrative structures) and no written language, let alone *belles lettres*.

In a country that spans two continents and stretches from the Arctic to the Central Asian deserts, the peoples of the Soviet Union are inevitably aware of their own and their fellow citizens' ethnic identity, and cannot ignore developmental trends. This fundamental factor in Soviet society poses intractable problems for the policy-makers, which will be further explored below.

Trends and Prospects

This chapter has demonstrated the social changes accompanying the Soviet Union's great economic transformation over the past half-century, changes that were an integral part of a total process of development. At the revolution, Russia had a backward, somewhat primitive, traditional society, characterized by a peasant economy and a harsh, poor, dull and ignorant way of life for the masses. The Soviet Union today possesses a developed industrial economy with a well educated and diverse social structure, characterized by a sophisticated role division and multifarious opportunities for different occupational and leisure pursuits, and supported by material wealth and social welfare provisions undreamt of by all but a few visionaries at the beginning of the century. In this, the Soviet Union is not unique: the advanced capitalist countries have likewise expanded welfare provision, enhanced the general wealth of society and experienced rapid changes in social structure as old industries have given way to new; similarly, the ex-colonial developing countries are now undergoing the same basic changes undertaken in the Soviet Union half a century ago. What is remarkable and even impressive about that transformation in the Soviet Union is its speed. A country that repeatedly in the last century was proved inferior to those powers against which it measured itself is now one of the world's richer societies, and claims a role in shaping the world.

These processes of social development are not complete. In common with all other modern societies, change continues at a rapid pace, as technical innovation in the economy renders old occupational positions and social categories obsolete or less applicable. The rise in the skill levels among sections of the industrial working class has been mentioned, together with the increased 'mental labour' content of productive occupations, which brings them closer in their characteristics to the intelligentsia. This is seen as evidence of the development of Soviet society towards the goal of a classless society. Indeed, it has been suggested that the traditional characterization of the intelligentsia as a distinct stratum is now less valid in consequence of these developments.

On the one hand, it is argued, there is a 'growth of the intellectual, creative content of the labour of all workers', while simultaneously the engineering and technical intelligentsia ... is fusing with other categories of industrial workers, is steadily becoming an intellectual contingent of the working class'. What is taking place, some Soviet observers conclude, is 'the fusion of the intelligentsia with the working class'; moreover, common lifestyles are already developing for workers, peasants and members of the intelligentsia; and the level of social mobility is still such that the process of developing a socially homogeneous society continues. Families that are 'purely worker', 'purely peasant' or 'purely intellectual' are less and less frequently encountered, so that by a process of 'social diffusion' the prerequisites for a classless soiety are being created (Kosolapov, 1972, pp. 63–5; also *Razvitoi sotsializm*, 1978, pp. 250–4; Senyavskii, 1982, ch. 2).

In response to some of these points, one might observe that for some segments of the working class the advent of new technology based on the assembly-line means less and less creative input into the job. In the electronic era this is already hitting the Soviet working class as in other countries, and is manifest in low job satisfaction, high labour turnover and rural-urban migration (*Razvitoi sotsializm*, 1978, p. 251). Moreover, the uniformity of lifestyle can partly be explained by the lack of attention to consumers' needs, rendering it more difficult for different social groups to express their distinctive values through their expenditure and consumption patterns, so displaying a special lifestyle.

Even so, significant differences still exist in the opportunities available to urban and rural dwellers, and this cuts across the official line of the working class, which (as noted above) includes state farm workers. The 'industrialization' of agriculture, which some Soviet commentators say brings the peasantry closer to the working class, and rural life closer to urban (for example, *Razvitoi sotsializm*, 1978, pp. 244–9), still has far to go before it can truly be said to have 'proletarianized' the peasantry. It may be the case, as this source records (pp. 246–7), that one-third to one-half of peasants in some farms perform work requiring specialized training, that educational levels among the peasantry are rising, that their earnings are now closer to those of industrial workers, and that their pension and other social welfare provisions are being raised to the level enjoyed by their industrial cousins. Yet the village throughout most of the country remains culturally deprived poorly equipped, badly supplied with consumer goods and services.

An enormous economic and social transformation of the countryside doubtless has taken place and is continuing. But the gulf between town and village remains acute, and it has been argued that the peasants are aware of this, no doubt in consequence of the very developments in peasant cultural and educational levels that justly impress Soviet spokesmen. 'At the beginning of the 1980s', write two American observers of Soviet rural life, 'the Soviet peasantry, with its poorer compensation, lesser mobility, and fewer privileges, *is* relatively deprived, and is aware of its status' (Laird & Francisco, in Pankhurst &

Sacks, 1980, p. 139; original emphasis). The result is that, for many peasants, the village is still a place from which the younger generation flocks in substantial numbers, to joint the ranks of the real proletarians in the cities. The expanding influence of urban standards in rural areas—part of the process of 'urban expansion' analysed by W. Douglas Jackson (1974)—must have a long-term impact in promoting the erosion of traditional rural values, and thereby changing the peasant consciousness in the direction of the proletariat (the stated goals of social policy: *Razvitoi sotsializm*, 1978, p. 248). But the rediscovery of the traditional values by Russian nationalist intellectuals of the *derevenshchiki* or 'ruralist' school (Dunlop, 1984, ch. 5), coupled with the constant creaming-off of the bright, ambitious and mobile among the younger generation, may also help to perpetuate a resistance to proletarianization of the peasantry.

3 The Political System

The Ruling Party

The Bolshevik Party came to power, under Lenin's firm and imaginative guidance, in the revolutionary coup of October 1917. With that, as Soviet writers express it, the party became a ruling party. For some months it shared power in coalition with the left wing of the Socialist Revolutionary Party; but other parties were quickly outlawed, following the forcible closure of the Constituent Assembly in January 1918, and the Bolshevik Party alone survived the Civil War. Virtually since the revolution, therefore, the communists have enjoyed the position of unchallenged wielders of power.

In the intervening period it has modified its structures, its size has grown enormously, its composition has changed in consequence of economic and social changes instituted through its policies, and, indeed, its position in Soviet society has undergone significant development. Yet never has there been even a hint that the party should abandon its monopoly. Indeed, so central is this to the system that the word 'partocracy' has been coined to characterize the Soviet form of government (Avtorkhanov, 1966, 1973).

There is a standard justification for this political monopoly (presented, for example, in Farukshin, 1973, *passim*; Shvets and Yudin, 1980, pp. 306–7). It states that political parties in competitive systems represent the interests of different classes, or of different segments within a class; in the Soviet Union antagonistic classes no longer exist, having been abolished with the creation of socialism in the 1930s; hence, there is no further need for different parties. It is further asserted that this single party can perfectly represent the interests of all classes and social groups. 'The party's policy brings the required results', said Leonid Brezhnev at the Twenty-Fourth CPSU Congress (1971), 'when it precisely takes into account the interests of the whole people, and also the interests of the classes and social groups that compose it, and directs them into one common stream' (*XXIV s"ezd*, I, p. 97).

The modern party is very different, however, from the organization that took control of the Russian Empire in 1917, and its very role in society has undergone serious modification over its decades in power. In the years before and immediately following the revolution, it was rather like a tiny elite, a yeast of political commitment in a society characterized by political inexperience and broad indifference. At that stage, too, the party ruled through the organs of the newly established Soviet state: although the acknowledged *leader* of the party by virtue of his political acumen, his towering intellect and the force of his personality, Lenin held no party post, deriving his formal power from the position of chairman of the Council of People's Commissars, i.e. prime minister (see Brown, in Rigby *et al.*, 1980, p. 135).

Following Lenin's death in 1924, Stalin exploited his position as party general secretary, which gave him access to personal files on party members and accorded him enormous power over appointments within the apparatus. He came to dominate the party by his capacity to make and break careers, outwitting his colleagues in the party's leading bodies and having them removed from office. And in the 1930s, after the Seventeenth Congress (1934), he effectively destroyed the party as a ruling institution. Loyal party members and officials were put to death; committees ceased to function; party congresses became rallies of the sycophantic faithful; the Politburo, formally a subcommittee of the Central Committee and accountable to it, was composed of Stalin's creatures, who enjoyed no tenure of office. As Politburo members, they were rarely convened in full session, but instead were divided into overlapping groups that met casually at Stalin's whim. Stalin used party membership to impose discipline on important segments of Soviet society—the army, for example, or the rapidly expanding class of industrial and economic managers—and chose to rule through the state administrative organs. After Stalin's death in 1953, Khrushchev, who shortly became first secretary of the Central Committee, was determined to establish the party as the principal organ of rule. He succeeded in defeating Malenkov, the prime minister, and subsequently himself assumed the premiership. Although these two positions have been separated since Khrushchev's removal from office, his assertion of the party as the central institution in the political system has been retained, and is enshrined in Article 6 of the 1977 USSR Constitution:

The leading and guiding force of Soviet society and the nucleus of its political system, of all state organizations and public organizations, is the Communist Party of the Soviet Union. The CPSU exists for the people and serves the people.

The party's nature has meanwhile changed in other ways. First of all, it has grown enormously. At the beginning of 1917, the Bolshevik wing of the party comprised only some 24,000 members—in part, at least, a consequence of Lenin's insistence at the 1903 Congress upon only actively committed members ('professional revolutionaries'). Nevertheless, pursuing the policy of political activism during 1971, the party enlisted new recruits, and by October-November the Bolshevik leaders could claim a following of about one-third of a million (although estimates vary considerably: see Rigby, 1968, for the fullest historical account of party membership). A recruitment drive following Lenin's death in 1924—the 'Lenin Enrolment'—brought in approximately 200,000 working-class members. Further rapid expansion in the late 1920s and early 1930s brought within the sphere of party discipline the newly promoted industrial and economic managers, who otherwise might have constituted a political threat to the regime. By 1934, therefore, the total membership stood at 2,701,008, according to official figures (*Partiinaya zhizn'*, 21/1977, p. 21).

At that point, Stalin set about his systematic destruction of the party. Whatever the reasons for this devastating and socially debilitating policy, its effect was to reduce the total party membership by some 600,000 in the three years 1935–7. Moreover, a four-year moratorium on the recruitment of new members, initiated in January 1933, compounded the undermining of the party as an effective political institution. A period of rapid expansion at the end of the decade—with over one million new recruits drafted in during 1934 alone—completed the party's transformation. Formerly it had been a reservoir of political, administrative and technical knowledge and experience. In Stalin's hands, admission into the party became mainly a reliable means of disciplining important segments of the new industrial society.

This role continued through the Second World War. At the time of the German invasion, membership stood at some 3,900,000 (Rigby, 1968, p. 220). After a fall of 808,589 between January 1941 and January 1942 (many presumably killed on active service, some perhaps captured by German troops and so removed from Soviet control), a policy of rapid recruitment was adopted, both to replenish the ranks of the fallen comrades and to lend the party a patriotic image. By identifying the party with the *national* cause, Stalin harnessed the patriotism of the people and their old antipathy towards the Germans, while simultaneously demanding extraordinary sacrifices of those drawn into the party. Hence, even though party members in the armed forces were frequently sent on particularly dangerous missions (leading the attack against enemy forces, for example) many Soviet troops greatly desired to become party members. The Soviet president M. I. Kalinin expressed it thus: 'when the Red Army man sees that he is about to participate in a harsh battle, he puts in an application to join the party, wishing to go into battle a communist' (quoted in Rigby, 1968, p. 238). This was facilitated by a relaxation of the political entry conditions for soldiers who had distinguished themselves on the battlefield; moreover, losses were high, so that the turnover among the mass party membership stood at around 50 per cent throughout the war. Naturally, therefore, the party's *political* and *ideological* quality remained low. Indeed, the war had what Rigby (1968, p. 236) termed a 'cataclysmic' effect on the party.

The war similarly affected the party's 'officer corps'. They too were killed in substantial numbers, and replaced frequently by poorly educated, ill-trained, insensitive but politically reliable ignoramuses and bullies, whose qualities, however effective in maintaining discipline among the population in wartime, were quite inappropriate when it came to running an increasingly sophisticated society later in their careers during the 1960s and 1970s: that is but one element in Stalin's legacy to his successors. Furthermore, those who reached the top in Stalin's late years occupied such a peculiar position, and their experience was so unorthodox, that they were ill trained to run the great power that the Second World War had made their country. Indeed, their main preoccupation in the first months following Stalin's death was to secure their own positions against the threat from one another, and even over the next four years jockeying for position among the various contenders for supreme power was a constant preoccupation of the ruling circle, until Khrushchev's defeat of the 'Anti-Party Group' in 1957.

Having established the party's supremacy over the Soviet state in the political system, Khrushchev set about again transforming the party's nature by engaging in a massive expansion campaign. So rapid was the recruitment rate in the late 1950s and early 1960s that one scholar has applied the word 'heedless' to the process: certainly Khrushchev was concerned to bring CPSU membership to ever wider circles of the Soviet people, regardless of the impact that this would have on the party's internal structures, or on its capacity to perform its 'vanguard' role. Over the five-year period 1956–61, the party grew by 29.3 per cent, and by 33.2 per cent in the following quinquennium, with the proportion of the adult (i.e. eligible) population within the party rising from 5.7 per cent in 1956 to 8.6 per cent a decade later. Had that rate of expansion continued, the party by the early 1980s would have had 28 million members, or one in every six adults in the population (Miller, in Brown & Kaser, 1982, p. 6).

Under Khrushchev's successors, the expansion rate was cut drastically, and regular weeding out was engaged in, in order to maintain the 'purity' of the ranks: under Gorbachëv, indeed, the recruitment rate has been cut back still further, and following the nineteenth conference in the summer of 1988 a campaign of 'attestation' or verification of members (similar in its conception to the 'exchange of party documents' conducted by Brezhnev in the early 1970s) has been agreed on. Nevertheless, the party has continued to grow, and by 1 January 1989 (the latest precise figure to hand) stood at 19,487,822 (*Isvetiya Tsk KPSS*, 2/89, p. 138)—an increase of almost half a million in three years.

As the party has expanded, its social composition has also changed substantially, a phenomenon that has been most thoroughly investigated by Rigby (1968, 1976, 1977; see also Unger, 1977; Miller, in Brown & Kaser, 1982; Harasymiw, 1984; J. Miller, in Miller *et al.*, 1987). Originally a party of intellectuals with a mainly proletarian following, the party has become so catholic in its recruitment and membership policies that it feels confident in calling itself the 'party of the whole Soviet people' (Party Rules, 1961, Prologue). But there have been clearly marked trends and, at times, out of embarrassment at the overwhelmingly non-working-class complexion of its membership, even basic statistics were not made available. Moreover, there is a clear conflict of aims confronting the party managers in devising recruitment policies, which is relatively easy to define, but evidently exasperating to regulate (see Hill & Frank, 1986a, pp. 44–6).

The party sees itself as, first of all, a party of the *working class*—as that term was understood, moreover, in the late nineteenth century: those who sold their labour power to manufacturing industry. The implication of this image, if the party wishes to retain it, is that there must be recruitment among the industrial workers. The party is also a *ruling party*, implying that it requires access to the expertise needed in running a relatively complex and sophisticated modern society: in practice, that most likely means that the party will wish to have such expertise within its own ranks. Associated with this is the fact that party membership has long been used to bring potentially powerful sectional groups—those with technical and administrative expertise—under the requisite *discipline and control*. Party membership also conveys a range of *privileges and political rights*, which have come to be regarded as a 'normal' element in the more responsible and high-status jobs: indeed, Hough (1977, p. 131) has calculated that every second male over the age of thirty with higher education is a party member—an astonishing ratio, if accurate. As a party *of the whole people*, it obviously has to draw into its ranks suitable representatives of all significant groups in Soviet society: that means in particular 'minority' groups such as women, members of the smaller nationalities, and the whole range of eligible age groups, as well as the fullest practicable range of occupations. Yet the party also presents itself as the *vanguard* of the Soviet people, containing (in the words of its own Rule Book) only 'the more advanced, politically more conscious section' of society. It cannot accept the whole of society—nor, indeed, everyone who might wish to be admitted, since some of these might do so for careerist reasons; instead it has to be restrictive, otherwise that image would be swiftly eroded. Devising a recruitment and membership management policy to satisfy these various aims is proving a difficult, perhaps impossible, task.

To some extent the changes in party membership patterns have been a reflection of changes in the social structure of Soviet society, in turn the product of economic change induced since the late 1920s, as the figures in Table 3.1 indicate. In this table, the striking absence of

Table 3.1 Party composition by social class, 1917–82 (per cent)

Year	Workers	Peasants	White collar, etc.
1917	60.2	7.5	32.2
1927	55.1	27.3	17.6
1947	33.7	18.0	48.3
1957	32.0	17.3	50.7
1967	38.1	16.0	45.9
1977	42.0	13.6	44.4
1982	43.7	12.6	43.7

Sources: 1917, 1927; Rigby, 1968, p. 85, Table 1, and p. 116, Table 2; 1947–57: *Partiinaya zhizn'*, 21/1977, p. 28; 1982: *Partiinaya zhizn'*, 10/1982, p. 36. No figures available for 1937.

figures for the 1930s reflects the embarrassment of a supposedly working-class party in which the bulk of members were white-collar administrative, managerial and similar employees, as revealed in the figures for 1947 and 1957: in the latter year, this category constituted a majority of the membership. Under Stalin's successors, there has been a policy of boosting the party's proletarian ranks, which is reflected in the trend contained in the figures in Table 3.1. It is also revealed in recruitment statistics, which show that workers constituted 52.0 per cent of new entrants in the years 1966–70, and 57.6 per cent in the following five-year period (official figures, quoted in Hill & Frank, 1986a, p. 37); in 1986 the figure was 59.3 per cent (*Partiinaya zhizn'*, 21/87, p. 8). With the rise in the working-class strength in the past three decades, there has been a commensurate decline in the white-collar contingent—although it still constitutes virtually the same proportion of members as does the working class. The social group that has most clearly been reduced is the peasantry, and this certainly is a response to the decline of the rural work-force as industrialization and urbanization make their impact. It should also be remembered, however, that the *number* of 'peasants' (that is, collective farmers) within the party continued to rise, from 1,023,903 in 1946, when they accounted for 18.6 per cent of the membership, to 2,248,166 in 1986, when their proportional strength had fallen to 11.8 per cent (*Partiinaya zhizn'*, 14/86, p. 22); in 1987, however, their number had fallen slightly, suggesting that they may have passed their peak numerical strength.

However, these official figures present a number of difficulties. One is that their meaning is uncertain: whether they apply to current occupation, occupation on admission into the party, or social origin (i.e. parents' class). The interpretation of this particular variable can be seriously affected by this in a population characterized by rapid development and high social mobility. Rigby (1968, p. 116, Table 2), for example, gives figures which suggest that in 1927 a mere 17.6 per cent of members were classified as white collar, etc., whereas 46.9 per cent of party members were employed in such jobs; similarly, 55.1 per cent of the party was said to comprise workers—yet only 39.4 per cent were actually on the shop-floor, and 13.7 per cent were working as peasants, compared with a claimed peasant strength among the party members of 27.3 per cent. Harasymiw (1984, pp. 54–60) makes a similar point in a more sophisticated up-to-date analysis. By such a statistical sleight-of-hand, the party has in the past attempted to establish and reaffirm its working-class credentials, while nevertheless satisfying some of the other criteria of its role requirements, outlined above.

An associated difficulty relates to the 'worker' recruits. The discrepancies in the meagre figures available for class origin and current occupation imply that the kind of 'worker' accepted into the party has in many cases been one judged ready for promotion from the production-line into management (Rigby, 1976, pp. 331–2). Indeed, given the established association between party membership and managerial or administrative responsibility (for which it is almost axiomatic that party membership is a necessary qualification), this is a natural consequence. The political question, then, is how far these 'leading' workers can be seen as representing the class they are about to leave.

A related question concerns the impact of technical advance as the country experiences the 'scientific and technological revolution'. As we saw, the present period of technical innovation is reducing the demand for the traditional skills of the manual labourer and creating completely new industries based on the application of the natural sciences and in particular electronics. This faces the party managers with classifying the more highly trained workers in modern industries. Coal-miners, train drivers and steel smelters are manifestly of the working class: but what of the white-coated computer maintenance technician, or the repairer of a robot-controlled assembly-line? The former groups are declining in numbers, while the latter are on the rise. The evidence appears to be that the party has recognized that changes have taken place in the social structure of the working class, and its recruitment practice is indeed to concentrate on the prestigious advanced edge of the work-force: the highly skilled workers in chemicals and petrochemicals, electronics, automobiles, machine-building, instrument-making and the like (Kadeikin *et al.*, 1974, p. 168; Harasymiw, 1984, p. 66). Hence, although the official statistics indicate a sharp 're-proletarianization' of the party's ranks since the mid-1960s, the CPSU is rapidly losing its former image as the party of the 'cloth-cap' working class.

Underlying this discussion of trends in the party composition is an important point related to Lenin's insistence on active membership, which all communist parties insist upon. That is, membership is not open as membership of political parties in pluralist systems usually is. So, although the party rules state that 'Membership of the CPSU is open to any citizen of the Soviet Union who accepts the Programme and Rules of the party, takes an active part in communist construction, works in one of the party organizations, carries out all party decisions, and pays membership dues' (Rule 1), recruitment is more a matter of co-option by the party than of volunteering to join.

The party says there are more people wishing to join than can be accommodated, and it is very selective about whom it admits. The screening procedures accompanying admission are laborious and extended: the procedure takes over a year, and entails the submission of an application form, a curriculum vitae, a personal letter and three references from party members of five years' standing (one may be from the Komsomol committee). These are discussed by the monthly meeting of the primary party organization at the applicant's place of work, at which his or her character, political reliability and qualities as a worker are assessed, prior to admittance on a two-thirds vote of the members present (non-members may attend the meeting). After confirmation by the next higher committee, there follows a year's probation as a 'candidate member' before repeating the whole process for admission to full membership. Only the members proper enjoy the right to participate fully in the party's life, plus the unwritten privileges of greater access to job promotion, opportunities for a political career, and other benefits that accompany the undoubted burden of party membership.

This burden begins immediately: paying membership subscriptions (a small percentage of monthly salary), attending Marxist-Leninist study groups and party meetings, perhaps helping to prepare these, and undertaking a range of 'party assignments'—tasks ranging from single obligations (writing an article, giving a talk to a Komsomol group or arranging for May Day banners to be prepared) to more onerous burdens, such as serving as secretary of a parent-teachers' association at the local school, holding trade-union office, or sitting as a local council deputy.

In fact, the party not only requires its members to be active, but itself determines where they shall be deployed. It keeps detailed records containing the information supplied in the original application, regularly updated as circumstances change. Through these records the party deploys its 'troops' to leading positions, and in principle the ordinary member has to comply with whatever posting the party determines. A member may not change jobs without the party's approval; when travelling away, the party organization must be notified, and if the absence is for more than a few days, temporary attachment to an appropriate organization at the destination is usual.

Thus, the primary party organization (PPO) is the central institution in the life of the ordinary party member. This body, of which there were 441,851 on 1 January 1987 (*Partiinaya zhizn'*, 21/87, p. 15), 'conducts its work directly among the working people, rallies them round the Communist Party of the Soviet Union, organizes them for carrying out the task of building communism and actively participating in applying the party's personnel policy' (Rule 58). They are formed in every place of work employing at least three party members, and may also be formed on a territorial basis, say, in a block of apartments where pensioner and housewife communists live. There are by now no significant work places in the state sector without a PPO. They vary in size and structure from a handful of members, well known to one another—like the party 'cell' in pre-revolutionary Russian factories—to some very large organizations of over a thousand members. These are given special rights with regard to recruitment and have a complex organizational structure, often comprising departmental sectors and party groups that meet according to work shift; party groups within the one PPO may be spread across a city in the case of a major industrial works—a steelworks or a car assembly plant, for example (see Figure 3.1). Such an organization is a microcosm of the party's overall structure, with hierarchical chains of authority up to the *PPO Secretary*. He or she (women quite frequently hold party office at this level: see Harasymiw, 1984, pp. 146–50) is an important individual in the works managerial team, who enjoys prestige in the locality (frequently sitting on the district party committee, and often the local soviet), politically—and sometimes physically—remote from the rank-and-file members.

Official statistics for 1987 indicate that 39.5 per cent of PPOs contained under 15 members, 40.2 per cent had 15–49, 12.9 per cent had 50–100, and 7.4 per cent had over 100. Hence, the number with over a thousand was very small, and the bulk of primary organizations—over four-fifths—have under 50 members (although the tendency is for the average size to increase). In industry the average PPO contained 107 members, in construction, 40, in the state farms, 69, and in the collective farms, 61 (*Partiinaya zhizn'*, 21/87, p. 16).

According to Rule 55, the PPO's highest organ is the monthly meeting, responsible for admitting new members and carrying out party policy 'on the ground'. At this level the significance of the PPOs becomes apparent, for quite obviously the Kremlin's policy decisions have no practical value until implemented, and it is the PPO that arranges the application of policy. This usually means that the PPO allocates responsibilities to individual members in carrying out the latest policy edicts, which may involve instructing party members who work in state administrative offices as to what they should do in that office: this is part of the triple problem known as parallelism, *podmena* and petty tutelage (see below). Ideally, party members volunteer their services for the specific assignments, according to their individual talents, skills and inclinations: quite often, though, there is probably some inducement or compulsion, the willing workhorses burdened

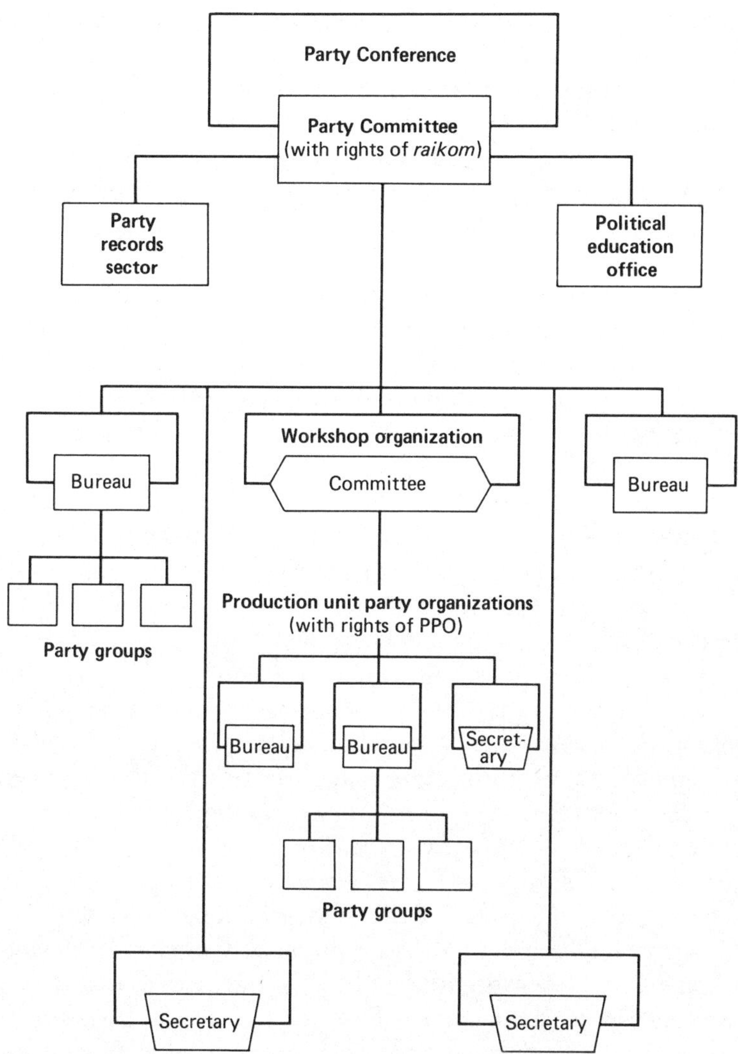

Figure 3.1 Large industrial plant PPO structure

Source: Adapted from *KPSS–naglyadnoe posobie po partiinomu stroitel'stvu* (Moscow, Politizdat, 1973), pp. 116–17.

with an array of time-consuming obligations by the secretary or party group organizer responsible for recording policy implementation through the assignments.

Each autumn, an 'accounting and election' meeting elects the secretary, plus a small committee or bureau. In fact, these elections have not been the open contest implied by the word, since the posts have always been subject to *nomenklatura* (see below), and the elections take place in the presence of a representative of the district committee whose opinion carries great weight, and helps to avoid the 'danger' of spontaneity. Nevertheless, as Rigby (1964, pp. 432–3) argued, the very presence of the elective principle is symbolically very important, given the lack of democratic traditions in the political culture: and some nominees have been defeated—eighty-eight in 1979, according to the official figure (*Partiinaya zhizn'*, 3/80, p. 28)—attesting to some political vitality at that level, even in the years of Brezhnevite stagnation.

In 1988, the Nineteenth Party Conference moved to establish the principle of contested elections to all party committees and official posts, following on speeches by Gorbachëv in the previous year calling for democratization of Soviet political life. A new Central Committee *Instruction on Elections* was issued on 12 August 1988, which made 'broad discussion' of candidates and a secret ballot mandatory, and permitted the inclusion of more candidates than places available (without requiring this as a norm). It is not yet clear to what extent these provisions are to be applied in practice, although after the idea of contested elections was first broached, in January 1987, the press carried reports of party secretaries being elected through contest.

At the same reporting and accounting meeting, every second or third year, the PPO elects delegates to the district party conference, which discusses the work of the district committee (*raikom*) over its term of office, elects the new *raikom*, and also elects delegates to the next higher conference, at the city or province level. In this way, moving steadily up the hierarchy, conferences of delegates elect party committees and delegates to the next higher level, up to the CPSU congress, which since the 1960s has been held every five years (the last—the twenty-seventh—in February 1986). The indirect method of election means the ordinary party member has practically no influence over the composition of the CPSU Central Committee (CC). Since the CC elects the Politburo and the general secretary, even the party members—let alone those outside the party—have no meaningful say in selecting the party's leader and ruling body.

The Politburo is indisputably the most powerful body of men in the country. As an institution, it defines broad policies, decides priorities and allocates resources, tasks that make it functionally equivalent to the cabinet in a parliamentary system. It consists of some two dozen individuals (only two women have ever been members), about half of whom are 'full' or voting members—the 'super-elite' of the Soviet political system (Löwenhardt, 1982, p. 74). The Rules say they are answerable to the CC, which in turn is answerable to the congress; but in practice, policy is determined by the Politburo, approved retrospectively by the CC, and endorsed—with acclaim—by the five-yearly congresses. Other bodies, such as the Council of Ministers, individual ministries, the CC and the party's central organs, may influence the policy-making process in an advisory capacity (the six 'commissions', established in the autumn of 1988, are intended to do precisely that): but the Politburo takes final decisions of broad policy. It may produce a limited and even distorted picture of Soviet reality to concentrate almost exclusively on the Politburo, as analysts in the 'Kremlinological' school tend to do: examining 'who eats before whom' (Bell, 1962, p. 341) in order to establish whose star is on the rise and whose is falling; however, in such a centralized political system it is obviously important to study the top leadership group, if only for the practical reason that they are the individuals with whom the rest of the world has to deal.

The inner workings of the Politburo are largely unknown (as is true even of cabinet government in liberal democracies, despite 'leaks' and the occasional memoirs of former members): indeed, it was one delegate's complaint at the 1988 party conference that the party members and the public did not know what the responsibilities of individual Politburo members and CC secretaries were—so they did not know whom to blame for failures or to praise for successes. Under Stalin, the Politburo functioned in an unbusinesslike and haphazard fashion. During Brezhnev's period in office greater order was brought into the administrative apparatus, and the Politburo came to meet regularly, usually weekly on Thursdays, preceded by a Wednesday meeting of the CC secretariat: this has evidently continued under his successors. Andropov instituted the publication of brief newspaper accounts of these meetings, allowing the public to glimpse the range of issues discussed by the leaders, although vague phrases such as 'other topics of national and international significance' mask detail when this is deemed appropriate.

The Politburo's composition has varied, although no clear pattern emerges. In the early 1970s, there appeared to be a trend towards an institution of the Western cabinet type, incorporating major regional and sectoral interests: the Ukraine and Belorussia, the Baltic, Transcaucasus and Central Asia; Moscow and Leningrad; agriculture, defence, foreign affairs, security and the trade unions. This 'principle' became eroded, however. This may be a political strength from the leader's point of view: the Politburo is flexible in both size and composition, allowing the incumbent general secretary to bring in his own supporters and fashion a team of like-minded colleagues. After all, as pointed out by Archie Brown (in Brown & Kaser, 1982, p. 228), unlike a British prime minister or United States president, a newly selected Soviet party leader inherits the colleagues chosen by his predecessor, and there is no evident tradition of placing seals of office at the disposal of the victor in a power struggle following a leader's demise.

A key feature of Politburo membership is the overlap with the Central Committee secretariat, led by the general secretary (who heads both bodies). The secretaries hold portfolios in specific areas of administration. Six of them (all either full or candidate members of the Politburo) chair the new Commissions on party organization, agriculture, ideology, international relations, social and economic policy, and legal policy; another is at present first secretary of the Moscow party committee, and another coordinates the various areas connected with the defence industries. The Politburo also contains the prime minister (that is, the chairman of the Council of Ministers), the minister of foreign affairs, and the president of the Russian republic; among its candidate members are two deputy prime ministers (one of them a woman, Aleksandra Biryukova), each with a further specific portfolio, the minister of defence, the Russian republic prime minister, and the chairman of Gosplan (the state planning committee). In the recent past, the chairman of the security police (KGB) has been on the Politburo, as have the first secretaries in some of the republics. Following a general secretary's death or removal from office, a successor is usually selected from those secretaries who are on the Politburo (often designated 'senior secretaries' in Western writings). The new general secretary then sets about refashioning his team, dropping rivals and opponents or placing them in uncontentious posts, and bringing in supporters and like-minded colleagues in an exercise akin to cabinet-making, but frequently spread over several months and even two or three years (see Hill & Frank, 1986b). In any case, whether or not they depend for advancement on their loyalty to the general secretary, all these individuals in the Soviet political elite are powerful figures in their own right.

The Politburo and secretariat members are all drawn from the voting members of the CC, elected by the party congress for a five-year term. The size of the CC (as of other party committees) is not fixed, and in 1986 the Twenty-Seventh Congress elected a CC of 307 members and 170 candidates (a reserve of non-voting members). Places on the committee—among both membership categories—are normally 'reserved' for the occupants of key positions in the party, state and other segments of the administrative apparatus: what Robert V. Daniels calls the 'job-slot' (in Cocks, Daniels & Heer, 1976, p. 78; see also Gehlen & McBride, 1968). It therefore contains significant numbers of central administrators (10.1 per cent of the full members were central party officials and 21.2 per cent were drawn from the USSR government apparatus in 1986) and provincial officials (33.2 per cent party and 4.9 per cent state); there are also foreign service officials, including ambassadors (3.6 per cent), representatives of the military (7.5 per cent), the security services and the law (2.3 per cent), trade unions and economic management (2.3 per cent), and a range of other groups totalling 14.0 per cent of the voting members: writers and artists, scientists, workers and peasants, the last combined category accounting for 7.8 per cent of the members (figures for 1986 full members based on John H. Miller, in Miller, Miller & Rigby, 1987, p. 77). In short, the CC incorporates a wide range of expertise and experience on which the Politburo and central secretariat can draw in formulating policy. The principle of contested election to the

Committee, when implemented, is not likely to have a substantial impact on the broad lines of this composition, although conceivably the category of representatives of 'ordinary' members might increase in size at the expense of officialdom. The Committee normally meets twice a year, in May–June and November–December, although it occasionally meets more frequently, say, on the death of the leader, or in response to an international or internal crisis: in 1988 it met at the end of July and again at the end of September to agree on measures (including personnel changes) stemming from the Nineteenth Party Conference, held at the end of June.

At the lower levels, provincial committees (*obkoms*), city and town committees (*gorkoms*), and urban and rural district committees (*raikoms*) replicate the CC in terms of membership patterns and functioning, but meeting more frequently (four or six times a year), and frequently taking as their lead the latest Central Committee statement and identifying its implications for the locality (Stewart, 1968, pp. 58–9; Hill, 1977, p. 90; but, for a slightly different view, Moses, 1974, pp. 22–6).

As with the general secretary at national level, at all other levels the key person is the party committee first secretary. He is carefully selected by superior organs, usually trained in a special party school in Moscow or in the provincial or republican capital city, and allocated to this formally elective post through the party's leadership recruitment system known as *nomenklatura*. This system is supposedly secret, although there has been considerable reference to it in recent years and the principle is well understood. All party committees from the *raikom* level upwards maintain two lists: one consists of posts over which that committee has a deciding voice (either making the selection directly, issuing a 'consultative' recommendation, or confirming the choice of another body); the other contains the names of individuals holding such positions or deemed suitable to hold them (including persons holding *nomenklatura* posts at lower levels). Thus, PPO secretaryships are on the *nomenklatura* of the appropriate *raikom*; *obkom* secretaryships are on the CC *nomenklatura*, as are republican central committee positions (all the union republics apart from the largest, the RSFSR, have nominally separate communist parties). *Nomenklatura* helps to link the party into a unified structure, with switching of personnel between levels of administration and across republican party organizations, particularly from the RSFSR into other areas (see Miller in Rigby & Harasymiw, 1983, pp. 77–87; also Miller, 1977). The principle extends beyond the party to posts in the state apparatus, the trade unions and most other organizations and institutions. This is how the party maintains its self-appointed prerogative of the 'selection, training and allocation of cadres', as part of its 'leading and guiding' role, so that the members of the *nomenklatura* form a single pool for allocation to wherever the party deems appropriate (Harasymiw, 1969, remains the best short exposition of *nomenklatura* in English; see also Voslensky, 1984). The wide extension of real elections to all party positions, which is being adopted following the 1988 party conference, is likely to encroach slightly on the *nomenklatura* powers of party committees, although these will still be able to maintain a veto over who will be permitted to run for election; their powers over appointments outside the party structure may be more seriously affected.

To summarize the CPSU's position: it is, in its own image and in reality, the central political institution in the system. A body of over 20 million men and women (approximately 10 per cent of the adult population), it is a significant employer, both of its own full-time officials and also of auxiliary staff such as chauffeurs, cleaners, typists and other office staff, and indirectly through party-owned publishing and other enterprises. A recent estimate puts its annual income at approaching 2 billion (2,000 million) roubles—one-tenth of the admitted defence budget (see Hill, 1988, p. 20). Millions of people depend on the party for their very livelihood; adding dependants, many more millions rely on party membership or employment for their social status. As an institution, it deploys its members in all other institutions, setting up a hierarchical network of organizations and organs that culminates in the CC, central secretariat and Politburo. This last-named body holds ultimate responsibility for the fate of the nation, as policy-maker for the entire country. Hence, the significance of the party and its role cannot be overestimated.

However, it continually asserts that it is a *ruling* but not a *governing* party: it decides policy, but it is not directly involved in administration. That governmental function is performed by the administrative apparatus of the Soviet *state*, to which we now turn.

The Constitutional Arrangement

The Soviet Union's constitutional arrangements are broadly comparable with those of other countries in establishing 'conventional state machinery' (Scott, 1969, ch. III). Indeed, the requirements of administering a complex society are similar no matter what the form of economic ownership or which social class is said to be dominant: certain things must be done to keep the society running smoothly, according to accepted standards, and foreign states have to be dealt with in a relatively businesslike fashion. This applies even to revolutionary governments, which frequently inherit a tradition of public administration going back several generations, if not centuries. So, it is perhaps not surprising that administrative structures look similar across the 'East–West divide'.

Initially, the revolutionary Bolsheviks intended to establish a different type of state, according to the decidedly utopian view expressed in Lenin's theoretical work, *The State and Revolution* (written in 1917). The state was viewed as an instrument used by the ruling class (in capitalist society, the bourgeoisie) to oppress the non-ruling class, the proletariat. The 'representative' parliament and other legislative bodies passed laws that enshrined the rights of the ruling class, largely against the interests of the exploited classes, and the state's rule-application agencies (the bureaucracy, the courts, the police) enforced that law, using coercion if necessary. Under communism, however, antagonistic classes would no longer exist, so there would be no further need for an instrument of class rule. The state would become superfluous and, in Engels's classic phrase, it would 'wither away'.

Attaining communism would, however, be a long-term goal. Meanwhile, argued the Marxists, a state-like apparatus would be necessary, through which the new ruling class (the proletariat) would exercise its dictatorship over the former ruling classes. Marx did not describe the form this would take, and into the theoretical gap Lenin slotted the *soviets of workers' deputies.* As spontaneous creations of the working class in revolution, strike committees of representatives who met to coordinate revolutionary activity, they held real power in competition with the Provisional Government during 1917. The impending Second All-Russian Congress of Soviets determined the date of the Bolsheviks' seizure of power on the night of 25–6 October 1917, and the Soviets immediately became the organs of state power of the proletariat, under Bolshevik guidance. The All-Russian Central Executive Committee (VTsIK), elected by that Congress, became the organ of government. Through this 200-strong body Russia was ruled during the Civil War; day-to-day administration was carried out through the eighteen ministerial organs which it appointed, their heads meeting as a council, under Lenin's chairmanship. It looked rather like a cabinet form of government, with one significant symbolic innovation: 'ministries' and 'ministers' were replaced by 'people's commissariats' and 'people's commissars', a term for which Trotsky (1960, pp. 337–8) claimed credit. Control over the VTsIK was to be exercised by the Congress of Soviets, which would continue to meet quarterly for that purpose. In all this, the separation of legislative and executive powers was rejected as a 'negative side of parliamentarianism' (Carr, 1966, p. 158). Soviets were to be set up in cities and rural communities across the country, and delegates from these would constitute the Congress of Soviets, the supreme organ of state power. This arrangement was enshrined in the first Soviet constitution, adopted on 10 July 1918.

The Russian Empire contained many ethnic strains, from major nations to minute national groups. Handling these had been one of the tsarist government's most testing tasks, and its Russification policy had contributed to provoking the collapse of authority in the peripheral regions. The Bolsheviks inherited this delicate problem, and Stalin (himself a Georgian—his family name was Djugashvili) was appointed people's commissar in charge of nationality affairs as a token of Lenin's earnestness in approaching this question (von Laue, 1966, p. 180).

During the Civil War, soviet republics were established in the Ukraine, Transcaucasia and Central Asia, each one adopting a constitution like that of Soviet Russia. On 30 December 1922, a federal state was established, the Union of Soviet Socialist Republics, for which a new constitution was ratified on 13 January 1924. This only trivially altered the provisions of its 1918 Russian predecessor: it allocated foreign relations, defence, the budget, transport, the judiciary, economic planning and similar basic functions to the federal (i.e. All-Union) government, also allowing it to establish fundamental principles of legislation for enactment by the republican governments, with possible modifications to take account of local traditions and conditions. This principle still holds, as does the 1924 Constitution's main institutional modification: the restructuring of the Central Executive Committee as a two-chamber body, one chamber handling affairs of federal significance, the other concentrating on issues of interest from the perspective of the national republics. The annual Congress of Soviets formally retained supreme authority.

The Stalin Constitution

Further constitutional development came on 5 December 1936 when the Stalin Constitution was introduced. The promulgation of this new fundamental law symbolized the attainment of socialism through the five-year plans: Article 1 stated that 'The Union of Soviet Socialist Republics is a socialist state of workers and peasants'. That constitution is to all appearances an impeccably democratic document, and it made certain changes.

The Congress of Soviets, elected indirectly by the lower-level soviets, and the VTsIK were replaced by the USSR Supreme Soviet as the highest organ of state power, a bicameral quasi-parliament, directly elected by the adult population in a secret ballot in single-member constituencies. The soviets at low levels—union and autonomous republic, *oblast, krai*, city, *raion* (district), settlement and village—were now named 'Soviets of Toilers' Deputies' (*Sovety deputatov trudyashchikhsya*), and the franchise was extended on the basis of one man, one vote. (Previously, priests, former landowners and some other categories had been disenfranchised, and the peasants had a restricted level of representation.) In other ways, too, the Stalin Constitution gave all the appearances of enshrining the ultimate in democratic principles, particularly Chapter X, Articles 118–28. These guaranteed basic rights and freedoms: freedom of the press and of assembly, freedom from unlawful arrest and inviolability of the person and the home, plus a range of other individual and collective rights—balanced in Articles 130–33 by certain duties, including military service. This was, of course, the very Constitution under which Stalin conducted the Great Purge trials: indeed, the trial of Zinov'ev and Kamenev in August 1936 was held as the finishing touches to the new Constitution were being made, and that of Rykov, Bukharin and nineteen other prominent defendants took place in January 1937, barely a month after the adoption of the document.

In fact, the changes were largely cosmetic, particularly as far as the representative institutions were concerned. Even in the Supreme Soviet, and more particularly at the local level, the representative functions were not allowed to develop, so by Stalin's death the soviets were as unfulfilled as when he came to power (Friedgut, 1978, p. 464). By contrast, the state's administrative organs burgeoned, with the Commissariats (renamed ministries in 1946), state committees and the state planning commission accumulating enormous power through their control over substantial economic empires. In this apparatus the security organs—notably the State Security Committee (KGB) under Stalin's compatriot Lavrentii Beriya—played a key role, and through it Stalin chose to exercise his power, eclipsing not only the 'organs of state power' (the soviets) but also the communist party.

After Stalin's death, and alongside the reassertion of the party's central role, efforts were undertaken to breathe fresh life into the representative bodies (see Hill, in Jacobs, 1983, pp. 18–33). These culminated in a proposal, adopted at the Twenty-Second Party Congress (1961) to draft a new Constitution, which was eventually drawn up and adopted, with much fanfare and following nation-wide discussion at meetings and in the press, on 7 October 1977 (which replaced 5 December as the public holiday, Day of the Soviet Constitution). This is the current Constitution and is said to incorporate legal and institutional changes appropriate for a society at the stage of 'mature' or 'developed' socialism.

The 1977 Constitution

The currently valid 1977 Constitution (and Constitutions for the union and autonomous republics, adopted during 1978) originally consisted of a preamble and nine chapters, containing 174 articles in all (for a lawyer's exposition, see Butler, 1983, ch. 8). Subsequent amendments will be outlined below.

The Preamble recounts the country's history from the revolution to 'developed socialism', defined as 'a society of mature socialist social relations . . . a natural, logical stage on the road to communism'.

Part I, 'Principles of the social structure and policy of the USSR', briefly defines the *political system* as a socialist state of the whole people, in which all power belongs to the people. The concept of 'political system' was an innovation, reflecting important intellectual developments in the way Soviet political life was viewed inside the country (see Hill, 1980a, p. 164; Brown, in Harding, 1984, pp. 73–81). The key article in this chapter—in fact, the most revealing article of the whole document—is Article 6:

> The leading and guiding force of Soviet society and the nucleus of its political system, of all state organizations and public organizations, is the Communist Party of the Soviet Union. The CPSU exists for the people and serves the people.
>
> The Communist Party, armed with Marxism-Leninism, determines the general perspectives of the development of society and the course of home and foreign policy of the USSR, directs the great constructive work of the Soviet people, and imparts a planned, systematic and theoretically substantiated character to their struggle for the victory of communism.
>
> All party organizations shall function within the framework of the Constitution of the USSR.

That article defines the system's major institutional elements: the Communist Party, the state organizations and the non-state 'public' organizations; it indicates the party's general role, defining broad policy for the society; it identifies the role of the ideology in guiding the party's policy-making activity, claiming the legitimacy imparted by the ideology's 'scientific' character; it indicates the party's method of rule, providing the leading nucleus in non-party organizations; and it repeats Lenin's dictum that the party operates constitutionally. This is a far more honest and realistic representation of power relations than was found in any previous constitution.

Article 5 allows for referendums to be held on 'major matters of state', something called for in the scholarly literature fifteen years earlier (see Hill, 1980a, pp. 100–3). A referendum may, indeed, be a means of introducing new legislation (Article 108), although so far this has not been done. Article 3 states that the organizational principle that governs the functioning of the state is *democratic centralism*. Finally, Article 9 holds out the future hope of greater democratization, promising ever broader citizen participation in managing the affairs of society, through continuous improvement of the machinery of state, strengthening the legal basis of public life, greater openness and publicity, and constant responsiveness to public opinion.

The next chapter, 'The Economic System', identifies state property as the main form of socialist property in the country, adding collective farms and other forms of jointly-held property, and the personal property of citizens derived from earned income. Article 15 identifies the supreme goal of the economic system as 'the fullest possible satisfaction of the people's growing material and cultural and intellectual requirements', and the following article establishes the principle that the Soviet Union constitutes a single economic complex: this is challenged by the aspirations of Estonia and perhaps other republics. Individual self-employed labour for the benefit of society is permitted under Article 17, and has been expanded by legislation in the Gorbachëv period.

Chapter 3, which reads rather like a manifesto, proclaims 'the unbreakable alliance of the workers, peasants and intelligentsia', and declares that the state promotes social homogeneity by eliminating class differences, and provides opportunities for citizens to apply their energies, abilities and talents, and to develop their individual personalities.

Chapter 4 declares that the country's foreign policy is 'a Leninist policy of peace', intended to establish an international climate favourable for the building of communism in the Soviet Union (Article 28). The same article establishes the principle of peaceful coexistence between countries with different social systems, and formally bans 'war propaganda'. Articles 29 and 30 outline the principles governing relations with other states, referring specifically to other countries in 'the world system of socialism'. Articles 31 and 32 (Chapter 5) declare defence of the Socialist Motherland to be one of the state's most important functions, adding that the state provides the armed forces with 'everything necessary for that purpose'.

Part II (Chapters 6 and 7, Articles 33–69) proclaims the equality of citizens' rights, and enumerates citizens' obligations towards the state and the rights that the state undertakes to uphold. Uniformity of Soviet citizenship, equality before the law, equality between women and men, and equality among different nationalities are granted in Articles 33–6.

The rights to work, rest and leisure, health protection, maintenance in old age or sickness, housing, education and access to cultural benefits are all written into Chapter 7, as are freedom of scientific and artistic work, and the right to take part in state and public affairs, together with other civic or political rights, such as the right to form organizations; some of these rights were new in 1977. Freedom of conscience ('the right to profess or not to profess any religion, and to conduct religious worship or atheistic propaganda'—Article 52) is backed up by the prohibition of incitement to hostility or hatred on religious grounds; the article also contains the Leninist declaration of the separation of church from state and of school from the church. The family is afforded state protection; inviolability of the person and the home, and privacy of correspondence and telephone conversations, are assured. Then, in a constitutional innovation, citizens are granted certain rights of complaint against public bodies and state officials, with provision for compensation for damages resulting from unlawful actions.

The chapter then identifies certain civic obligations: to work conscientiously in a socially useful profession; to protect socialist property; to safeguard and enhance the interests, power and prestige of the state; to undertake military service; to respect other citizens' rights and interests; to protect and conserve nature and historic monuments; and, finally, the 'internationalist duty', to promote international friendship and co-operation and help maintain and strengthen world peace.

The state's federal nature is described in Chapter 8, listing the union republics in Article 71—following the order decreed in 1947: descending population at that date (see *Sovety*, 8/1977, p. 23). Article 72 affirms the republics' right to secede from the Union, and subsequent articles define the relationship between the federal jurisdiction and that of the individual republics, with the specific rights and powers of republican authorities and autonomous regions identified in Chapters 9, 10 and 11.

In Part IV the basic state institutions—the Soviets—and their functions are introduced (Chapter 12); the principles of the electoral system are elaborated (Chapter 13); and the deputy's role is broadly defined (Chapter 14). Parts V and VI elaborate the various sets of state bodies, describing their constitution and spelling out their general powers, rights and obligations. Part VII establishes the legal system: the court, the judges and people's assessors ('independent and subject only to the law'), the principle of equality of citizens before the law, the principle of open courts *except* 'in cases provided for by law' (in practice, cases with political overtones), and the arbitration machinery for resolving economic disputes between state enterprises. The procurator's office, headed by the procurator-general, is established by the provisions of Chapter 21.

The symbols of statehood—the emblem (coat-of-arms consisting of 'a hammer and sickle on a globe depicted in the rays of the sun and framed by ears of wheat, with the inscription "Workers of all countries, unite!" in the languages of the Union Republics', the whole surmounted by a red five-pointed star), the flag, the national anthem and the capital city (Moscow)—are described in Part VIII. Finally, Part IX identifies the Constitution as the supreme legal document in Soviet legislation, and makes provision for amendments.

The name of the representative institutions was again altered, to 'Soviets of People's Deputies', emphasizing the universal nature of the Soviet state: it is now classless (whereas the *society* is not), and serves all nationalities. The range of civil rights formally accorded to citizens was expanded; but more explicitly than before it states that 'Enjoyment by citizens of their rights and freedoms must not be to the detriment of the interests of society or the state, or infringe the rights of other citizens' (Article 39). Article 59 observes that 'Citizens' exercise of their rights and freedoms is inseparable from the performance of their duties and obligations', and the constitution enumerates ten specific duties required of all Soviet citizens. The size of the Supreme Soviet's two chambers was equalized at 750 deputies each (formerly, the Soviet of the Union had been elected according to population, and hence had a propensity to expand), and the powers of the Supreme Soviet presidium were extended to include ratifying treaties, declaring war or a state of emergency, and supervising the constitutionality of laws.

In terms of the system's everyday functioning, however, the new Constitution brought about little change, and the institutional arrangements remained essentially as laid down in the Stalin Constitution and subsequently developed through legislation. The state institutions are classified by function: representative 'organs of state power' (or 'state authority'), and executive 'organs of state administration'.

Amendments to the 1977 Constitution

In the autumn of 1988, a series of major changes to the Constitution were proposed and adopted (on 1 December), following a brief nationwide debate during which the republic of Estonia defied the existing Constitution by proclaiming virtual autonomy from the authority of the federal legislature (this claim was rejected). The changes stemmed from the resolutions of the Nineteenth Party Conference, aimed at 'democratizing' the political system.

Chapter 12 establishes the system of Soviets, headed by a new body, the Congress of People's Deputies (see below). A new electoral system is set out in Chapter 13, extending the experience gained in an experiment in 1987, when multi-member constituencies were created and more candidates competed than the number of seats available. The text of Chapter 15 sets out the new institutional arrangements. The first is a Congress of People's Deputies, comprising 2,250 deputies elected on three different bases: population, national territory, and public organizations. Next is a bicameral Supreme Soviet, composed of 542 deputies elected by the Congress of People's Deputies, to meet for two terms of three to four months each year, and to exercise effective powers on behalf of the population *vis-à-vis* the executive arm: for the first time, Soviet citizens will henceforth be represented by professionals.

A new post is established, which is echoed at lower levels in the hierarchy: Chairman of the Supreme Soviet, with virtually presidential powers to speak on behalf of the Soviet state internally and internationally. For example, the chairman nominates the prime minister (chairman of the Council of Ministers) and other leading figures for appointment by the Congress of Deputies or the Supreme Soviet, heads the Defence Council, and formally represents the Soviet state in negotiations with foreign governments. This is a new departure, possibly associated with the need to have formal state (rather than party) authority in dealing with foreign heads of state, perhaps also connected with the desire to demarcate the functions of party and state more clearly—although whether it will do so, given the intention that the party leader should normally be elected to that position, is open to doubts (which were duly expressed at the 1988 party conference, when the proposal was first moved).

This chapter also establishes, again for the first time, a Constitutional Review Committee, to advise the Congress of People's Deputies on the constitutionality of legislation. These provisions—along with the previous provision for independence of the judiciary—are intended to bolster the development of a so-called 'socialist *Rechtsstaat*' (a state based on law—*pravovoe gosudarstvo* in Russian). Certain enhanced rights of representatives in controlling the administration are also set out, and other amendments have the effect of adjusting the powers of the Council of Ministers and other executive organs.

At the time of writing (early 1989) it is not yet clear what the practical effect of these constitutional amendments will be, apart from enhancing the prestige and power of the country's leader. The crucial political question is whether the incumbent will use that undoubted power with the restraint that is required in a democratic system, which the Soviet Union claims to be. Past experience is not encouraging: but it is also true that the main restraint on a *British* government with a secure parliamentary majority is the political culture, rather than any legal impediments. In this field, Gorbachëv is pushing the Soviet Union across borders that the society has never previously attempted to traverse, and it must, at best, be seen as a positive experiment in building democracy'.

Organs of State Power

The organs of state power, as indicated above, are the Congress of People's Deputies and the Soviets of People's Deputies, bearing the name but little of the character of the revolutionary soviets of 1905 and 1917. These are highly formalized bodies of deputies that hitherto were selected according to certain social criteria rather than for their political acumen, skills in representation, administrative flair or even desire to serve their fellow citizens (although, of course, some may possess these qualities). They are formally elected by the population, but there is no doubt whatsoever that until very recently the party authorities effectively controlled the electoral process. The system has come under severe fire under Gorbachëv, and a limited experiment in the local elections in 1987 was deemed a success and is being extended (see Hahn, 1988b).

The Electoral System

The election of deputies to serve on the soviets is one of the few political events in which the population can participate; they may, moreover, perform a directly political act, so it is inappropriate to be too dismissive, despite the existence of a single party and its acknowledged influence, and the broadly unconvincing results. The system is in transition, so our discussion has to be somewhat guarded; it is based on the new legislation adopted on 1 December 1988 (text in *Pravda*, 2 December 1988).

Elections are administered by local soviet executive committees, which are responsible for compiling the lists of voters and defining the constituency and polling precinct boundaries. Electoral commissions, one in each constituency, comprise representatives of works collectives and public organizations and supervise the conduct of the election, scrutinizing the legality of all proceedings, registering the nominated candidates, running the polling stations, counting the votes, and declaring the result. They also issue certificates of eligibility, which allow absentee electors to vote at any polling station in the country. Ballot boxes are taken to hospitals and maternity homes, and polling stations at airports and railway termini and on long-distance trains afford every Soviet voter the opportunity of exercising this civil right.

Candidates are nominated by public organizations and work collectives, and once duly registered they campaign to persuade their constituents to vote enthusiastically on polling day. They are assisted by party workers and other volunteers attached to campaign headquarters—termed an *agitpunkt* (literally, 'agitation point')—located in the constituency. During the campaign a public meeting is held, at which electors give agreed 'mandates' (*nakazy*) to their future representative, whose formal obligation is to strive for the implementation of these mandates: indeed, greater attention has been paid to these of late as a means of feeding demands into the political system (see Hill, 1980a, pp. 95–100). The workers of specific enterprises o certain public organizations are evidently allocated identified constituencies for which to nominate candidates, and a point to note is the common practice for each constituency to adopt two candidates, including a Politburo member who withdraws before polling day, leaving one registered candidate.

On election day—Sunday, a rest day for most voters—the streets are decorated with bunting and banners, and lively music plays from loudspeakers, to create a festive atmosphere. Families and groups of workers are encouraged to turn out and vote together, thus transforming a private act of voting into a social event. Newspapers appear with exhortatory leading articles, and coloured inks splash the front page with the headline, 'Everyone to the polls!' 'Agitators' (canvassers) call on voters to persuade them to vote for the candidates of the 'unbreakable bloc of communists and non-party candidates', a designation introduced by Stalin in 1937.

At the polling station, the voters identify themselves and are given a ballot paper for each level for which they are selecting representatives. Normally, under the new law, each paper is expected to bear several names, and electors are instructed to 'cross out the names of the candidates against whom you are voting'. The previous practice, with only one name (which still continues), required no more effort to vote for the one approved candidate than dropping the ballot paper unmarked into the ballot box, whereas deletion required a visit to the booth to cross out the name 'secretly' (a form of 'inertia voting', rather like inertia selling, which requires effort to reject the merchandise). The electors are now supposed to pass through the booths and mark the ballot, although a proposal to require them to endorse or reject *single* candidatures by marking a box 'For' or 'Against' the name was not incorporated into the final law.

Henceforth, therefore, voters will in many, if not most, cases be offered some real choice between candidates—all approved by the party, as in the past, but at least offering different personalities, energies and capabilities, if not distinct programmes. Voting is not compulsory, but there is tremendous pressure to turn out and support the system by endorsing regime-approved candidates. Most Soviet citizens apparently do that. Even in the partially contested elections of 1987, there was almost saturation turnout, according to official figures, with practically total support for the candidates of the 'bloc', although in a number of cases local party and state officials failed to top the poll, and some even failed to secure the requisite 50 per cent of the vote to secure election. Thus, while old practices of ballot-rigging by those who manned the polling stations eventually continued, out of 120,449 candidates who submitted themselves to competitive election 599 failed to secure the requisite 50 per cent of the poll; 133 seats remained unfilled (Hahn, 1988b, p. 442, citing *Pravda*, 27 June 1987).

Under the new system, all candidates who receive a 'majority' are deemed elected, and places are filled in descending order of votes cast; when all available seats are taken, the remaining candidates who receive a 'majority' become 'reserve deputies'; as such they perform representative functions and may later take the place of deputies who die, retire through illness, move from the area or are removed. That status was attained by 25,127 individuals in the partially contested local election of June 1987 (Hahn, 1988b, p. 442).

Finally, at the USSR and republican levels, a category of deputies is elected by public organizations—the trade unions, creative unions, sports and similar associations—at their conferences or plenary meetings, by secret ballot of the delegates. In the spring of 1989, for the first time within memory, the Soviet Union was gripped by something akin to 'election fever', as candidates vied for nomination, frequently against the nominees of a bureaucracy that had much experience in behind-the-scenes manoeuvring; some leading political figures were obliged to choose where they might run for election against locally-known candidates.

These new arrangements give the electors a greater say in choosing their representatives, since it is now considerably easier not to endorse the approved candidates. In the bulk of cases, perhaps, the result will still be predictable: most Soviet citizens will still be voting for the Soviet regime, as they were a quarter of a century ago (Mote, 1965, p. 87). But the chance to reject mistrusted and despised officials brings a new dimension to the electoral process. This modestly but significantly alters the relationship between rulers and ruled by introducing a measure of uncertainty that scarcely existed in the past. The count will become a more interesting event than it has traditionally been, and the voters can now render a slap in the face to disliked *apparatchiki*, and, of course, to any of their own colleagues deemed to be over-ambitious or otherwise undesirable. Time will tell whether this potential is realized, or is stifled by careful manipulation of the nomination process. The national election results of 26 March 1989, when even senior party and state figures failed to win seats, despite running unopposed, may signal a decisive turn in the importance of Soviet elections.

The Deputies

The 'products' of the electoral system are the people's deputies, who serve a term of five years. In principle, they represent their electors' interests, although in practice their role is severely circumscribed by political tradition and custom: they have never been expected to emulate public representatives in parliamentary systems. Indeed, as noted above, their selection was normally based largely on sociological criteria rather than on their political qualities. Research by Western scholars revealed patterns in the make-up of the body of deputies that suggested a policy of using the soviets as part of citizens' civic training, rather than as an effective element in the policy-making process: their role was further hampered by the nature of the institutions in which they served (see, for example, Taubman, 1973; Jacobs, 1970, 1972, 1983; Friedgut, 1979; Hill, 1973, 1977; Hahn, 1988a). These points were raised in the public discussions initiated by Gorbachëv in 1987 and continued during 1988 as the process of 'democratization' unfolded. One aim of this process is to make the deputies effective, rather than nominal, representatives.

There are at any one time over two million deputies: candidates were elected to 2,251,273 places in local soviets alone in 1987; allowing for some overlap, there are still about two million individuals serving. There is a turnover rate of approximately 50 per cent at each election (a 'renewal' rate of 54.7 per cent was recorded in 1987: Hahn, 1988b, p. 438, note); so several million citizens experience deputy service in a decade. (The number will decline, since the term of office of local soviets was previously half of what it now will be.)

Studies of their composition, based on official statistics, reveal certain policies in candidate selection which seem unlikely to change radically in the short term. Every soviet contains, first of all, the local dignitaries—leading party officials, local government officers, industrial or agricultural managers: these form a core of deputies who often enjoy repeated election. A second category includes similar individuals of lesser status, who serve intermittently. Then come large numbers of 'ordinary' members of the public, probably distinguished by their fine work record or their political devotion (rather than their political acumen), most of whom serve for a single term of office. The extreme uniformity of their social characteristics revealed the care with which deputies were selected according to guidelines issued by the central authorities, with individuals picked out so as to produce a set of figures that testified to the 'representative' quality of the deputies and hence of the soviets in which they served. As Jeremy Azrael (in Cornell, 1970, p. 207) put it, 'the soviets are composed so as almost perfectly to replicate the ethnic, sex, and other demographic differences in society'. In other words, the Soviet form of representative government has traditionally stressed the *sociological* representation of groups by inclusion in 'representative' bodies, rather than representation by the advocacy of causes that reflect group interests (see Table 3.2).

A result of the preoccupation with producing 'representative' statistics is that the individuals selected have not always possessed the qualities required for *effective* representation: the ability to argue a case persuasively, to intervene energetically with the authorities in pursuit of a constituency problem, or otherwise to serve as a 'middleman' between the citizen and the authorities. Deputy service has been regarded as an honour, a form of public recognition for deserving individuals, while the deputies' *political role* of interest articulation was ignored or deliberately played down.

In the 1960s Soviet research began to reveal some of these glaring weaknesses in the quality of the representatives. In consequence, some attempts were made to improve their calibre, by stressing the importance of all-round education, experience of life, and specific training in such fields as the law: deputies are, after all, supposed to be law-makers. Much was done, by publishing handbooks full of helpful advice to newly elected deputies, by establishing seminars and courses to assist them in improving their performance, and by being supportive in other ways. In particular a 'Law on the Status of Soviet Deputies', introduced in 1972, clarified the representative's rights in dealings with the administration.

The results were disappointing, but at least the deputies themselves appear to have had a vision of the role they could play: a survey conducted in the late 1960s revealed that deputies felt a need to spend seven hours minimum each week in order to perform their duties adequately (see Hill, 1980a, p. 50). Yet, even in the USSR Supreme Soviet, deputies were not full-time representatives, but continued their regular work. There was little chance that they could amass the expertise and experience needed to examine legislative proposals effectively: that is but one reason for their traditional role of rubber-stamping policies decided elsewhere. The reforms of 1988 are intended to enhance the role of both the deputies and the institutions of which they are members. But for that to happen, more serious obstacles in the nature of the soviets themselves need to be overcome.

The Soviets of People's Deputies

The soviets today are complex structures combining representative and executive segments that perform a variety of representative, legislative and administrative functions. Legally each soviet is master within its own territory, making all the necessary decisions to run local affairs, within guidelines established at the centre and subject to confirmation by the next higher soviet (according to the principle of democratic centralism). The pinnacle of the system is the *Congress of People's Deputies*, defined in Article 108 of the Constitution as the highest body of state authority in the land, with the competence to discuss and decide any question relating to the running of the USSR. Among its special prerogatives are adopting the USSR Constitution and introducing amendments to it, determining the basic directions of domestic and foreign policy, confirming long-term developmental plans and broad social and economic policies, electing the deputies of the USSR Supreme Soviet (see below), the chairman of the Supreme Soviet (i.e., the country's President) and his first deputy, and confirming the appointment of the prime minister and a number of other leading officials; it may also amend legislation when judged unconstitutional, and call for a referendum.

The Congress comprises 2,250 deputies, elected in three blocks: 750 from territorially based constituencies of equal numbers of electors; 750 from the national territorial units; and 750 from all-Union public

Table 3.2 Composition of local Soviet deputies elected 1987 (per cent)

	Workers	Peasants	Women	CPSU	Komsomol	Under 30
By republic						
RSFSR	45.2	18.4	49.7	42.8	19.9	31.8
Ukraine	33.7	37.9	49.2	43.7	21.0	32.1
Belorussia	38.9	27.8	48.6	44.5	20.6	31.0
Uzbekistan	35.7	27.7	47.8	44.6	20.8	33.1
Kazakhstan	59.5	8.7	49.4	42.2	21.7	33.7
Georgia	39.8	28.7	50.7	43.2	23.0	34.0
Azerbaidzhan	44.5	23.3	48.1	44.9	21.4	34.1
Lithuania	33.8	30.3	48.2	46.0	21.0	32.9
Moldavia	36.6	30.3	49.1	43.4	24.5	36.0
Latvia	33.2	27.2	48.7	45.7	18.2	28.9
Kirgizia	43.6	22.9	48.6	43.6	24.3	34.6
Tadzhikistan	44.1	26.7	49.0	42.9	25.1	36.8
Armenia	50.2	18.7	49.5	43.5	24.0	34.0

Turkmenia	31.0	36.5	48.4	43.5	21.7	35.5
Estonia	44.7	20.5	49.0	45.0	22.1	34.9
By level						
Krai	47.5	10.6	48.7	54.6	25.3	35.6
Oblast	42.9	13.7	47.2	55.9	25.5	34.7
Autonomous *oblast*	48.8	8.4	47.4	52.6	24.2	34.7
Autonomous area	46.5	8.8	45.7	54.0	21.9	35.2
Rural *raion*	37.5	24.0	47.5	50.9	22.2	33.6
Town and city	60.7	0.9	48.9	46.7	22.9	35.0
Urban *raion*	61.3	0.04	49.2	47.3	23.5	35.3
Urban settlement	57.1	4.9	49.8	40.7	19.8	31.8
Village	34.5	35.1	49.8	40.8	19.6	31.3
USSR (Summary figures)	42.1	24.2	49.4	43.3	20.7	32.4

Source: *Sovety narodnykh deputatov*, 8/1987, p. 15.

organizations, including the party, trade-union and co-operative organizations (100 deputies each), young communists, women, veterans and other groups (75 each), and 75 from a variety of further organizations. The first elections to this newly created institution took place (under the provisions of the new electoral law) on 26 March 1989, and the first session—lasting a few days—was scheduled to take place within two months of the election, to elect from among its members by secret ballot 542 deputies to the *USSR Supreme Soviet*, whose membership is to be rotated by one-fifth annually.

This body, comprising two chambers of equal size and of equal constitutional weight, dealing with all-Union and nationality concerns respectively, is intended to be 'a permanently functioning legislative, executive and monitoring organ of state authority'. It is to hold two regular sessions a year, in spring and autumn, each of three-four months' duration, with the possibility of convening extraordinary sessions as the situation demands. The two chambers may meet separately or in joint session. It formally appoints the prime minister (on the recommendation of the President, subject to ratification by the Congress of Deputies) and the ministers and heads of other state bodies, and creates and abolishes ministries and state committees, and also the Defence Council. In principle, deputies have the rights and prerogatives enjoyed by parliamentarians in other systems, including the power to regulate through legislative acts virtually all relations between citizens, groups, organizations and institutions, and the Soviet Union's relations with other states. Deputies are to be encouraged to exercise their right to question ministers, and the Supreme Soviet—like the Congress of Deputies—has the power to amend regulations issued by the Council of Ministers.

Political tradition, if nothing else, long ago established that Supreme Soviet debates were not occasions for challenging policy fundamentals, or even proposing serious alternatives. At most, deputies would make minor suggestions or requests for a slight re-deployment of resources, or a modest amendment to draft legislation. No Supreme Soviet deputy could propose, for example, improving the health service by spending less on missiles, or abandoning the space race in favour of developing water supplies for Central Asia. Such broad questions of development strategy have always been decided elsewhere—specifically in the top party bodies, the Politburo together with the Central Committee apparatus. Even the voting procedure in the Supreme Soviet has been perfunctory: instead of secret voting, or by means of a machine-recorded vote (as in many modern legislatures) or by tellers (as in the British House of Commons), Soviet deputies record their assent by a show of hands on the floor of the house, with little opportunity to vote negatively or abstain. They have been expected to support every motion unanimously, which is what the official record showed until 1988. Disagreements on the floor of either chamber or between the two chambers were virtually unknown. Then, perhaps inspired by Gorbachëv's rhetoric on the need to upgrade the role of representative institutions, small numbers of deputies began to oppose legislation—including the proposed amendments to the Constitution—in what may turn out to have been a foretaste of their future role.

In the past, the most useful work of the Supreme Soviet probably took place in the permanent or standing commissions. Each chamber forms from among its own deputies a number of commissions—seventeen in 1984, each consisting of thirty-five or forty-five members. These convene outside the sessions and examine specific areas of administration, concentrating on the scrutiny of draft legislation prior to its introduction into the Supreme Soviet chambers. In the past the work of these commissions was, by common consent, so hedged around with restrictions that they had no opportunity to monitor or control the work of the ministries. However, a major reform of the system in 1967 led to a considerably more effective role for these bodies in checking on the functioning of the administration (Vanneman, 1977, ch. 6; also Little, 1972; Minagawa, 1975). Some of that role may now be taken over by the deputies in the sessions, but the work of the standing commissions as 'watchdogs' is likely to retain its importance. Special or *ad hoc* committees may also be formed to examine specific policy issues.

These features of the functioning of the Supreme Soviet reflect a modest revival and upgrading of its political significance over the past thirty years or so. The calibre of deputies has been enhanced; the standing commissions meet more regularly; and the technical and informational back-up services have been improved, with better all-round support for the deputies. These developments will surely be augmented as the reform process advances.

The new constitutional stipulations concerning the Supreme Soviet certainly appear to give deputies far greater opportunities than they had in the past to exercise supervision over everyday government and to challenge executive actions at the time of implementation, rather than, as previously, up to several months later. Moreover, as virtually professional representatives, residing in the capital for much of the year, they will be able to accumulate experience and confidence that will permit them to perform their role more effectively with time. This meets repeated criticisms in the past that the essentially amateur representatives, who spent most of their time away from their legislative and representative functions, were no match for the full-time employees of the apparatus, which led to a system dominated by the administrators. Whether they will develop an effective role in practice only time will tell. This is something quite new in modern Soviet politics, and must be viewed as an experimental attempt to overcome the legislature's political impotence in what is seen as a redistribution of power at the summit. It is also part of an attempt to establish a firm basis of law as a social regulator in Soviet society, after half a century or more in which law was seen as subordinate to politics. The political effectiveness of the Supreme Soviet and its deputies will depend in part on how the party performs its self-appointed 'leading and guiding' role (see below), and on the performance of other institutions associated with the Supreme Soviet: the Supreme Soviet Presidium, and the Chairman of the Supreme Soviet (President).

The Supreme Soviet Presidium, until now a body with extensive formal powers to run affairs while the Supreme Soviet was not in session, comprises (as before) *ex officio* officers of the top state bodies of the USSR and the union republics. Its chairman acted as a non-executive head of state: signing legislation, receiving foreign ambassadors and performing other protocol functions. Now it is to be chaired by the Chairman of the Supreme Soviet, with extensive powers of his own. The Presidium services sessions of the Supreme Soviet and the Congress of Deputies, and retains the right to institute and award orders, medals, ranks and titles, to declare amnesties and grant pardons, to appoint and recognize diplomats, and, when the Supreme Soviet is not in session, to mobilize the armed forces, declare war, or take emergency powers to secure the national defence.

The new permanent post of Chairman of the USSR Supreme Soviet—expected to be taken by the party General Secretary—accords sweeping 'presidential' powers to its occupant in representing the Soviet state at home and abroad. Elected by secret ballot for not more than two consecutive five-year terms, and subject to possible recall, this officer supervises the preparation of all matters brought before the Supreme Soviet and the Congress of Deputies, both of which he chairs. He nominates his own first deputy, the prime minister, the members of the Constitutional Review Commission and certain other top officers (subject to formal election or confirmation), heads the Defence Council, negotiates with foreign heads of state and signs international treaties, and exercises 'other powers accorded to him by the Constitution and laws of the USSR'. While on paper these powers appear to be equivalent to those enjoyed by a president in other types of political system, their combination with the prerogatives of CPSU General Secretary renders the USSR President a very powerful figure indeed: such concerns were expressed in the debates surrounding the creation of the post in the autumn of 1988. At the very least, if these innovations are to be seen as part of the process of 'democratization', the leader will have to act with exemplary self-restraint—something that experience and the political culture do not encourage the world to expect of Soviet leaders.

Local Soviet Deputies' Role

As hitherto at the Supreme Soviet level, the deputies sitting in full session meet so infrequently that it is impossible to supervise current events effectively. In these circumstances power slips away from the 'organs of state authority' and accrues to the executive bodies (see below). With such restricted time in each session, the 'debates' frequently turn into formalities. Few deputies have a chance to speak, and those who do are sometimes instructed to do so, even down to being told what to say, so the discussion of the 'report' is more like a parade. Meetings have often been poorly prepared: deputies were sent no background papers or even a draft agenda, so they could hardly make valuable contributions, and simply turned up to raise their hand in an affirmative vote at the appropriate moments (on these points see the sources discussed in Hill, 1980a, pp. 51–4, 69–75; also Hahn, 1988a, ch. 6).

In such circumstances, assuming this uncritical kind of performance suits the political authorities, the more significant part of the deputy's role lies outside the legislative session: working in the constituency on behalf of the electors (arranging school entrance for a child, mediating in neighbourhood disputes, intervening with the amenities department to have a leaky roof fixed before winter, and so forth), or participating in the work of the *permanent commissions*, local equivalents of those in the Supreme Soviet. They survey particular areas of administration, usually under the chairmanship of an expert. They have wide formal powers to scrutinize official records of the enterprises and state departments that they oversee, and may conduct fact-finding 'raids' in preparing a report. Their work is often used as a counterpoint to the administration's report when a particular department is under debate, although there is little direct evidence of their effectiveness in checking the administration. Nevertheless, like general participation in the soviet's work, involvement in a permanent commission serves a valuable educative function for citizens who are otherwise largely excluded from the business of running the country.

Far more powerful are the *executive bodies*: the ministries and state committees at federal and republican levels (see below), and the executive committees in local soviets. Formally elected by the deputies from among themselves (but in fact controlled by *nomenklatura*), they consist of state employees supplemented by deputies who always include representatives of the 'ordinary' workers and peasants. Although answerable to the soviet that elected them, the executive committee members gain substantially in power by virtue of their more regular meetings and of their control over the administrative departments, which they supervise. The bulk of their members are launched on a political career, and the executive committee chairman at any level possesses substantial power (although less than the equivalent party committee secretary): in cities that post is commonly equated with that of mayor, although the duties are far more than ceremonial. Moreover, there is a close interaction with the party organs at all levels (see below). Finally, in this highly centralized political system, the authority of all local government is circumscribed by the power of superior organs, up to all-Union level, to countermand decisions and to remove officers from their posts.

Constitutional innovations introduced in 1988 for subsequent implementation are intended to boost the authority of the elected body against that of the executive organs. Local soviets are henceforth to have a presidium to organize their affairs, so as not to rely on the administration; administrators are forbidden to serve as deputies on the soviet to which their administrative body is subordinated, a common feature in the past (although they may serve at different levels in the hierarchy); and as a rule the newly created permanent post of chairman of the soviet is to be taken by the party secretary, provided he or she wins a ballot of deputies. The purpose of this last controversial innovation is supposedly to lend the political prestige of the party to the representative body, as a counterweight to the power of the state administrators.

The Government Structure

Despite the ideological differences between the Soviet Union and Western governments, the state machinery looks remarkably similar and 'conventional'. This is partly explained by the nature of modern society, whose complexity requires an extensive bureaucratic structure to promote the smooth functioning of the various social, economic and political institutions.

In addition, popular *expectations* of the modern state are such that a formidable array of administrative procedures is required for it to perform its expanded functions adequately. The whole world now tends to look to the state to provide a range of services dependent on the transfer of resources from the wealthy to the less well-off: educational provision, health services, unemployment and other benefits associated with the 'welfare state'. Equally, the state has been relied on to introduce protective legislation for workers against exploitation by entrepreneurs, and for other members of society against the absolute freedom of the market. Legislation to protect women and juvenile workers and, more recently, to guarantee consumers' rights, has become part and parcel of the modern capitalist industrial society. Even those bastions of capitalist liberty, the banks and stock exchanges, have been brought under state supervision in many countries and in the leading capitalist nation, the United States of America, the state uses its power to enforce the competition that is supposedly a basic characteristic of capitalism (Lenin's views on monopoly capitalism and imperialism notwithstanding).

Although more developed in some parts of the world than in others (and with tendencies in the 1980s to revert to less state intervention in society's affairs), the welfare state is substantially different from the 'instrument of class rule' identified by Marx in the Prussia of the 1840s. Hence, even outside the Soviet-inspired 'socialist' countries, the state has become heavily involved in economic activity, and directly or indirectly employs many millions of workers, frequently in those industries—mining, transport, steel and so forth—regarded by Lenin as the 'commanding heights' of the economy. Hence, the Soviet Union has not been unique in manifesting the tendency towards 'big government'.

For Soviet Marxists the state, a transitional phenomenon between capitalism and communism, is an instrument for effecting the transformation of society in the direction indicated by the ideology. Stalin demonstrated that, rather than being simply part of the superstructure reflecting the economic base, the political system was capable of stimulating massive changes in that base. This required the creation of a powerful, centralized administrative structure, backed up by a network of coercive agencies, the like of which has rarely been experienced. In this it can be seen as a pioneer, and it has served as a model for rapid industrial development in newly independent countries.

Whatever the explanations for the universal rise of the modern bureaucratic state, the Soviet Union quite consciously developed the state apparatus as a vital element in the 'transitional' society. In the early years, cosmetic attempts were made to disguise the similarities with 'bourgeois' state institutions (including those of the pre-revolutionary Russian Empire). But the word 'state' (*gosudarstvo* in Russian) has long been a central element in Soviet analyses of that political system, and for decades Soviet political rhetoric has talked of *strengthening* it, rather than inducing its 'withering away' in conformity with Marxist predictions and prescriptions (see Hill, in Harding, 1984).

In fact, from the very origins of the regime there was little real effort to dispense with the state apparatus. Although leader of the Bolshevik Party, Lenin chose not to attempt to rule through the rather sparse party membership, placing himself instead at the head of the governmental apparatus, as chairman of the Council of People's Commissars. His closest party colleagues also assumed important offices in the emerging Soviet state: Trotsky, for example, was People's Commissar for War, responsible for establishing the Red Army; Stalin, as a leading non-Russian in the central party institutions, became People's Commissar for the Nationalities; the writer Anatolii Lunacharskii headed the People's Commissariat for Enlightenment.

Other state bodies were established, including the Cheka (after its Russian initials, standing for Extraordinary Commission), the forerunner of the KGB (State Security Committee), charged with combating 'sabotage', counter-revolution and other subversive activities: this came into its own in the 1930s and has never thrown off its horrific image (although it functioned with greater finesse under Andropov's chairmanship from the late 1960s). Since the introduction of the Five-Year Plans in the 1920s, Gosplan, the State Planning Commission, has always enjoyed a special position among the highest state bodies, with local branches at republican and lower levels (where the equivalent body goes under an appropriate acronym: *gorplan* in cities, *raiplan* in districts, and so forth). The state apparatus works closely with the communist party, and even as he headed Russia's first communist government, Lenin proclaimed the party's political supremacy over the state, which has never enjoyed an independent existence (see below). Nevertheless, it performs important administrative functions, it undoubtedly plays some role in advising the party authorities in policy formulation, and indeed in Stalin's day the ministerial system eclipsed the party as an institution.

In the Stalin system at its apogee, the state revelled in performing two main functions: directing the exciting process of the country's rapid industrialization, and rooting out and destroying alleged subversives and enemies of the state. The burgeoning power of the industrial ministries and the state security provided much ammunition for hostile critics: there was no sign here that the state was 'withering away'.

Partly with this in mind, Khrushchev moved to reduce the power of the ministries, some of which functioned like industrial empires in their own right. In 1957, he abolished the central economic ministries, replacing them with 100 or so regional economic councils (*sovnarkhozy*), which ran the Soviet economy until after his removal from power in October 1964. In 1965, the *sovnarkhozy* were themselves abolished, to be replaced by a revived ministerial structure, augmented with state committees. A further scheme favoured in the Khrushchev era was to abolish the local administrative departments completely, transferring their functions to the soviets' standing commissions: this was actually attempted in some places, but not widely adopted before being abandoned in recognition of the need for professionally competent administrators (see Hill, 1980a, pp. 79–80). So the Soviet Union still carries the full panoply of administrative structures to be expected in such a socially and economically advanced country. The Council of Ministers, headed by its chairman (prime minister), is defined as 'the government' of the Soviet Union, and consists at the present time of some eighty ministries and state committees. (Under Gorbachëv, the ministerial structure is being altered and reduced.) Also considered as members of the government are the chairman of the state bank, the head of the main statistical administration and one or two other senior officials. These individuals, responsible for the everyday running of the country and supervising the detailed implementation of laws by subordinate bodies, are appointed by the USSR Supreme Soviet at its first session, held within two months after its election (however, the appointments are controlled by the party, through *nomenklatura*).

Ministers of the Soviet Union are important and powerful individuals, and their office frequently carries membership of the party Central Committee; a small number are in the Politburo. However, unlike ministers in parliamentary systems, Soviet ministers are not directly *political* figures. They are not responsible ultimately for policy formulation—or at least, for policy *decisions*—although they have some influence in the process because of their access to technical information in their sphere of responsibility. In this they are comparable with the permanent heads of the civil service departments in the British system. In fact, the parallel can be carried further, since Soviet ministers and state committee chairmen are not normally subject to the frequent turnover in office common in parliamentary systems: a well-known example of such ministerial longevity is Andrei Gromyko, who became foreign minister in 1957 and retained that portfolio until July 1985.

Behind these special peculiarities lies an administrative organization broadly comparable with those of other modern states. It is, however, more centralized than other countries' structures, with the principle of 'democratic centralism' dominating the lines of authority. One result is an almost complete lack of horizontal communications between different ministries, which has resulted in a tendency for each ministry, responsible for managing a particular section of the national economy, to expand its activities into peripheral areas, rather than relying on other sectors for supplies. Under Stalin, in particular, ministerial empires flourished, and enormous power of control accrued to individual ministers. Today, in the absence of significant structural reforms, long-established economic ministries are given new tasks to which they may or may not be suited: industrial building concerns construct housing, radar factories and automobile plants produce television sets and refrigerators (Colton, 1984, p. 25). This extends the ministers' *responsibility*; and since the satisfaction of these new consumer needs is now given a higher political priority, their power, too, is increased.

Below the all-Union administration located in Moscow stand ministries at the republican and autonomous republican levels. Certain areas are reserved for all-Union dispensation, notably the defence and security-related fields; others are subject to administration at both levels in collaboration—education, for example; while still others are left to the republics—specifically areas where local cultural traditions are of significance. In local government, the chain of command passes to the administrative departments of local soviet executive committees, which are subject to *dual subordination*: they are answerable both to the soviet to which they are attached and which appoints their heads, and also, through democratic centralism, to the equivalent department of the next higher soviet and ultimately to the appropriate ministry or ministries.

Soviet theorists and politicians have paid much attention to the organs of state administration, and increasingly to the calibre of the staff employed. Apart from their concern about the bourgeois state's police functions, Marx, Lenin and their successors were particularly critical of its bureaucratic tendencies. Thus, in *The State and Revolution* Lenin wrote of the need to 'smash' the old bureaucratic machine and replace it with one that would permit the gradual abolition of all bureaucracy; during the transition from capitalism to communism the economy would be administered rather like the postal service (that is, according to straightforward rules and procedures), and eventually the tasks involved in running society would be so simplified that any literate citizen ('any cook') could competently perform them, and would in fact do so. Under Stalin the opposite happened. The representative institutions in which citizens could both exercise their rights and develop their administrative skills were prevented from developing, while the administration burgeoned, staffed by professional state employees and backed up by unprecedented coercive agencies.

Khrushchev's abolition of the ministries was in part an attempt to reduce the bureaucracy's power at a stroke (see Cattell, 1964), and was accompanied by the transfer of certain welfare functions to bodies such as the trade unions—'public' organizations theoretically distinct from the state. He also attempted to revitalize the soviets, comprising representatives of the population at large, as a counterweight to the power of the administrators, at the same time giving the people experience in administration. The soviets, therefore, could eventually become *non-state* institutions through which, alongside other non-state public organizations, the Soviet people would engage in 'communist self-administration'. Khrushchev's long-term vision of political development, therefore, entailed the 'withering-away' of the state by transferring its administrative functions to the soviets, which would cease to be organs of state; meanwhile, mass participation in public affairs would take place within this branch of the state.

Nevertheless, despite apparently genuine attempts to upgrade the soviets and to formulate a positive role for them, the task of administering the Soviet Union's complex society has increased, not decreased. The technical sophistication required of decision-makers continues to grow, and places an enhanced burden on those charged with policy-making and policy implementation. The 'masses', as such, are not equipped to judge the technical merits of a policy of shifting from coal- to oil-fired electricity production, or the relative merit of using fuel from one part of the country rather than another (or from abroad) in a particular area. Nor, indeed, are the masses likely to decide spontaneously to migrate and establish new industrial centres in the far east to exploit newly discovered mineral deposits. As a leading soviet scholar expressed the problem in 1968:

> In present-day conditions the technical complexity of government, planning and the preparation of well-founded decisions (with scientific calculations, computations, statistics, etc.) is growing significantly. ... This raises the question: how can all this be combined with the necessity of further developing democracy, with widening the participation of the masses in government, with raising the level of activity of the electors, the deputies and the broad masses, when many questions of government are practically within the power only of specialists? (Chkhikvadze, 1968, quoted in Hill, 1980b, p. 164.)

Part of the solution is to raise the administrators' technical qualifications, a point elaborated by scholars and political leaders. The crude bureaucrat whose function is to push through the implementation of state policies has no placed in modern Soviet society. Brezhnev repeatedly called for 'leaders' to display tact and sensitivity, courtesy and responsiveness, in their dealings with the public, as well as greater administrative skill and technical competence. In what came across as a fit of exasperation, at a Central Committee plenum in November 1979, he denounced those officials (of whom there must have been many thousands) who refuse to change their ways 'no matter how much you speak to them, how much you appeal to their conscience or sense of duty'. The time had come, he added, 'to replace those who cannot cope with their assigned work' and to promote 'energetic and creative comrades, [those] with initiative'; as a warning of his earnestness, he criticized eleven ministers by name (*Pravda*, 28 November 1979, p. 2).

Yet, for all the rhetoric, the central authorities have not succeeded in tackling the problem effectively. In his last years, Brezhnev achieved very little in remedying what remains one of the crucial tasks facing the new generation of leaders later in the 1980s. Andropov attempted to weed out those whose services were no longer required, and there was a sharp rise in turnover among party and state officials (see Brown, 1984, p.135). Gorbachëv has identified bureaucratic inertia and resistance as one of the principal obstacles to effective reform of the system, and has been waging a vociferous campaign against all manner of maladministration, including corruption, favouritism, padding of statistics and reports, and other evils identified over many years, and brought fully into the open under the policy of *glasnost'* (openness). Where Brezhnev uttered condemnatory speeches, Gorbachëv has been acting to weed out the incompetent and the corrupt. After the widespread revelations of such evil practices in the recent past, no one can be unaware of the scale of the problem that has to be overcome.

It is not clear, though, what effect such a policy has. It is one thing to sack a minister or a provincial party secretary; but are they personally responsible for all the maladministration within their own bailiwick? At the very least, of course, they set the tone, and together with their colleagues who control the *nomenklatura* they can influence the selection of subordinates. The person who actually engages in coarse behaviour towards citizens is, say, a town's housing manager, or a hotel reception clerk; the person who accepts bribes is the restaurant manager, the school director, the doctor or dentist who prefers lucrative practice to state hospital work, or the theatre manager who dispenses scarce tickets. The individuals who frustrate economic reform are the Gosplan officials, the industrial managers and ministerial bureaucrats, whose established way of doing things provides a comfortable existence that would be disrupted by reform (see Ryavec, 1975).

The fact is, of course, that the Soviet Union is a long way from the glorious state of 'communism' when professional administration will, it is supposed, be able to 'wither away'. There is still a clear need for a large administrative apparatus, and it is obviously desirable that it should be as well designed for its task as is practicable, and that it should be staffed by skilled officials trained to the highest standards of technical competence and imbued with the appropriate values and attitudes both towards their work and towards the public whom they ostensibly serve. The practice of the past sixty-odd years, with its legacy in the present, means that at least for the foreseeable future there is a need for the state administration. Moreover, it must change with the times, and the theoretical underpinnings of this state need to be updated. As one recent booklet expressed it, there have been many changes in the role and place of local administrative departments over the years of Soviet power, yet the basic prescription of their character has remained unchanged since Lenin wrote of the lack of a need for such bodies (Nikolov, 1981, p. 3).

In order to achieve these developmental goals, much literature has been published in recent years, aimed at developing the correct attitudes on the part of the officials themselves, and also at educating the Soviet public to appreciate their own proper expectations of the state administration, and their role in relation to it. In this connection, Soviet commentators have shown much interest in the concept of *culture* (political culture, administrative culture), arguing that what is needed is the development of a 'state service ethic' and greater professionalism among bureaucrats (see, for example, the sources cited by Hill in Harding, 1984, p. 125, notes 70–6). Gorbachëv, too, has pointed to the low level of political culture of Soviet society (Gorbachëv, 1987, p. 82). But if an important dimension of the problem is changing the *culture* of the administrators (see Hill in Potichnyj, 1988), then it requires a long and sustained effort, perhaps spread over several decades. It will mean recruiting and training new generations, while taking steps to ensure they do not succumb to the mores of the existing incumbents (who are, of course, mostly their superiors). There is no easy solution to the problem, which is manifestly hampering the new generation of Kremlin leaders in stimulating a more rational and responsible ethos in Soviet public administration.

Party-State Relations

Relations between the ruling party and the state organs in communist systems are fraught with difficulties, both to regulate and to understand. This point has been made by such eminent Western scholars as Leonard Schapiro (1961, p. 111) and Merle Fainsod (1959, p. 93), and by leading Soviet scholars such as Georgi Shakhnazarov (1974, p. 64). In the West, the relationship has been identified largely as one in which the party 'controls' or 'dominates' the state, which, as a kind of façade (Armstrong, 1973, p. 157), enjoys no independent existence. Many Soviet statements appear to support such an interpretation, including a well-known quotation from Lenin: 'No single decision is taken by a single state organ in our republic without the guiding instructions of the party Central Committee'. This seems to imply that such is the desired relationship.

The difficulty can be conveniently resolved by seeing the 'party' and the 'state' as a single set of interconnected institutions (see M. McAuley, 1977, p. 186). It is to some extent a matter of definition, and the way these sets of institutions *function* in relation to one another is undeniably one of both collaboration and confusion; there may also be a degree of rivalry. In practice, firm lines of separation cannot be drawn between party and state. However, certain aspects of the relationship cannot be adequately appreciated by such an approach, in particular some of the 'problems' identified by party and state leaders themselves. One may conclude, with Waller (1982), that what is a political problem for Soviet officials need not be an analytical problem for Western students trying to identify the system's essence; but this question attracts so much attention that it is at least important to discover what the fuss is about.

In fact, to some extent the Soviet concern appears to be related to a desire to convince the world that the Soviet 'state' is comparable with other states with which it has dealings. There is a particular sensitivity to charges of party domination, reflected in the insistence that the relationship between the two sets of institutions is *political*, based on *persuasion*, rather than the administrative method of commanding or giving orders (see, for example, Barabashev & Sheremet, 1967, p. 34; Paskar', 1974, p. 79).

However, Western students of the Soviet Union cannot accept such statements at face value. For one thing, the very same writers (e.g. Paskar', 1974, p. 79) also assert that 'All decisions of the communist party on the most important questions of public life are obligatory for all state organs, including the soviets'. One might quibble over what constitute 'the most important questions' of public life: but in practice, the party exercises minute control and influence over the work of all state bodies, whether representative or administrative, reducing to zero the scope for an independent role for the state.

Constitutionally, CPSU decisions and edicts are formally binding only on party members, and they become binding on the bulk of Soviet citizens (and acquire validity in international law) only when duly processed by the Supreme Soviet. However, the *political* relationship is such that the state organs must comply with the party's wishes, and the party has a number of means to ensure this compliance (see Hill & Frank, 1986a, pp. 109–18).

Elections

As noted above, the party is heavily involved in the conduct of the campaign for election of representatives to the soviets (see also Hill, 1976). The whole campaign is directed by the party raikoms, which effectively control the selection of candidates and the compilation of their 'mandates'. They ensure that all duly registered candidates are party or Komsomol (Young Communist League) members or at least loyal supporters, who will dutifully implement the party line. Unapproved individuals would never be permitted to stand for election—as was demonstrated in the spring of 1979, when two dissidents, Roy Medvedev and Lyudmila Agapova, failed to secure registration as election candidates; even under the new system introduced in the winter of 1988–9, there is no general freedom to run for election unless nominated by an approved organization. The party in fact uses the campaign to present propaganda in favour of its own policies, and to train propagandists among its own members and recruits (Hill, 1976, p. 598).

The Deputies

This control over elections means the party also enjoys effective influence over the elected deputies. Official statistics indicate that, taking all soviets together, the party is in a minority of some 44 per cent (see Table 3.2). However, the figures also show that the party is in a clear majority at any level of administrative significance, rising to 71.4 per cent in the 1984 Supreme Soviet. Only at the relatively insignificant village level does the party not enjoy a majority among deputies, and in fact the large number of deputies to such low-level soviets distorts the global figure. Furthermore, the Young Communist (Komsomol member) deputies are also under party control, and they usually boost the strength of the formally 'committed' deputies to a majority.

This deployment of party members among deputies, which is likely to persist, is justified as an important aspect of the party's exercise of its obligation—sanctioned by the Constitution—to provide 'leadership and guidance' in all state and other organizations.

Party Groups

In every soviet, the party members and candidate members form a party group, to co-ordinate the work of the party core within the state organ. They function under the direction of the local party committee, and plan a coherent approach in advance of the soviet sessions, probably also selecting speakers for the debates and briefing them on what points to make in their speeches. The party groups strongly influence the allocation of deputies to the permanent commissions (Vinogradov, 1980, p. 265), and they most likely have a say in the selection of officers—although the superior party committee has a stronger influence through *nomenklatura* (see below). This means that party member deputies have an obligation not only towards those whose interests they legally represent (their constituents) but also—and primarily—towards the party. As representatives of the party in the organs of state, their obligation is to ensure that the state carries out party policy.

Similar party groups exist within the state administrative apparatus, alongside formal PPOs (formed, it will be recalled, where three party members are employed). Ministries, state committees, Gosplan, local soviet administrative departments and the like each have their party group or organization, embracing all party members employed there. They regularly discuss the department's business and the work of individual party-member employees. These meetings may be seen as forums at which the party members are given their working instructions. If a party member in the state apparatus felt any conflict between the party's wishes and what, say, administrative procedures or efficiency—or even the perceived needs of the electorate—indicated, then party discipline should ensure the party's desires were carried out. For CPSU members, the party's decisions have the force of law (Ukrainets, 1976, p. 65), which implies that even if a soviet declined to give legal force to a party policy the communist deputies would have to carry it out anyway.

Overlapping Membership

This imposition of discipline on its members, regardless of how they might perceive their other commitments, is obviously a very powerful instrument of party control over the state. It is enhanced by interlocking or overlapping membership of state and party positions. Party committee members frequently serve as soviet deputies (or, conversely, deputies sit on party committees), and there is overlapping among members of the executive bodies as well.

The party first secretary is usually a local soviet deputy (and henceforth will normally be elected chairman of the soviet), while the soviet executive committee chairman habitually serves on the party committee and often on its executive bureau. At the Supreme Soviet level, there is overlap with the CPSU Central Committee, and among members of the Politburo and central secretariat (party bodies) and the Supreme Soviet presidium and the Council of Ministers and its presidium. In February 1989, for example, the Politburo contained the prime minister (Ryzhkov), the minister of foreign affairs (Shevardnadze), the minister of defence (Yazov), the first deputy chairman of the USSR Supreme Soviet Presidium (Luk'yanov), two USSR Council of Ministers deputy chairman (Biryukova and Talyzin), the chairman of Gosplan (Maslyukov), and the Russian republic's prime minister (Vlasov); all are, by definition, CC full members (for a complete listing of the Politburo and party Secretariat membership, see Table 3.3). Similar principles apply at lower levels (see Hill, 1977, ch. 6), and will also be applicable in the new Congress of People's Deputies and in the local Soviet presidiums.

This practice means that, to a significant extent, those involved in adopting policy decisions are also responsible for passing the laws that give statutory authority to the policy. Indeed the party committee usually meets immediately in advance of the relevant soviet, so that members can go more or less directly from one meeting to the next, perhaps pausing for a meeting of the party group (which includes those communist deputies not on the party committee): Supreme Soviet sessions are normally preceded by a CPSU CC plenum, where personnel changes or policy innovations to be given legal endorsement are agreed. Probably the same will apply in future to the annual sessions of the Congress of People's Deputies. So overwhelming is the political

Table 3.3 CPSU Politburo and Secretariat, February 1989

Name	Age	Nationality	Offices held
* Gorbachëv, M. S.	57	Russian	CPSU CC General Secretary; Chairman, USSR Supreme Soviet Presidium
Vorotnikov, V. I.	62	Russian	Chairman, RSFSR Supreme Soviet Presidium
Zaikov, L. N.	55	Russian	First Secretary, Moscow city party committee
* Ligachëv, Ye. K.	68	Russian	Chairman, CC Commission for Agriculture
* Medvedev, V. A.	59	Russian	Chairman, CC Commission for Ideology
* Nikonov, V. P.	59	Russian	Deputy Chairman, CC Commission for Agriculture
Ryzhkov, N. I.	59	Russian	Chairman, USSR Council of Ministers (Prime Minister)
* Slyun'kov, N. N.	59	Belorussian	Chairman, CC Commission for Social and Economic Policy
* Chebrikov, V. M.	65	Russian	Chairman, CC Commission for Legal Policy
Shevardnadze, E. A.	60	Georgian	Minister of Foreign Affairs
Shcherbitskii, V. V.	70	Ukrainian	First Secretary, CC, CP Ukraine

* Yakovlev, A. N.	65	Russian	Chairman, CC Commission for International Affairs
Biryukova, A. P.	59	Russian	Deputy Prime Minister; Chairman of the Council of Ministers Bureau for Social Development
Vlasov, A. V.	56	Russian	Chairman, RSFSR Council of Ministers
Luk'yanov, A. I.	58	Russian	First Deputy Chairman, USSR Supreme Soviet Presidium
Maslyukov, Yu. D.	51	Russian	Chairman, Gosplan
* Razumovskii, G. P.	52	Russian	Chairman, CC Commission for Party Construction and Personnel Policy
Solov'ev, Yu. F.	63	Russian	First Secretary, Leningrad obkom
Talyzin, N. V.	59	Russian	Deputy Chairman, USSR Council of Ministers; USSR Permanent Representative at CMEA
Yadov, D. T.	65	Russian	Minister of Defence
Baklanov, O. D.	56	Russian	CC Secretary (Responsible for Defence Industries)

Note: Names appear in the official order, alphabetically in Russian, with the exception of Gorbachëv, and according to rank. Gorbachëv to Yakovlev are Politburo full members, Biryukova to Yazov are candidate members; the Secretariat consists of those Politburo members marked * plus Baklanov.

authority of party committee meetings, and so effective the discipline they can impose on their members, that the soviets in session have hitherto acted as little more than rubber stamps (see Hahn, 1988a, ch. 6).

Nomenklatura

The party exercises its greatest influence over the work of the state, however, in the staffing of the administrative apparatus, achieved through the formal but essentially confidential recruitment arrangement of *nomenklatura*. As explained in relation to the party, the *nomenklatura* lists include posts in the party apparatus itself and in other organizations, including the state institutions. Some of these positions are nominally elective, including such important posts as chairman of a soviet executive committee, chairman of a city planning department, and so forth. Party committees usually meet before a newly elected soviet's first session, and arrange the allocation of these posts; the party's wishes are communicated to the first session by the party committee first secretary (himself a deputy), who makes the nominations to the key posts; the deputies oblige by 'electing' those nominees.

In practice, therefore, the CPSU—through its committees—influences the staffing of key segments of the state apparatus, and so should ensure the competence and political reliability of its nominees. In practice, it does not always succeed, and it can use what amounts to a party veto over state appointments to shield the incompetent: in Georgia in the early 1970s, for example, over 120 out of 313 *nomenklatura* officials lacked the educational qualifications for the job, and 280 ordinary workers were in posts that nominally required higher education (Kharchev *et al.*, 1976, pp. 59–60).

The Effectiveness of Party Control

The last example raises an important question: what is the political impact of this elaborate array of party controls? There is much evidence of failure to have party policies implemented by the state. The party authorities pass resolutions year in, year out, calling for tighter state discipline and incessantly bemoaning incompetence, inefficiency, red tape, corruption and other administrative failures. A standard justification for such heavy involvement has been that the party's superior experience, knowledge and wisdom befits it to exercise such a 'leading and guiding' role throughout society. Also, a certain logic derives from the system's ideological underpinning: the party's understanding of the ideology supposedly enables it to devise 'scientifically correct' policies for building communism; those policies must therefore be implemented, and the party has a right and a duty to ensure compliance, by influencing the selection of the personnel directly responsible for policy implementation, and then supervising their performance. With that in mind, the party's organizing principle of democratic centralism has been applied to the state structure, and indeed all other organizations (see Vasil'ev, 1973), ensuring that effective supervisory power is vested in the centre; and, in 1971, at the twenty-fourth CPSU congress, the rights of PPOs to supervise the day-to-day work of state bodies were expanded.

Party Interference

The party does not directly admit its own responsibility for the deplorable state of affairs in the administration. However, it has long acknowledged the tendency to supplant the state organs, taking over their work and interfering in purely administrative tasks that are the state's proper concern. Known in Russian as *podmena*, this has long been regarded as a serious problem preventing the development of an appropriate working relationship between party and state.

Soviet spokesmen explain *podmena* in terms of a lack of respect by both party and state officials for each other's legitimate area of competence. Indeed, the vague phrase of 'leading and guiding' is a very imprecise guideline for the local party officers responsible for exercising that function. Their own success is largely measured by the success of policies within their own district, yet they have to rely on officials in the state apparatus, or in economic management, to arrange for those policies to be implemented. Not surprisingly, they tend to issue direct instructions to the responsible officials, or over their heads—particularly when, as in the 1930s when the present system was being devised, the party officials might legitimately be said to possess skills, expertise and experience lacking in the state apparatus.

Equally, state and economic officials have every incentive to avoid taking decisions, knowing that the penalty for a faulty decision in the past has been dismissal or worse, and sensing that ultimately the party officials will intervene in any case. Local state officials tend to refer even trivial matters to the local party committee, overburdening it with administrative details when it should be responsible for general policy guidelines and political supervision: hence the view of party and state as a single entity, in which roles are confused and duplicated. In everyday practice, the party engages in 'parallelism'—setting up a duplicate apparatus that so closely supervises the work of its 'state' counterpart that the latter is capable of performing only in an auxiliary administrative capacity.

Complications to the Picture

So far, this discussion has emphasized the subordinate nature of the state: the state is politically subservient, subjected to supervision and control under the guise of leadership and guidance. However, the state organs do not simply execute party policy without question, and the relationship is more complicated and complex than the traditional notion of domination would allow for.

One dimension of this complexity can be explained by modern administrative theory (see, for example, Downs, 1967). Policy implementation is not just a matter of applying specific instructions. The CPSU's central organs do not issue millions of directives saying what needs to be done in carrying out the latest policies: that would be quite impossible in any society, let alone one so populous, dispersed and diversified. Instead, fairly broad statements are issued in the name of the Central Committee, which are interpreted as they pass down the administrative hierarchy to where individual communists or citizens put the policy into practice. At each stage, opportunities exist for distortion or misunderstanding, because, after all, bureaucratic systems are run by human beings, not yet by reliable computers that simply store and transmit information.

All officials have their own perspectives and interests, which affect their performance. This question has come to be recognized in recent years by Soviet social scientists, who are paying attention to the matter (see, for example, Obolonskii, in Kerimov *et al.*, 1979, pp. 72–81;

Lebedev, 1980, pp. 156–210). For example, apart from serving as representatives of central authority in a system governed by democratic centralism, party and state officers in the localities have responsibilities towards the area where they serve, particularly native administrators in the minority nationality areas, who must be aware of the pressures of their populations for advancement. As individuals, moreover, they know their own careers depend on their being able to report 'success' to a political centre that is physically remote (and therefore limited in its capacity to check up): so they may engage in selective emphasis in their interpretation of central policy.

Secondly, the centre needs information on which to base its policies. As society grows ever more diverse, the task of governing it by adopting appropriate policies becomes vastly more difficult. An effective policy is carefully devised to change the existing situation—but that presupposes the maximum information about the situation. Even though the long-term goal ('building communism') is derived from the ideology, Marxism-Leninism is not a blueprint, and the society must be kept running reasonably smoothly in the present. In fact, the guardians of the ideology require information on the present situation, in order to gauge how far the society has travelled towards communism.

The state organs, forming a bureaucracy, possess much information relevant to the policy-makers in the central party apparatus. The bureaucrats, after all, are responsible for *running the country*, whereas the party ostensibly is not. The CPSU could hardly devise policy without the expertise of the Council of Ministers, which bears ultimate responsibility for administration. It in turn can call upon the experience and information accumulated by bureaucrats, economic managers and state officials right down to the localities, collate and aggregate this, and place it at the disposal of the party. Such political communication is facilitated by the overlap between state administrative bodies and party committees. Not only can the party authorities *require* their own members in state offices to disclose information, by invoking party discipline, but equally those same state officials have a chance to present their own perspective on information, as they feed it into the decision-making process.

Moreover, even the soviets may have a role in this. The system of 'electors' mandates' to deputies has been identified as a significant means of feeding information into the political process (see Hill, 1980a, pp. 95–100). The deputies also are seen as performing a useful input role, since they are in contact with the interests, needs and aspirations of their constituents, or at least of those alongside whom they work.

If these arguments are at all valid, therefore, the relationship between party and state becomes not simply one in which the state is subservient to the CPSU: rather there is a degree of complementarity in their relations. The Soviet state is not an independent repository of power; but neither is it simply the dutiful handmaiden of the politically dominant CPSU.

Furthermore, at local level, relationships among officials are complicated by *hierarchy*. The state institutions themselves constitute a structure in which power resides at the top, in Moscow, among individuals (ministers, state committee chairmen, Supreme Soviet officers and so forth) who are prestigious party members in their own right, many of them on the Central Committee. This gives local state officials a channel of influence to counteract a local party secretary's overbearing 'authority', since a minister who is on the CC ranks far ahead of a district or city secretary whose highest party office is provincial committee membership (Hough & Fainsod, 1979, pp. 505–6).

These considerations help to explain some of the exasperation voiced by Gorbachëv at the unresponsiveness of state and party officials to respond to his policy of *perestroika* (for an elaboration of this point, see Hill & Dellenbrant, 1989, ch. 10). While easily pilloried as selfish and obstructive, bent on maintaining their privileged position in the system—sentiments that undoubtedly do inspire a good deal of the bureaucratic resistance—many local officials in party and state are perhaps fundamentally perplexed by the competing demands made upon them. They are now expected to display initiative—but they are also subject to party discipline and democratic centralism; they are expected to change radically their mode of operation—yet they are not given training in new managerial techniques; they are also charged with keeping the society running as efficiently as possible—which means responding to a population that is itself imbued with certain expectations of the role of government and administration. Moreover they recognize the imperatives imposed by the continuing tradition of the party's 'leading and guiding' role and by the power that superiors have over their careers. So long as it is politically impermissible to make mistakes, state officials will continue to play safe and let the party take the rap if things go wrong; and so long as a principal reward of party officials derives from the power of influence over state officials, they are unlikely to forswear such satisfactions. The problems of local administration are just as much associated with the complexities of party–state relations as they are with bureaucratic obduracy and bloody-minded resistance.

Conclusion

Party–state relations remain beset with difficulty, both for Western students and for those trying to devise an 'appropriate' relationship and attempting to make it work as intended. So far, they have failed, as witness their continuing concern about *podmena*, parallelism and petty supervision, and the anguished comments about the 'conservatism' of the bureaucracy. There is an aspiration to delineate the spheres of competence of the two sets of institutions, and Gorbachëv has taken some steps to enhance the law-making institutions of the state, to place the administration under more effective democratic control, and to get the party to abandon its 'infallibility complex' and step back from day-to-day involvement in the running of the country. So far, though, the impact has been modest. There is still, apparently, every intention that laws adopted by the Soviet Soviet will embody what the party's leaders deem appropriate as Soviet society continues its development towards 'communism'—although those leaders may be a little more responsive than in the past to demands emanating from the masses. The Soviet state institutions, too, particularly the revamped representative bodies, have a contribution to make in attaining the long-term goal, and may have an enhanced influence—however modest it remains—over policy details. However, the party's 'leading and guiding' role means that institution retains the prerogative of determining which policies are 'correct': to that considerable extent—and to the extent that its own officers still abuse their political authority in dealing with state and other non-party institutions—the CPSU is still the dominant political force in Soviet society.

Mass Organizations

In addition to the Communist Party and the state, there is a further element in the institutional framework within which Soviet political life takes place. Article 7 of the Constitution refers to 'Trade unions, the All-Union Leninist Young Communist League [the Komsomol], co-operatives, and other public organizations, [which] participate, in accordance with the aims laid down in their rules, in managing state and public affairs, and in deciding political, economic, and social and cultural matters'. The Communist Party itself has been identified as a social organization that occupies a unique position in the system, as have certain types of economic association, such as collective farms, fishing co-operatives, housing co-operatives, hunters' co-operatives (even 'summer cottage-building co-operatives') (Yampolskaya, 1975, pp. 49–51). These are obviously quite different from sports societies, creative and trade unions, blind and deaf welfare societies and so forth, and will be omitted from the present discussion.

The Komsomol

The most obviously political of such organizations is the Komsomol, effectively a junior branch of the Communist Party. Enrolling young people from the age of 16 through the politically formative years up to their early twenties (and sometimes up to 28), it is run mainly by recent party recruits, and its rulebook is virtually indistinguishable from that of the CPSU. It fulfils an important socializing function for the majority of Soviet young people (Komsomol membership stood at almost 41 million in 1987: *Yezhegodnik*, 1987, p. 20), and it prepares young people for membership of the party itself, which draws some 70 per cent of new recruits from among Komsomol members.

Younger children pass through the Little Octobrists (in Russian, *Oktyabryata*—Children of October), for 6- to 9-year-olds, and the Young Pioneers who, with their white shirts and distinctive red neckerchiefs and hats, often perform guard-of-honour duties at war memorials or in polling stations. By involving practically the whole of the rising generation in such officially sponsored mass organizations, the authorities are attempting to inculcate the value of collectivity, rather than individual development (see Riordan, in Avis, 1987, ch. 6). They are simultaneously preparing future citizens for involvement in the adult political world, by familiarizing them with structures and organizational principles encountered in adulthood. For the small proportion of highly devoted and politically keen citizens (plus perhaps some ambitious cynics), that could mean party membership, or experience as a soviet deputy. For the masses, an array of other institutions exist to channel their energies and enthusiasms, thereby pursuing their intellectual interests and involving themselves in public organizations. Moreover, under Gorbachëv, the opportunities for participation in new, unofficial organizations have expanded greatly.

Trade and Creative Unions

Distinguished among the mass organizations are the trade and professional unions, to which almost the whole Soviet work-force belongs—an impressive 140.8 million men and women in 1987, organized in some 707,100 primary branches and 640,800 workshop organizations (*Yezhegodnik*, 1987, p. 19). Their special position derives from the sheer mass nature of their membership, from their character and from their very close relationship with the political system.

Unlike trade unions under capitalism, Soviet unions are engaged less in defending the workers' interests against factory owners or managers than in promoting the perceived common interests of all engaged in the productive process: attaining the greatest output as effectively and efficiently as possible, consistent with certain principles of labour protection, safety, and so forth. As Yampolskaya (1975, p. 52) puts it.

> the trade unions are called upon to mobilize the masses for carrying out the country's main economic task—to create the material and technical basis of communism, to work to further strengthen the economic might and defence potential of the Soviet state and to ensure the steady improvement of the well-being and culture of the working people.

The connection with the political authorities is even closer than this. It is openly stated that 'the unions perform their tasks under the direct leadership of the CPSU and in close contact with the system of soviets and the sectoral apparatus of state administration' (Yampolskaya, 1975, p. 53). Many officials in the trade-union organization serve as deputies in soviets, or sit on CPSU committees. The head of the national trade-union committee, the All-Union Central Council of Trade Unions (VTsSPS) is invariably a member of the Central Committee. Past occupants of the position have been in the Politburo, which nominates them to the post; the same applies at republican level. The ordinary union member therefore belongs to a highly politicized, if not directly political, organization.

In return for the monthly subscription—a small percentage of earnings—the member gains certain benefits. In addition to services at the work-place, the unions run subsidized sanatoria, vacation camps and trips for their members, and since Khrushchev's day they have administered certain social welfare schemes on behalf of the state. The so-called creative unions, for writers, composers, architects, artists and other members of the creative intelligentsia, and other unions organized at republican level, operate somewhat differently. They are not jointly organized or affiliated to a co-ordinating council, and their major function is to ensure copyright protection, proper remuneration and similar professional concerns for their members. They are also responsible for maintaining appropriate artistic standards. In view of the delicate subject matter of creative works, this often means that they police their members' output on behalf of the authorities. They wield the ultimate right of expulsion, thereby—as in the case of Solzhenitsyn—depriving their members of the right to practise their craft. The marked relaxation under Gorbachëv in what may be produced and published has somewhat undermined that particular function, but it remains in reserve.

Other Organizations

Apart from the directly political and quasi-political organizations already referred to, there exists a plethora of special-interest groups to which Soviet citizens adhere in their millions. These range very broadly, and can almost match the variety of bodies that cater for citizens' intellectual interests and organize their leisure time in other modern societies. Stamp collectors and numismatists, basketball and tennis players, cinéastes and choral singers, radio hams and target shooters, nature lovers and protectors of the architectural heritage, and quasi-charitable associations for the welfare of the disabled: these and other sometimes surprising pastimes and pursuits are catered for, all under the auspices of one or other officially sponsored and registered organization. There are also what in other countries would be seen as professional associations, such as the Soviet Political Sciences Association, or the Paediatric Doctors' Society. Like the Soviet Red Cross and Red Crescent societies, these may be affiliated to international organizations, in which their members sometimes serve as officers. Although largely unknown or ignored in the West, since they are clearly not independent in the way that their Western equivalents are, these organizations do cater for the interests of Soviet citizens, they offer a chance of involvement in social life, and they can occasionally open foreign travel opportunities—particularly the various societies for friendship with foreign countries.

The lack of independence among those institutions is a fact, nevertheless; however, under Gorbachëv there have been marked changes in the range and type of public organizations in existence. Alongside the officially sponsored bodies there are now a plethora of 'independent' bodies whose existence seems reasonably secure. Until this new development, no matter what the peculiar needs of each public organization, they were virtually identical organizationally and administratively. All were governed by the principle of *democratic centralism*, and all were strongly influenced by the political authorities—specifically the party, which had control over the selection of officers and other leading personnel through *nomenklatura*. In addition, at the enterprise level, the party primary organization always established party groups within the societies to ensure conformity with the appropriate standards, as determined by the political authorities, and generally acted as a coordinator among them. The role of the public mass organizations was often seen, therefore, as one of disciplining the masses, by channelling their interests in approved directions.

Similarly, their role can also be seen as one of controlling the expression of opinion in the given area. Cases such as the volleyball section of the all-union sports association or the chess federation carry little political significance, except when Soviet policy becomes implicated: for example, in a chess tournament involving Israeli or South African players. A theatre group, by contrast, may deal with politically sensitive materials, so from the regime's perspective the repertoire and interpretations should be controlled, and the officially approved artistic canons of 'socialist realism' should be inculcated into the players. In other ways, too, the party uses these organizations, most obviously in giving party members and other approved citizens administrative experience, to be used later in a more directly political role.

However, such associations may not be simply the tools of the political authorities: they may have some political input. As Soviet society grows more complex and sophisticated, the range of issues requiring policy decisions expands considerably, into areas of human activity with which the writings of the 'founding fathers' are little concerned. Lenin had nothing to say about the needs of hang-gliding enthusiasts or even about the desirability of developing such a sport; yet, in a country where nothing is left to spontaneous market forces, introducing such a novel activity into Soviet society requires a series of authoritative decisions, if only at the level of deciding to manufacture or import the equipment. There may be many pursuits and interests, therefore, about which the government as such has no firm opinions, and on which it may be willing to heed advice and respond to demands. It seems more likely to do so if those demands are expressed through a channel that it itself has sponsored, and one that is run by individuals who enjoy party confidence.

Furthermore, such an attitude may even on occasion extend to more contentious policy areas. It has been argued, for example, that public opinion, expressed through the society for nature conservation, has influenced the introduction of protectionist legislation since the mid-1960s (Safarov, 1975, p. 169). There may be little direct evidence of a link of this kind (see Kelley, in Ryavec, 1978, pp. 88–107; Gustafson, 1981); and one might argue about the effectiveness of such measures as have been introduced (see, for example, Perry, 1973). Undeniable, however, is the rising tide of public attention paid to this issue in the Soviet Union, as elsewhere, with a section of the party leader's congress speech now regularly devoted to the issue, and a steady stream of conservationist legislation. All this has taken place in the face of the traditional emphasis on heavy (which usually meant dirty) industry, and the well-entrenched industrial ministry and Gosplan lobby.

In other cases, there may be a still more clearly political overtone to the society's pursuit: the All-Russian Society for the Preservation of Historical and Cultural Monuments is a body that appears to have laudable and innocuous goals, but has become in fact a vehicle for Russian nationalist sentiments—a clear political purpose in some ways contrary to the regime's values. It is believed, moreover, to enjoy the support of leading figures in the cultural world, and also to have influenced the thinking of some highly placed politicians (see Dunlop, 1984, ch. 3).

If this analysis is correct, the Soviet Union is experiencing the beginnings of a genuinely political process, in line with the notion of 'socialist pluralism of opinion' expressed by Gorbachëv. It has been argued inside the country for some years that the role of such organizations is growing, in terms of membership numbers, the range of interests catered for and problems tackled, their extension throughout the country and society, and the expansion of their funds, which enables them to improve the facilities and services offered to their members (Yampolskaya, 1975, pp. 166–75); such enhancements may have made them more effective as interest articulators. In the late 1980s, however, they have been joined by an array of independent—or quasi-independent—organizations that express a further variety of interests and attempt to influence the course of events (see Hosking, 1988a, 1988b): there were some 60,000 of such associations by the end of 1988, including dozens of political discussion clubs in the major cities.

Quite obviously, the party is not about to offer lobbying facilities to the mass organizations and associations; it still attempts to control the major ones by appointing reliable officers, and it carefully (although now far from rigidly) prescribes the boundaries both of the interests that they pursue and of permitted forms of expression. For quite a long time, though, a clear emphasis has been placed on the mass organizations as a third institutional pillar of the Soviet political system, alongside the party and the state, in analyses of 'developed socialism', and they are being given an enhanced position in the political rhetoric, and to some extent the practice, of *perestroika*. There appears to be a move under Gorbachëv towards institutionalizing channels for interest articulation, as a means of giving the citizen a sense of genuine involvement in the country's political system.

For the moment, the shackles have not been removed entirely; there remain limits in the extent to which such channels and other means—including the enhancement of the role of the soviets and their deputies—can facilitate effective interest articulation. Yet the boundaries of what is possible are now broader than they have been for well over fifty years, and this has had a marked effect on the fate of one of the country's most important political developments over the past quarter of a century: the rise of a wave of dissidence, indicating a clear feeling of the inadequacy of the system's capacity to respond to demands for opportunities for self-expression.

Political Dissent

A consequence of an official ideology that identifies a 'correct', scientifically accurate understanding of society is that its values must be accepted by everyone. A parallel is the adoption of a state religion, to which all must adhere—a phenomenon well entrenched in Russian and European history. Furthermore, the 'totalitarian' model stressed that the Soviet regime strove to ensure conformity with the values of Marxism-Leninism, and assumed that the regime would fully use its powers to destroy competing sources of information and prevent simple dissatisfaction from coalescing into dissent or opposition. The Russian word for dissident—*inakomyslyashchii*—simply implies one who thinks differently.

The Soviet government does indeed possess an impressive array of devices for controlling information flows, and hence the circulation of competing ideas. From the education system to organizations for children and adults, from censorship of publications and broadcasting to the control of foreign travel (including travel by foreigners into and within the country), the authorities in principle possess the means of ensuring ideological and political conformity. Where different ideas do infiltrate the Soviet public mind, a security apparatus exists to root them out. Indeed, the massive terror apparatus characteristic of Stalin's

Soviet Union was a fundamental part of this model, effectively eliminating political opposition and dissent, by physically destroying those found guilty of expressing critical thoughts; this inevitably inhibited their development. There was no identifiable dissidence in the Stalin era, yet this is hardly because the whole population really was firmly behind the leader.

By contrast, a remarkable feature of Soviet life in the past twenty years has been the rise of political dissidence, which has been given enormous publicity in the West, usually accompanied by strong anti-Soviet rhetoric, since to the liberal conscience a regime that forbids the voicing of opposition to the government and its policies contradicts the basic values of 'democracy'.

Sources of Dissidence

Given the control over the circulation of ideas, it is somewhat surprising that, half a century after the revolution, such a wave of antipathy—even hostility—to the system's values and institutions should have arisen. Despite massive efforts over several decades at politically re-educating the population, inculcating the notion that the party always serves the best interests of the entire people, that message has still not been assimilated by at least some sections of the population.

There have been two traditional explanations for this. First, dissidence reflects bourgeois prejudices that have lingered on since before the revolution: but the longer the present system persists and influences the socialization of new generations, the less plausible such an explanation becomes. Secondly, dissent reflects the subversive activities of external agents, particularly the hostile bourgeois states of the capitalist West and their agencies such as Radio Liberty (broadcasting to the Soviet Union from Munich) or Voice of America: this implies a failure by the heavy-handed Soviet national security agencies, and a vulnerability to alien ideas that calls into question the ideology's alleged 'scientific' character. These interpretations both contain a grain of accuracy, but other explanations provide a more comprehensive understanding.

The Family

As the primary socializing agent, the family establishes the individual's initial orientation towards society. Through it, unapproved beliefs and values may have been transmitted across the generations—for example, religious faith, passed on from *babushka* to grandchild in a society where the grandmother has traditionally been the baby-minder. Similarly, details of family history may amplify and contradict the official line—say, of an uncle who disappeared in the purges, an event well known to everyone alive at the time, but about which until the past few years there was a notable official reticence. The family may thus help to educate about the past differently from the history books.

Religion

Organized religion, despite the official creed of atheism, has also been associated with the rising tide of dissent. In recent years interest in religion has surged, despite multiple forms of pressure amounting to virtual persecution, as revealed in the researches of the British-based Keston College, and chronicled in the College's journal, *Religion in Communist Lands*, and in the books of its director, Michael Bourdeaux (1965, 1971, 1975, etc.). This embraces both recognized denominations such as the Russian Orthodox Church, Baptists, Roman Catholics, Islam and Buddhism, and unofficial and secret sects such as the Jehovah's Witnesses and Seventh-Day Adventists. Moreover, whereas until the mid-1960s religious observance was increasingly becoming the preserve of poorly educated, elderly rural women, more recently younger and relatively well-educated citizens have developed an interest in religion (Biddulph, 1979). A number of sociological explanations for this have been put forward (see, for example, Christel Lane, 1974, 1979), among which the curiosity factor must play some part, stimulated by the knowledge that 'official' society disapproves of it; in addition, an increasingly educated society seems less prepared nowadays to accept official teachings without question.

Religion challenges the authorities since by definition it rejects Marxism-Leninism, especially its materialism, assuming that there are spiritual values more important than material values, and forces in the universe beyond those of physics and the human intellect. There has been a policy of forcibly closing church buildings, and in law congregations must register with the civil authorities, which can take over church property for profane use (most notoriously, cathedrals are used as anti-god museums, but more prosaically a delightful little church on Moscow's Kalinin Prospekt now houses an aquarium). Nevertheless, church buildings still exist, often prominently positioned on a hill in the centre of a village, a visible symbol in stone and gilt of values distinct from those the regime wants citizens to uphold. In the past two decades, many old churches have been designated historical monuments, and the state has lavished significant funds on refurbishing them, even re-gilding faded cupolas in Moscow and other cities.

Under Gorbachëv, this trend has been taken further, with the return to the various churches of cathedrals and monasteries earlier confiscated by the communist state. In 1988, indeed, the General Secretary and his wife participated in the celebrations marking the millennium of the Russian Orthodox Church. In what appears to be an attempt to win the support of religious faithful, Gorbachëv has repeatedly observed that they too can be patriotic citizens, and a new law on freedom of conscience is in preparation. Such moves—whether mere concessions or sincerely intended efforts to create a more pluralist society—have been inspired in part by the Russian nationalist movement, identifying Russian Orthodoxy as an essential national characteristic, with shades of the nineteenth-century conservative slogan, 'Autocracy, Orthodoxy, Nationality' (Dunlop, 1984, chs 3, 7).

National or Group Grievances

The last point combines religion with nationality, a feature evident also in the case of the Jews, Lithuanians (traditionally Roman Catholics), Kalmyks (Buddhists) and certain other groups. National identity has become a further element in promoting dissidence. Some aspects of the nationalities issue were explored above: here we consider its impact on the rise of dissent. In some cases, there is an antipathy towards Russians that may recede for generations or even centuries. Ukrainian nationalism, for example, is based partly on the knowledge that the cradle of East Slavic civilization was Kiev, long before Moscow rose to prominence and expanded to incorporate the rich Steppe lands into the Empire. There is a feeling that 42 million Ukrainians could and should enjoy greater freedom of action without the 'leadership' of the Russian nation.

Other nationalities hold specific grievances against the Soviet regime, particularly groups that suffered deportation under Stalin: the Crimean Tatars, deported to Central Asia in 1944 from the Crimean peninsula where they had resided for generations, and never permitted to return; the Meskhetians, deported from southern Georgia; and the Volga Germans, descendants of a colony established in the eighteenth century, who until the Second World War enjoyed the status of a distinct Volga German Autonomous Soviet Socialist Republic, before being deported a thousand miles south-east. Nationalist movements have sprung up round these nations, seeking permission to return to their homelands or demanding permission to emigrate. A sense of group dissatisfaction is articulated by intellectuals, sometimes—as in the case of such Ukrainian nationalists as Ivan Dzyuba (1968) and Vyacheslav Chornovil (1968)—under the patronage of leading regional politicians, in that case Petro Shelest (see Krawchenko, 1983, pp. 4–5).

The Intelligentsia

The intelligentsia is an important element in the emergence of dissent. It consists of people trained to use their minds, who may assess official claims in the light of their own observations and sometimes reach unorthodox conclusions. Some have indeed become 'dissidents' themselves—the writers circulated in *samizdat*; the poets who give clandestine readings of critical verse; the artists who privately exhibit works deemed contrary to the spirit of 'socialist realism'. Others have supported identifiable branches of the dissident movement: Major-General Piotr Grigorenko, who took up the cudgels on behalf of the Crimean Tatars; Andrei Sakharov, the nuclear physicist, who became a spokesman for the cause of political rights and more open democracy. Still others—the Marxist historian Roy Medvedev is perhaps the best known—have very carefully trodden on the legal side of what is approved. Many other intellectuals—identified by Friedgut (in Tökés, 1975, p. 116, n. 2) as 'reform communists'—function within the system, adopting nevertheless a somewhat critical stance towards it, and occasionally coming out with astonishing proposals for reform (see the survey in Hill, 1980a).

Contact with the West

For the intelligentsia, in particular, the outside world—principally the West, but also Eastern Europe—is a significant source of alternative information and ideas. Quite apart from 'subversion', there is now much international contact, affecting Soviet citizens at numerous levels. Many of them listen to foreign radio and television broadcasts, and the better educated read foreign newspapers which, even when published by pro-Moscow communist parties, contain far better news coverage and opinions on more diverse topics than the regular Soviet press. There is a constant stream of foreign tourists into the Soviet Union, whose standard of dress and spontaneity of behaviour contrast markedly with the official portrayal of the oppressed masses in capitalist countries. The presence of foreigners as a source of materials and information has been particularly significant in establishing Moscow as an important centre for democratic dissent (Tökés, 1975, p. 127). And, in increasing (although admittedly still tiny) numbers, Soviet citizens themselves have opportunities to visit the outside world. There is also now substantial trade with the West, including consumer goods that are distinctly superior to the home-produced equivalent: this, too, contradicts the image of capitalism in crisis, and must lead many to question the official line.

The Propaganda Apparatus

Finally, therefore, failures of the propaganda apparatus itself contribute to the growth of dissent, or at least scepticism. The official figures of 47,635 million copies of newspapers printed in 1987 (*Narkhoz, 1987*, p. 538), and over 1,000 million political lectures of one kind or another, say nothing about their quality or effectiveness. The party authorities frequently decry the unimaginative and unconvincing presentation of political education that has no perceptible impact on the listeners; the dullness of journalists' style is another source of regular complaint (see White, 1979, ch. 6; White, in Potichnyj, 1988, ch. 4). Scepticism at the regime's ideological commitments is hardly to be wondered at.

The development of a uniform set of values and beliefs poses a further, rather special problem: for, although Marxism-Leninism supposedly contains eternal scientific truths, its interpretation changes, as does the official line on many issues, including, for example, individual politicians, so the official sources of information are rife with inconsistencies over time. One day *Pravda* writes of the party first secretary as a true son of the people, a devoted exponent of Marxism-Leninism; the following day it announces his sacking, and a few days later criticizes him for lack of vision and hare-brained schemes. Children learn different interpretations of historical events from what their parents or elder siblings were taught, and some of them respond with scepticism, if not cynicism, about the so-called eternal truths and claims that the party is always right. From there it is a modest step to reject the party's teaching more generally.

Domestic Changes

An underlying precondition for all of this, however, is the change that occurred after Stalin's death. The removal of secret police head Beriya dealt a severe blow at that agency's power in the system. More significantly, Khrushchev's anti-Stalin campaign, launched in February 1956, had devastating international repercussions and internally confirmed the swift and effective abandonment of terror as a normal part of the process of government. Thousands of victims were rehabilitated and, if still alive, released from camps, and Soviet society grew to accept and expect a degree of personal security not enjoyed by the previous generation. The expression of dissentient opinions became 'easier', in two senses: the risks involved were less than they had been; and the likelihood of having some impact on political life appeared greater. As David Kowalewski has put it (in Kelley, 1980, p. 151), the de-Stalinization process opened the prospect of 'change in the rules of the political game', which 'made more likely both the possibility of winning the game and, thus, the mobilization of collective action in pursuit of group interests'; it signalled a 'shift in the cost-benefit calculus of political protest'.

Forms of Dissent

The rise of dissidence as a politically relevant phenomenon has been dated from the arrest and trial in 1966 of the writers Yuli Daniel and Andrei Sinyavskii, in a post-Khrushchev wave of attacks on intellectuals in the Ukraine and elsewhere from late 1965 onwards (see David Kowalewski, in Kelley, 1980, p. 151: Kowalewski sees this as a catalyst in the development of a human rights movement; for details of the trial, see Labedz & Hayward, 1967). This trial, seen as a *cause célèbre*, seemed to signal a return to tighter control over culture after the relatively relaxed atmosphere that had allowed the publication in 1962 of Solzhenitsyn's *One Day in the Life of Ivan Denisovich*, the first officially published fictional memoir of the Stalin labour camps. For publishing their critical and satirical works abroad, under pseudonyms and without permission, Sinyavskii and Daniel ('Abram Tertz' and 'Nikolai Arzhak') were sentenced to seven and five years' detention and later exiled in the West. In 1968, a small group were detained for mounting a demonstration in Moscow's Red Square against the Soviet-led intervention in Czechoslovakia.

From then onward, facing pressure from the authorities, groups of critical intellectuals produced a clandestine journal, *The Chronicle of Current Events*, to record and circulate information about the arrests, trials and prison whereabouts of detainees. Handmade copies were circulated, some of which reached the West, where they were translated and published by Amnesty International (see also Reddaway, 1972). Peter Reddaway's characterization of the *Chronicle* (in Brown & Kaser, 1978, p. 126) can scarcely be bettered: 'It avoided value judgements, it reported factually and objectively on events connected with human or national rights, and it summarised new works circulating in *samizdat* . . .' It became an indispensable source of information, and enabled the world (including thousands of Soviet citizens) to glimpse at the realm of Soviet courtrooms and prison camps, and to assess the methods and the successes of the regime in handling a problem that the leaders had never experienced and for which they were unprepared to deal through a *political* process.

The security police (the KGB, or State Security Committee), under Andropov's direction from 1967, gradually penetrated this and other informal groupings, relying on clauses in the penal code that outlawed 'anti-Soviet propaganda and agitation' and similar imprecise categories of quasi-political activity. In the autumn of 1972, in a wave of police pressure, the *Chronicle* ceased publication, but it reappeared in May 1974, and has continued fairly regular publication.

The *Chronicle* is the best-known *samizdat* journal, which served to focus attenion on Soviet dissidence, and to reassure its adherents that they were not isolated. Thousands of other privately circulated documents have become known, many of them collected and catalogued in the *Samizdat Archive* at Radio Liberty in Munich. From these self-published documents, and through other, informal channels, it has been possible to assess the scope of such activity, and to identify several clear strands.

Varieties of Dissent

National Dissent

National grievances are a feature of the political culture, and have been reflected in hostility to the present regime and its policies. The Jews, in declaring their desire to emigrate, have captured much media attention in the West, as to a lesser extent have the Germans, for similar reasons. (This issue became an important factor in East–West relations during the 1970s, when some 200,000 Soviet citizens, many of them Jewish, were allowed to leave the Soviet Union.) But nationalist sentiment is encountered in the Ukraine and the Baltic republics (Lithuania, Latvia and Estonia), among the Meskhetians and Crimean Tatars (see above), and among Russians who feel their own culture has been suppressed in favour of a bland 'internationalism'.

The demands of national dissenters vary, from challenges to Russian 'leadership' or hegemony within non-Russian areas, to expressions of dismay at the fate of the native language in publication, education and the arts in competition with Russian as the country's lingua franca, to calls to exercise the constitutional right to secede from the Union.

These various grievances have come into the open in the new opportunities for expression afforded by the circumstances of *glasnost'*. In the spring of 1988, festering animosities between Armenians and their neighbours in Azerbaidzhan flared into street demonstrations and riots which continued intermittently throughout the year. The focus of attention was the status of the autonomous area of Nagorno-Karabakh (an Armenian enclave under Azerbaidzhani jurisdiction since 1923), but linguistic, cultural and religious differences stoked the fires of hostility. The intermingling of different populations, in some cases ancient, but also boosted by the Soviet policy of encouraging migration, has been such that there exists much potential for racial, linguistic or cultural strife if national relations are not handled with care. Violent street demonstrations in Kazakhstan in December 1986 greeted the appointment of a Russian, Gennadii Kolbin, as party first secretary in the republic (even though ethnic Russians are in a majority there). In late 1988, the Baltic republics—Estonia, Lithuania and Latvia—also began to flex their nationalistic muscles, calling for far more effective autonomy from Moscow's rule than they have hitherto enjoyed.

These manifestations of nationalist dissent are branded as 'bourgeois nationalism', a reactionary step backward to a stage of social development preceding the attainment of socialism: as such it must be rooted out. It also has disintegrative implications, and so runs counter to the instincts of *any* politician responsible for governing that territory, no matter what his ideological identity: the tsar, too, was concerned with this problem—as are European governments in relation to nationalism in Northern Ireland, Scotland or Wales, Brittany or the Basque country.

Religious Dissent

A second variety of dissidence embraces religious groups, whether or not under the auspices of an organized church. Examples are the Jews, Russian nationalists who identify with the Orthodox Church, Lithuanians, whose concern is for the Roman Catholic Church, and adherents of the Uniate (eastern-rite Catholic) Church in parts of the Ukraine. Elsewhere, notably in Moldavia, illegal sects such as Jehovah's Witnesses refuse to acknowledge the symbols of the Soviet state or to perform their constitutional duty of military service.

As noted by Reddaway (in Brown & Kaser, 1978, p. 146), religious groups as such have not been particularly active as collective dissenters;

yet there is a vast wealth of information indicating how seriously the Soviet authorities treat citizens who insist on exercising the freedom of conscience granted by Article 52 of the Constitution. Religious believers in general seek greater opportunities to practise their faith, and this links them with a further strand in the movement, from which they draw support: those demanding greater civil liberty.

Civil Liberties

Dissidents seeking a broad range of specifically political change form a heterodox grouping that includes reformist Marxists and neo-Marxists along with liberals and democrats. Some are believed to have been tacitly supported by individuals in or close to the ruling circles. This strand, comprising 'those who advocate general political change in the Soviet Union and express their opinions outside the framework of the Communist Party' (Friedgut, in Tökés, 1975, p. 116, n. 2), has been referred to separately from other dissident elements as 'the democratic movement' (e.g. by Friedgut, and by Barghoorn, 1976); others refer to the 'human rights movement' (e.g. Kowalewski, in Kelley, 1980).

While not necessarily constituting an organized 'movement', they are broadly united under the civil rights and civil liberties banner. A general account of their origins and aims is to be found in the well-known work by the late Andrei Amalrik, *Will the Soviet Union Survive until 1984?* (1970). Their high level of literacy and articulateness, coupled with the expulsion from the Soviet Union of many of the leading figures since the early 1970s, prompted a massive output of works in *samizdat* and *tamizdat* ('published there', i.e. in the West). These reveal a variety of programmes and immediate and long-term aims for political reform, away from the Stalinist model that until very recently remained intact in its essentials.

Calls for freedom of information, the right to travel freely, the right to demonstrate *against* Soviet government policies, and in general to give citizens a more effective voice in the political process and to protect them from the unbridled power of the politically controlled state, have all been identified in the dissident movement.

These various dissident strands are not entirely separate, and individuals who begin their dissident 'careers' identifying with particular causes—say, religious freedom—may expand their range of interests towards civil liberties in general, or may demand to emigrate; similarly, the scope of nationalists' demands may broaden to include various rights for self-expression that have fundamental implications for the whole system (see Friedgut, in Tökés, 1976, pp. 120–3). There is, indeed, some evidence of cross-support from one group to another (see Kelley, 1980, pp. 168–74).

Official Responses to Dissidence

The regime's reponse has varied over time and from place to place, and also according to the kind of dissidence—either in its demands or in its forms of expression. Some were arrested, brought to trial (usually in effectively closed courthouses) and sentenced to periods in labour camps, often of strict regime, sometimes followed by internal exile. In other cases, particularly during the 1970s, persistent critics were bundled on a plane and flown to the West: the most renowned case was the writer Solzhenitsyn, who, after expulsion from the Writers' Union followed by several years of harassment, was exiled in 1974 and has settled in the United States. For others, such as the cellist Mstislav Rostropovich, deprivation of Soviet citizenship (and thereby removal of the right to return to Russia) followed a period of residence in the West. The Nobel Peace Prize winner, the physicist Andrei Sakharov, and his wife Yelena Bonner were exiled to Gorky, a city that is closed to foreign visitors, in January 1980.

Thousands of alienated Jews have been permitted to leave the country, mostly on Israeli visas, although many eventually moved to the United States. Similarly, thousands from the German community have been allowed to emigrate. In these cases, the authorities' response has fluctuated with the state of East–West relations, and specifically relations between the Soviet Union and the United States. The United States' decision to link emigration with enhanced trade (the so-called Jackson–Vanik Amendment of January 1975), and the subsequent deterioration in relations between the superpowers, caused the flow of emigrants to dwindle to a trickle, only to expand again with improved relations under Gorbachëv.

A notorious ploy of the Soviet government has been the use of enforced psychiatric treatment, often involving mind-changing drugs, and most notably in the Serbsky Institute of Forensic Psychiatry in Moscow (see Bloch & Reddaway, 1977). Resort to such treatment has been scaled down in the Gorbachëv period, with some legal protection adopted, although caution is evident (see Reddaway, 1988).

In general, the recent treatment of offending dissidents has been far more sophisticated and even lenient than in the heyday of Stalinism, and in the post-Brezhnev era changes in the political climate have aimed to classify as 'dissident' principally political actions and beliefs that would be regarded as marginal in most modern societies. Under Brezhnev, indeed, as even the most passionate opponents of the Soviet government acknowledge, the tendency was to use methods of persuasion and dissuasion before resorting to the courts, psychiatric hospitals, labour camps, internal exile and banishment, or expulsion. One such critic, Peter Reddaway, observed in the mid-1970s that certain groups of dissenters had made some modest, if reversible, gains (in Brown & Kaser, 1978, p. 151). Reddaway later attempted to identify the characteristics of official policy towards dissent, and concluded that 'The Politburo has in fact been forced to tolerate a gradually rising level of unpunished or weakly punished dissent' (in Rigby, Brown & Reddaway, 1980, p. 183).

There is much scope for argument about the scale of dissent, if only because its illegality means such dissident sentiment remains unexpressed, and certainly is unsupported by documentary evidence. It is clearly an exaggeration to claim, as does Shtromas (1981, pp. 99, 23 and *passim*), that 'the whole history of the USSR was (and is) the history of the regime's continuous struggle against dissent'; but it is equally wrong to dismiss dissidence as politically irrelevant. The various strands of the movement may have no direct impact on policy, or on the political structures they wish to change. Nevertheless, the Soviet government expends substantial resources in monitoring, controlling and punishing dissidents, and has to sustain the world-wide adverse publicity. Konstantin Chernenko (1981, p. 5) may assure his Western readers that 'The Soviet conception of human rights in no way contradicts the principles of the most important international documents. . . . In fact, Soviet legislation in this sphere goes much further than the international covenants, for it provides for broader guarantees of the rights and freedoms of the individual.' But in international politics the Soviet Union is vulnerable on this score, and this enhances the political significance of dissent.

Yet times have changed. No matter how distasteful the liberal conscience may find the pressure on dissidents, there has for more than three decades been no widespread terrorism in any meaningful usage of that word: there was nothing equivalent to the *yezhovshchina*, the purges and trials of 1936–8, when N. I. Yezhov was in charge of the security apparatus. Even so, as successive groups of dissidents complained, 'political change in the Soviet Union over the past twenty years is not yet sufficient to guarantee that Stalinism cannot return', so 'the shadow of Stalin still broods over the consciousness of virtually the whole intelligentsia' (Friedgut, in Tökés, 1975, p. 119). Even well into the period of *perestroika*—an attempt to restructure not only the institutions of Soviet society, but also the mentality and culture of the whole population—that statement remains valid.

Gorbachëv has moved faster and farther than most would have imagined in creating objective circumstances where dissent and dissidence will no longer be valid responses to society's problems. The idea of the socialist Rechtsstaat, or state based on the law, has become part of the official rhetoric, and the CPSU now seems more willing than ever before to *trust* its citizens, to rule by the force of *argument* rather than simple *assertion*, to use the persuasion that it loudly proclaims as its method of leadership. Yet, as one of the country's leading reformist social scientists, I. V. Bestuzhev-Lada, observed in 1988, in a discussion of the concept of 'socialist pluralism' ('Sotsialisticheskii plyuralizm', 1988, pp. 8–9), enforced political monopoly ('monism') inevitably leads to dissidence: 'pluralism' he saw as 'unpunished dissent'—unconsciously echoing Reddaway's use of the same term. That scholar's preferred long-term position was the evolution of a multi-party system, something that has been expressly ruled out by the country's present leadership. Moreover, such is the apparent vulnerability of the reformists that the ruling party remains under the suspicion that it might revert to the methods that Khrushchev in the 1950s went a long way towards suppressing. Stalinism is a memory for ever-fewer Soviet citizens, yet its values are still rife in Soviet society, as the passionate defence of its principles published in a daily newspaper by Nina Andreeva (1988) bears witness. The dissidents' fervent hope—and that of those formerly branded as such who are finding a constructive role in Gorbachëv's Soviet Union—is that the younger generations will not live to experience its substance under a different name.

4 The Economic System

Economic Structures and their Development

To a great extent, the Soviet regime has based its claim to legitimacy on its economic performance. This is understandable. After all, the central element in the ideology is Marx's and Engels's critique of capitalism as an economic system, further developed by Lenin in his theory of imperialism, 'the highest stage of capitalism'. The question of control over the means of economic production is at the heart of the ideology, so this aspect of their philosophy impelled the Bolsheviks to adopt a form of economic management radically different from the free market system of private entrepreneurship. The socialist basis of ownership is incorporated into the very name of the state.

The founding fathers of Marxism firmly believed also in industrial production as a rational way of organizing human activity, as opposed to what, notoriously, they saw as 'the idiocy of rural life' (*Communist Manifesto*, 1973, p. 71). So Marx's Bolshevik followers should logically set about industrializing the country. This imperative was further intensified by the ideological view of 'communism' as a society characterized by material abundance, rather than poverty and want, with resources and effort deployed in a rational manner, so as to serve society's needs rather than to pander to the capitalist's need for profit. Engels referred to the need for replacing 'anarchy in social production ... by conscious organisation on a planned basis' (quoted by Maurice Dobb, in Bor, 1967, p. 11). The idea of planned production is also implied in Marx's reference, in *Das Kapital*, to

> ... the need of society to calculate beforehand how much labour, means of production, and means of subsistence it can invest, without detriment, in such lines of business as for instance the building of railways, which do not furnish any means of production or subsistence, nor produce any useful effect for a long time, a year or more, while they extract labour, means of production and means of subsistence from the total annual production. (Quoted in McLellan, 1971, pp. 220–1.)

Soviet spokesmen have long extolled the virtues of centralized planning as a method of management that 'replaces the productive forces, accelerates their development and makes possible immense achievements within short periods of time' (Yesipov, 1975, p. 3).

In addition, the circumstances in which the Bolsheviks came to power—with the economy in a state of virtual collapse, following the First World War, then mass desertions from the army and the flight of former peasants from the cities back to the land—demanded drastic steps simply to keep the country going and to bring about a resumption of economic activity.

Thus, ideology and force of circumstances pushed the infant Bolshevik state into taking over sector after sector of the economy—services and light industry, as well as what Lenin called the 'commanding heights': the land and its minerals and forests, banking, basic industries, foreign trade. In adopting these measures in conditions of 'war communism', Lenin and his colleagues were devising a new way of running an economy, while also associating state ownership with 'socialism' and 'communism'.

With the promulgation in 1921 of the New Economic Policy, creating a modified free market in agricultural products, to entice the peasants to produce enough food for the towns, the Bolsheviks were engaging in a temporary, limited, but deliberate reversion to capitalism. However, the principle of state ownership was never abandoned, and later came to be seen as an integral and necessary part of 'socialism'. (In fact, heavy state involvement in promoting economic development had been a peculiar feature of Russia before the revolution, particularly in the late nineteenth century, but even going back to Peter the Great's reign.)

The development of the Soviet economic system really dates, however, from the late 1920s, following the adoption of Stalin's slogan of 'socialism in one country'. With the first Five-Year Plan (1928–32), the whole panoply of economic direction through Gosplan (the State Planning Committee), accompanied by a massive bureaucratic control mechanism to supervise plan implementation, became established as the Soviet method of economic management.

In the late 1920s came the collectivization of agriculture, with the incorporation of the bulk of the peasantry into *kolkhozy*, or formally self-governing agricultural co-operatives. In addition to the ideological preference for collective or social over individual and private ownership, there was a clear intention to bring the recalcitrant Russian peasants under political control, after several years when they had managed to place a stranglehold on the regime's industrialization ambitions by not producing enough food to cater for a growing industrial and urban population (for a thorough study, see Lewin, 1968). The collective farm has remained a central element in the Soviet system of economic institutions, accompanied by state farms or *sovkhozy*, owned and managed directly by the state, frequently as experimental enterprises. These are regarded as ideologically superior to the collectives, and are the form of agricultural organization that were expected to dominate as Soviet society developed towards 'communism'. Reforms under Gorbachëv, however, involving a return to greater private enterprise in agriculture, reminiscent of the NEP (New Economic Policy) period, raise questions about the long-term structural development of Soviet agriculture.

Industry has remained largely in state hands, with individual factories and plants owned by ministries that appointed the directors and supervised their functioning. In the rapid industrialization of the 1930s and 1940s, each ministry tended to develop a virtually self-contained industrial empire, expanding into peripheral areas of production in order to guarantee supplies to its own production units, without having to depend on the performance of other ministries. This led to considerable duplication, and seriously reduced the capacity of the state's representative organs to exercise their powers in governing their respective territory: the Soviet equivalent of the company town was the 'ministry town', in which local authorities were powerless in the face of the departmental plans of the big ministries (see Taubman, 1973; also Ross, 1987). In the 1970s, in an effort to rationalize production, new complexes were created, the 'production associations', combining a number of industrial units into a single, co-ordinated structure of factories and plants in related areas. These still function under the auspices of the ministries: they are not independent. So, whether for ideological, political, economic or other reasons, direct state involvement is the key to the Soviet model of 'socialism', and it has been imposed on or copied by other regimes around the world.

There are nevertheless certain significant exceptions to the state sector, which are increasing in significance, rather than being phased out. The first is the existence of small-scale private co-operatives and self-employed artisans providing consumer services such as tailoring, hairdressing, photography or shoe repairs. Although still small in number—they have long been too few to feature in Soviet statistics on class—these supply an important measure of economic provision in towns and cities, a branch of service that has been badly neglected in the state sector (see below). New laws on individual enterprise (adopted 19 November 1986) and on co-operatives (adopted in May 1988) have opened up this sector of the economy, and, despite manifest obstruction from traditionally-minded bureaucrats and some resistance to high prices on the part of sections of the Soviet public, these forms of economic activity appear set to supplement the state sector with which they are in direct competition. Co-operative restaurants and cafes now function in urban centres; street photographers and artists now ply their trade, thereby enlivening the formerly drab urban scene. Private medical practice, legal consultancies and educational coaching could be added to that category.

Secondly, there remains the very important private sector in agriculture, which is also expanding. All along—with greater or lesser toleration by the authorities—collective farmers' activity on their personal plots of land has been used to grow produce not only for their family consumption but also for sale in the *kolkhoz* markets existing in most towns. Selling at prices usually way above those in the state stores—a market price that reflects the balance of supply and demand—the collective farmers in their capacity as private producers provide a necessary supplement to the state and collective farms' output. According to one informed estimate at the beginning of the 1980s, while the private plots occupied a mere 3 per cent of agricultural land they produced a third of the country's livestock products and a fifth of its vegetable crops (Holzman, 1982, p. 35). Under Gorbachëv, this sector of agricultural production is being encouraged, with talk of long-term leasing of land for family production—a belated Marxist recognition of the attachment to the land that encourages peasant productivity: this is to be harnessed in an effort to solve the appalling food crisis facing the country.

Non-state enterprise is thus absolutely vital in sustaining the Soviet population, filling significant gaps in the socialized sector. However, it should be noted that this activity is almost exclusively in the fields of agriculture and service: industry is almost totally operated by the state—although it is preyed upon by private entrepreneurs in the 'second economy' or parallel market (see below).

Planning

State ownership of the means of production, plus collective ownership of some of agriculture, supplemented by a degree of individual enterprise, is thus the norm in the Soviet economy. These elements are brought within the ambit of the state planning mechanism, supervised by Gosplan, the State Planning Committee. Gosplan, whose chairman is a member of the Council of Ministers and at present a candidate member of the party Politburo, co-ordinates the activities of the economic ministries and state committees, each responsible for a particular sector of the economy, some very specifically defined. Alongside Gosplan is a second central agency, Gossnab, the state procurements agency, responsible for the allocation of commodities, 'tying' customers to suppliers (Nove, 1977, p. 40). The role of both of these agencies, particularly Gossnab, is subject to modification as the reforms of *perestroika* work their way through.

There is some argument among economists as to whether the term 'planned economy' is appropriate. John Wilhelm (1979, 1985) argues that the high significance of 'trial and error' in finding equilibrium between supply and demand, together with the use of administrative orders as 'the principal tool of central management', makes it an administered economy. He points to the significance of two areas not embraced by planning: the labour market and consumption. Soviet workers are not now directed into jobs, and consumers are free to spend their wages on whatever goods and services are supplied—or to refrain from doing so. (In fact, the maintenance of money—rather than, say, rationing—to regulate personal consumption implies that this area of economic activity will remain beyond the control of the planners.) Other scholars, such as Alec Nove (1980a), point to the role of the plan in allocating resources for such major products as the Baikal-Amur railway, the expansion of the fertilizer industry or land improvement schemes, or the tapping of Siberian energy resources. Whatever the philosophical arguments, what is not in doubt is that a great deal of effort is expended on producing economic plans, which are given the force of law by the Supreme Soviet, and must therefore be implemented.

Soviet economic plans are of two types, medium-term and short-term. The first category is basically for five years (supplemented by 'basic directives' that attempt to extend the projection over longer periods), the second for one year, further divided into quarterly periods in the operational and production plans of individual enterprises or ministries. The five-year plans are unveiled with great publicity at party congresses (now held quinquennially to coincide with the plans). As developmental plans (Nove, 1977, p. 31) they indicate major priority goals over the coming five-year period, and have a manifestly political purpose. In reflecting politicians' priorities, they indicate the general balance of investment and production within the economy as a whole. Frequently introduced after the beginning of the period they cover, they are of less significance in managing the economy than the annual plans, which are 'recognised as dominant by planning agencies, ministries, and association and enterprise managements' (Bornstein, 1985, p. 6).

The annual plans convert the medium-term goals into detailed balances, ultimately making provision for factories, plants or other enterprises to produce specific items or provide specific services, some of which become 'inputs' into the operation of other enterprises. The sheer complexity of producing a 'national plan' can be appreciated by considering the number and range of items produced (some 24 million), the number of different enterprises of various types, their geographical distribution, and the time dimension of production, plus the availability of labour with the appropriate skills (in a more or less free—that is, unplanned—labour market), the provision of transport facilities for the distribution of the products, the flows of finance to pay workers. All this is combined with a need to build into the plan means of ensuring that suitable standards of efficiency and quality are maintained throughout the whole economy, perhaps also making provision for accidents of climate or whatever.

It may seem an extraordinary way of running a highly complex society: is it indeed feasible to handle the vast quantities of information about what is required, what it is possible to achieve, what the current production levels are, and what the likely demand is for current and future products, plus all the other operationally vital information generated by the world's second largest economy, while still trying to control its general direction and performance? Can a planning mechanism effectively replace the silent hand of the market? At the very least, Nove (1977, p. 34) aptly comments, 'All this represents a vast challenge to the ingenuity of the planners', and he notes (pp. 38 and 52–9) that experienced Soviet experts are turning to think in terms of probability theory and mathematical modelling, rather than in terms of balancing a virtually infinite complex of specific material inputs and outputs (see below). To some extent, detailed production norms are nowadays set by production ministries rather than Gosplan. Even so, the complex economy of today still attempts to function according to a detailed co-ordinating document, the plan.

Plans are compiled on the basis of forward estimates of requirements by the production enterprises, aggregated by the ministries, co-ordinated by Gosplan, and adjusted towards balance, also taking politically determined priorities into account. In performing the co-ordinating task—balancing outputs from one branch or plant with the inputs of another in as rational a manner as possible, through a series of iterative operations—Gosplan together with Gossnab uses the expertise of its own departments, subcommittees and research institute, and the manipulative capacity of computers, and is no doubt also influenced by inputs from the central party apparatus. There is a measure of negotiation among the different institutional partners, but ultimately the plan is a document in which the central authorities instruct enterprises what to produce, on the basis of what inputs of materials, finance and labour, and at what prices, and to which receiving enterprise they shall deliver their product. These details do not necessarily coincide with the original estimates of input and output made some months previously.

A traditional economic plan has therefore been a highly complex document, and it has been argued that to view the plan as a co-ordinating document that in principle attempts to specify the vast majority of transactions in the economy is unreal, since 'perfect planning' is impossible. In practice, as argued by Millar (1981, p. 179),

> The success of central planning in the Soviet Union has depended upon the ability of central management to enforce the priority system. Despite an aspiration to plan the economy comprehensively and minutely, central planning proper in the Soviet Union has been confined to planning high-priority sectors' inputs and outputs. Central management and the principle of the devil take the hindmost has governed the remainder of economic activity.

Apart from obvious strategic decision on directing investment into particular sectors, 'planning' in practice has been 'from the achieved level': using past production ('the achieved level'), augmented by a growth factor, as a guide for future production (Birman, 1978). This method, with both the merits and the defects outlined by Birman in his article, *works*, in the sense that 'the plan does somehow operate. And it is more or less (mostly less) fulfilled. And the Soviet economy, despite our criticism, marches forward' (Birman, p. 161).

If the task of balancing material outputs is difficult, even more complex is the task of ensuring the quality of production. There is much disquiet on that score, and a good deal of discussion about the appropriate stimuli and indicators of success. A measure that may suit one industry may be quite unsuitable in another, and the evidence is that in very many cases the 'correct' indicators have not been found. The Soviet press contains many examples of efficiency criteria that lead to the production of unwanted products. Some have been the butt of Soviet cartoonists in such satirical magazines as *Krokodil*: the nail factory, whose efficiency is measured by the weight of its output, fulfils its annual plan by producing one giant nail; the shoe factory, required to produce a million pairs of shoes, does so—but all of the same size and design; the ploughman, required to plough as much acreage a day using as little fuel as possible, simply scratches the surface.

Equally deleterious to the quality of the final product is the supply of inferior materials—textiles of an old-fashioned design, produced in plan-fulfilling quantities and supplied to a factory that is obliged to turn them into clothing that will not sell because fashion and taste have moved on; electrical goods that break down through inferior transistors supplied to the assembly plant; moulded concrete staircases that crumble within a few months because of a wrong mix of ingredients. Again, many examples could be given, and the planners seem unable to cope with the task.

In fact, many professional observers of the Soviet economy have concluded that the planning system may serve its purpose well when its task is the 'large-scale planning of priority projects', whereas 'the routine of current planning, despite the help of computers, is too overwhelmingly complex' (*Cambridge Encyclopedia*, 1982, p. 358; see also below).

Industry

The planning system proved its worth in the 1930s in its clear ability to transfer resources from agriculture and invest them in industrial production, at its crudest by removing food from the rural areas to feed the expanding urban population. In contrast to the disaster of the Great Depression in that decade under capitalism, the Soviet 'planned' economy was industrializing by leaps and bounds, with new cities rising across the country, turning out iron and steel that were converted into machines that in turn established new industries, powered by electricity produced in an electrification scheme that had been one of Lenin's pet projects—he even produced a somewhat flippant but nevertheless highly symbolic definition: 'Communism equals communist power plus electrification of the whole country'. Official statistics suggest that, on an index of 1928 = 1, industrial production had expanded to 6.5 by 1940 and to 110 by 1975 (*Narkhoz za 60 let*, 1977, p. 13). In this sense, the plan works: the goods have been and continue to be produced.

The Soviet Union today possesses one of the richest industrialized societies in the world, claiming by 1982 to have a gross national income two-thirds that of the United States, with industrial production standing at over 80 per cent, electricity production at 55 per cent, steel smelting at 217 per cent, production of fertilizer at 134 per cent, of cement at 181 per cent, and of cotton textiles at 183 per cent (*SSSR v tsifrakh*, 1983, pp. 60–1); the same source (p. 63) claims the average annual growth in capital investments to have been 7.9 per cent between 1951 and 1982 (against 2.6 per cent in the USA), with industrial production growing by 8.4 per cent per annum over the same period. In volume of production of a whole range of industrial products—from electrical energy and oil to steel, coal, sulphuric acid, locomotives, tractors, cement, woollen textiles and leather footwear—the Soviet Union claims to occupy first place in Europe and first or second place in the world (pp. 64–5). Table 4.1 gives the official figures for a range of industrial products in selected years. In addition, of course, Soviet industry has proved itself capable of producing military hardware to match, if not surpass, that produced by her ideological and military opponents, and to manufacture sophisticated equipment to engage in an impressive programme of space research.

In many ways, the military and space research component of Soviet industrial production has been something of an exception, at least as far as the quality of production is concerned, although recent Western commentary has tended to downplay the notion of a 'dual economy'. It suffers some of the basic technical weaknesses of the economy—in electronics and computer technology, for example (see David Holloway, in Amann *et al*., 1977, ch. 9)—yet it is a privileged sector, provided for reasons of national security with the best brains, workers and materials. Indeed, the 1977 Constitution (Article 32) commits the state to supply the armed forces with 'everything necessary' to ensure the country's security and defence capability, a promise repeated by successive Soviet leaders—although now subject to the limitation of 'reasonable sufficiency' (for further argumentation, see Bova, 1988).

The success of the armaments industry and the rapid growth rates are the result of a long-standing emphasis on investment in producers' goods (essentially heavy industry), classified as Group A in the planners' jargon, at the expense of Group B, or consumers' goods. The priorities of the two sectors from 1928 are starkly revealed in the respective growth rates: with 1928 = 1, expansion figures for Group A were 10 in 1940 and 232 in 1975, while those for Group B were 4.2 and 38 (*Narkhoz za 60 let*, 1977, p. 13). Stalin established this priority in the early days of planned development, and it was something of a dogma until the 1970s: indeed, consumption has been called 'the stepchild of Soviet economic priorities' (Campbell, in Byrnes, 1983, p. 72). The ninth five-year plan, covering the years 1971–5, was the first to shift the balance of investment slightly in favour of Group B, in response to

Table 4.1 Soviet industrial production: selected years

Product	1970	1975	1980	1988
Electricity ('000m. kW)	740	1,038	1,295	1,705
Oil (m. tonnes)	353	491	603	624
Gas ('000m. cu.m.)	200	289	435	770
Coal (m. tonnes)	624	701	716	772
Pig iron (m. tonnes)	85.9	103	n.a.	116*
Steel (m. tonnes)	116	141	148	163
Mineral fertilizer (m. tonnes)	55.4	90.2	104	37.1†
Pesticides, etc. ('000 tonnes)	292	438	472	n.a.
Sulphuric acid (m. tonnes)	12.1	18.6	23.0	n.a.
Plastics (m. tonnes)	1.7	2.8	3.6	n.a.
Freight wagons ('000)	58.3	69.9	63.0	n.a.
Trucks ('000)	525	696	787	n.a.
Cars ('000)	344	1,201	1,327	1.3‡
Grain harvesters ('000)	99.2	97.5	117.0	n.a.
Paper (m. tonnes)	4.2	5.2	5.3	6.3
Cement (m. tonnes)	95.2	122	125	139
Fabrics ('000 m. sq.m.)	6.2	9.9	10.7	13.1
Leather footwear (m. pairs)	676	689	744	820
Clocks and watches (m.)	40.2	55	66.7	73.5
Radios (m.)	7.8	8.4	8.5	8.0
TV sets (m.)	6.8	7.0	7.5	9.6
Refrigerators (m.)	4.1	5.6	5.9	6.2
Washing machines (m.)	5.2	3.3	3.8	6.1

Sources: *Pravda*, 4 February 1971, 1 February 1976, 24 January 1981, 22 January 1989.
*Refers to 'rolled ferrous metals'.
† Million tonnes, reckoned at 100 per cent nutritives.
‡ The figure given was 1.3 million.

consumers' rising expectations, growing savings, and possibly the example of Poland, where popular revolt brought down the government of Wladyslaw Gomulka in December 1980 over consumer goods prices and availability. In the event, however, because of deficiencies in plan fulfilment, producers' goods still showed the greater growth in the course of that plan, expanding by the planned 46 per cent, while consumers' goods industry grew by 36 per cent, against the plan's 49 per cent (Byrnes, 1983, pp. 72–3).

These priorities lead to constant shortages ('deficits', in the Soviet phrase) of basic goods, from washing powder and toilet paper to clothing, lamp bulbs and domestic appliances. When deliveries of desirable products are made (including also food products), particularly in the provinces, queues form immediately and the item quickly disappears. Queueing has been identified (by Millar, in Cracraft, 1983, p. 176) as 'a major activity of adult Soviet citizens', who spend several hours a week waiting in lines to buy goods for which they have the ready cash, but which might not be available if they waited a day, or even an hour.

Apart from the inadequacies in quantity, the quality of goods has long been a serious weakness of Soviet industry. This is mainly associated with the difficulty of devising ways of encouraging the production of high-quality goods. There are few incentives for managerial efficiency, and when the key priority has been to produce *more*, the idea of producing *better* goods has been played down. In the absence of a market to regulate what is produced, in an economy manipulated by instructions, where price bears scant relation to production cost or to the market value of the good, and where there is no competition to simulate product improvement, there is every reason for management to adopt a strategy of producing more of the same. After all, the product is bound to be disposed of to another enterprise–ultimately to a retail outlet–while innovation demands effort and in any case interrupts production. Hence, Soviet industry produces goods of old-fashioned design, using outmoded techniques and materials, frequently of poor quality. The reports of shoes that lose the heel at the first wearing, electrical durables that break down within weeks of purchase, pens that leak, or furniture with ill-fitting doors or loose legs, are commonplace in the Soviet press. The quality of clothing, in terms of both design and materials, has almost become a joke, and it partly explains the avidity with which youngsters beset Western tourists with offers of inflated prices for jeans, shirts or jackets.

An element in the difficulty is that the plan largely *assumes* quality, which means that the intermediate consumer–the clothing, footwear or furniture factory–may be obliged to accept materials that are below specification, as the only way of filling its own production plan. There is no legal way of cancelling a contract and seeking another supplier, since transactions are prescribed in the plan. This also means that managements can shift the responsibility for shortcomings on to other enterprises, while in the retail sector the customer is faced with a 'take it or leave it' shrug of the shoulder.

Industry is beset with other difficulties stemming from the plan, particularly if it is 'taut' (i.e. allowing little spare capacity). Delay in the delivery of supplies often means plant and workers standing more or less idle, and that period is followed by intense production in order to fulfil the quarterly plan. This leads to inefficient use of labour, with managements obliged to keep on more workers than if the pace of production were more steady. In any case, since the state guarantees a job for everyone (and indeed requires everyone to work), industry is encouraged to employ workers rather than more efficient machines. Furthermore, the traditional extensive method of industrial expansion–using more workers to produce more output, rather than investing capital to raise worker productivity–has had the effect of depressing the skill level of the work-force, which was constantly 'diluted' by a flow of inexperienced and untrained workers from the countryside.

An equally significant cause of concern, repeatedly adverted to by Soviet politicians, is the tardiness with which scientific advances are incorporated into the production process. The links between research institutes and the industrial ministries are barely existent, and the bureaucratic channels between invention and production are so labyrinthine that important new discoveries or techniques are lost, or their application so delayed that their eventual impact is minimal.

Underlining the inefficiency was the fundamental lack of real incentives to efficiency, coupled with the knowledge on the part of managers and workers alike that financial losses did not matter: the state would sustain the loss, and an enterprise would never be declared bankrupt and closed down.

With some of these issues in mind, Western firms have been brought in over the past twenty years or so, the best-known example being the Fiat automobile works in the city of Tol'yatti, on the Volga, with a production capacity of 660,000 cars a year. Exporting one-third or so of its output, this plant is an undeniable success of Soviet industry.

However, it is based on Italian technology of the early 1960s, which has been rapidly superseded in the West and Japan. In fact, a judicious assessment of the technological level of Soviet industry suggested that it is below that of the advanced countries (Japan, North America, Western Europe, etc.), with defence industries more efficient than the civilian sector, heavy industry more so than light industry, and capital goods' production more than that of consumer goods (*Cambridge Encyclopedia*, 1982, p. 283; see also Amann *et al*., 1977).

This has its impact on other sectors of the economy that depend heavily on industrial output, as well as the individual consumer of industrial products. Agriculture needs high-quality fertilizer from the chemical industry and reliable and rugged equipment. The health service requires drug and medicines of consistent quality. The distribution network needs reliable trains and trucks. The food sector needs dry- and cold-storage facilities. The quality of production may be higher than in the past, and attention has indeed been paid to rising standards in both producers' and consumers' goods (Amann *et al*., 1977, pp. 58–9); it may also be significantly better in some sectors than in others—even individual plants may produce more efficiently and to higher standards (miners in Donetsk claim to know from which factory a bottle of beer comes, and even on which shift it was brewed). But quality is still an acknowledged concern of the planners and politicians.

In an era when the pace of industrial innovation—of both products and techniques—is being set by the advanced capitalist countries, the Soviet Union is manifestly not managing to maintain that pace, let alone overtake its rivals. The gross expansion rates of 10–15 per cent a year recorded in the 1950s, which caused Khrushchev to promise to overtake the United States on a whole string of agricultural and industrial products by 1981, had been replaced by near-stagnation by that date, after a steady decline: about 5 per cent in the 1960s, 3.8 per cent in the early 1970s, falling to 2.8 per cent and 1.2 per cent in the first two years of the present decade (Daniel Bond & Herbert Levine, in Bialer & Gustafson, 1982, p. 88). The eleventh five-year plan, covering the years 1981–5 inclusive, projected modest industrial growth of 4.7–5.1 per cent, but (as Western experts predicted) that proved optimistic, and the subsequent plan, following repeated redrafting, toned down the expectations substantially. With the slowdown in the rate of population expansion over the past generation, the traditional methods of increasing output by expanding the industrial workforce cannot be relied on, so that already at the beginning of the 1980s Western experts spoke of the Soviet economy as facing a period of stringency (see Bialer, 1980, ch. 15). Capitalism, too, has been less than successful at handling some of the problems of an advanced industrial society, particularly its need for employment; but without effective reforms (see below), Soviet industry is likely to lag further behind that of its rivals, with all that implies in terms of prestige and power.

Agriculture

This sector, long perceived as the Achilles' heel of the Soviet economy, was recently still identified as 'a most critical problem for the Soviet system and its leaders' (Robert W. Campbell, in Byrnes, 1983, p. 98). Its performance has been a constant source of disappointment and doubtless frustration for the Soviet leaders, and it has led to the abrupt termination of several political careers in the past quarter-century. In 1911, the tsarist minister of finance, Vladimir Kokovtsov, observed that Russia was directly dependent on 'His Excellency the harvest' (quoted in Vernadsky, 1961, p. 243). In the 1970s, the inability of the Soviet agricultural sector to produce sufficient food of adequate quality to feed the population led to the importation of massive quantities of grain, bought on the world market (principally in the United States); and in the 1980s, Soviet agriculture's poor performance still determines in a fundamental way the general performance of the economy. Butter, meat and other basic foodstuffs–not to mention more exotic products–are reported to have all but disappeared for much of the year in many provincial towns and cities, and supplies have been obtained (at bargain prices) from the European Economic Community's surplus stocks. The cost to the Soviet population–and indirectly to the economy's further performance–of standing in queues for long hours for food that may provide enough calories for subsistence but does not necessarily supply the full range of vitamins and trace elements for complete health cannot be accurately gauged or measured, but must be substantial.

Despite some clear successes, by practically any measure, Soviet agriculture falls far behind that of her ideological rivals, and in many cases behind that of her socialist allies, and in some products the trend has been downwards. Table 4.2 shows the output of basic agricultural crops in selected years. Grain is the best-known problem area, with planned (or rather, hoped-for) production rarely being attained, and up to one-quarter of requirements having to be imported (Goldman, 1983, pp. 64–5). In the six years from 1977 only in 1978 was planned production exceeded, by a record harvest of 237.4 million tonnes; this was followed by substantial shortfalls in subsequent years (D. Gale Johnson, in Cracraft, 1983, p. 201, Table 1); under Gorbachëv, excellent harvests in the three years 1985–7 were followed by a disappointing harvest of 195 million tonnes in 1988—16 million tonnes less than the previous year. Milk yields in 1981, at 2,040 kilograms per cow, were lower than in 1977 (2,260 kg.) and even 1970 (2,110 kg.) (Cracraft, 1983, p. 197)—a fraction of European production. Average

Table 4.2 Soviet agricultural production: selected years

Product	1970	1975	1980	1988
Grain (m. tonnes)	186.4	140	189.2	195.0
Cotton (m. tonnes)	6.9	7.9	9.9	8.7
Sugar beet (m. tonnes)	78.3	n.a.	79.6	87.8
Sunflowers (m. tonnes)	6.1	5	4.6	6.2
Potatoes (m. tonnes)	96.6	88.5	66.7	62.7
Vegetables (m. tonnes)	20.3	n.a.	25.9	29.3
Cattle (end year; m. head)	99.1	111.0	115.5	118.8
cows (m. head)	41.0	41.9	43.4	41.5
Pigs (m. head)	67.2	57.8	73.5	77.7
Sheep and goats (m. head)	143.2	146.9	147.0	145.9
Meat (m. tonnes slaughter weight)	12.3	15.2	15.1	19.3
Milk (m. tonnes)	82.9	90.8	90.7	106.4
Eggs ('000m.)	40.4	57.7	67.7	84.6
Wool ('000 tonnes)	415	463	461.7	476

Sources: as Table 4.1 except Grain, 1970: *SSSR v tsifrakh v 1970 godu* (Moscow, Statistika, 1971), p. 102.

hay yields have been only about half of those achieved in climatically comparable regions of North America, and the seeding rate (weight of seed per area sown) is more than twice that common on that continent (Cracraft, 1983, pp. 200, 202; Byrnes, 1983, p. 97).

A number of factors have been put forward to explain the continuing weakness of this sector, which must be quite perplexing for Soviet planners. The lack of the stimulus of a market is an obviously ideological point, but one that should not be discounted, given the clear evidence that the collective (and state) farmers do respond to that mechanism. Soviet sources have for some time acknowledged that while the share of production by value fell from 35.6 per cent in 1960 to 26.5 per cent in 1979, in quantity terms the private sector in 1979 contributed 60 per cent of the potatoes, 96 per cent of the rabbit meat, 42 per cent of the fruit and berries, 40 per cent of the pork, kid and poultry meat, 33 per cent of the horse meat (a figure queried by Nove in presenting these statistics: 1982, p. 118), 27 per cent of the venison and camel meat, and 17 per cent of the beef and veal. To a great extent, of course, these are products that command the highest prices. At the beginning of 1988, private herds consisted of some 23.4 million head of cattle, including 12.9 million cows, 13.6 million pigs, and 33.4 million sheep and goats (*Narkhoz 1987*, p. 213). These figures represented percentages of 18.6, 30.7, 17.6 and 22.7. While one may query the *efficiency* with which these are produced (frequently through the intensive cultivation of kitchen gardens by peasant women), the *effectiveness* is not in doubt. This clearly explains the benign view of private agricultural production adopted by Gorbachëv.

The climate is another common explanation, particularly for the failure of the main grain crop. Indeed, the disastrous harvest failure of 1972 must be principally attributed to that cause: a lack of sufficient snow cover in the Ukraine's grain-growing area meant that severe January frosts killed off much of the winter wheat and barley; drought in May scorched the spring-sown varieties; and early snow and hail interfered with the harvest in the country's second grain area, Kazakhstan. There is little that any system of ownership could do to counteract such harsh weather conditions. Moreover, one school of climatologists holds that the Soviet climate follows a cycle that began a downturn in 1975 (Holzman, 1982, p. 34)—which bodes ill for the success of the basic crops that affect agriculture, industry and the nation's health, and require the diversion of scarce hard currency needed in the industrial sector.

Other factors contribute to the continuing difficulties. The legacy of the past plays its part. Inspired by the nineteenth-century vision of Man's role as consisting of subduing Nature, and reinforced by political decisions taken in the Stalin era, Soviet political leaders since the 1920s have perceived agriculture as a resource to be used for the benefit of pursuing the country's principal goal—the creation of an advanced *industrial* society. The implicit assumption for decades was that agriculture could somehow produce food for an expanding urban population, without commensurate investment in infrastructure, including the training of the work-force. The brightest village-dwellers were (and still are) creamed off to the towns to become industrial workers, leaving behind the elderly, the unskilled, those with less drive and ambition, and with less appreciation of the need to change their ways to meet new demands. The rural work-force remains notoriously inefficient.

Added to that is the poor quality of equipment, the inadequate training in its use and servicing, and the lack of spare parts—all of these well-known and richly satirized ailments, that lead to millions of roubles' worth of essential machinery lying useless at critical times. Equally significant are the transport shortages, that cause grain to be left rotting in fields or railway sidings or blowing off open trucks, and the poorly developed distribution network that prevents the proper supply of cities with basic foodstuffs.

Still having an impact is the destruction of the science of genetics under Stalin, leading to inferior livestock herds and seed strains of low yield and pest-resistance—a problem that takes a long time to overcome. When climatic conditions destroy carefully nurtured orchards, or fodder shortage impels the slaughter of animals, the work of years in the steady improvement of breeding stock can be destroyed at a stroke. The lack of adequate pesticides, antibiotics and other chemical aids compounds the problem.

The incentive system and price structure, too, do not lead to the rational deployment of resources: for instance, because of the heavy subsidy on bread, farmers have found it more economical to feed this to their livestock than to purchase feed grains in short supply—hardly a rational use of food.

However, a fundamental problem, succinctly expressed by Johnson (in Cracraft, 1983, p. 203), is that 'the Soviet bureaucracy does not trust farmers; it does not believe that farmers have either intelligence or initiative'. But the bureaucrats, in their turn, do not understand agriculture and its needs, which they appear to have approached with the industrialist's mentality. Local initiative is stifled, and farms are instructed as to what crops they shall sow, what livestock they shall maintain, what fertilizers shall be applied and when. Johnson (p. 204) quotes the late Leonid Brezhnev in 1982 exhorting party comrades to 'get rid of administrative fiat and petty tutelage with respect to collective farms and state farms'. However, as we have seen, this tendency to engage in *podmena* is an ingrained part of party administration, which measures taken so far have barely affected.

This problem has taken on great political urgency in the late 1980s, as the queues for meat and bread have grown longer and sugar has been rationed. Gorbachëv warned the party at its nineteenth conference that it had neither the moral nor the political right not to solve the food problem.

Over the years, many initiatives have been undertaken to try to solve agriculture's perennial problems. Khrushchev in the 1950s sponsored the ploughing of over 40 million hectares of virgin and unused land in Kazakhstan and elsewhere. This failed to eliminate the problem, but the land has subsequently come to play an important role in supplementing the country's traditional breadbasket, the Ukraine (see McCauley, 1976, esp. ch. 4). His campaign to produce maize as the basic fodder crop came to little, since it was inappropriately administered, with farms being encouraged to sow it in totally unfavourable climatic conditions. Brezhnev after 1965 invested heavily in soil improvement, drainage, the application of more and better equipment, and other measures, so that by the second half of the 1970s one rouble in three was being invested directly or indirectly in agriculture (McCauley, 1981, p. 221). That undoubtedly had some beneficial effect, but over a very long time-scale. He was obliged to adopt a 'Food Programme' in May 1982, aimed at making the country basically self-sufficient in food by 1990, largely by using traditional methods.

Experiments in giving families direct control over production in some parts of the country have been reported, and a statement adopted in October 1984 promised to redouble investment up to the year 2000 in the old problems of soil reclamation and amelioration (very expensive to tackle effectively), through drainage, irrigation and anti-erosion schemes. This is seen as the way to reduce the marked fluctuations in production.

The tasks are enormous, further complicated by the rapidly growing population in Central Asia, a region prone to drought and hence not well suited to growing its own food in the quantities required without massive investment in a major project such as the diversion of one or more Siberian rivers to flow south into the Caspian Sea, using the water for irrigation purposes. Such a project was on the drawing-board from the mid-1970s (see Gustafson, 1981, ch. 5), but was shelved in 1986, for financial and environmental reasons. Yet some equally imaginative scheme has to be devised if the Soviet Union is to succeed in feeding itself over the longer term. The problems of agriculture were further exacerbated by the contamination of a large area in Belorussia and Ukraine following the Chernobyl nuclear accident on 26 April 1986; these effects are likely to remain for years, perhaps decades. There can clearly be no quick solutions to the weakness of Soviet agriculture.

The Service Sector

If consumption has been the stepchild of the Soviet economy, within it the service sector has been little more than a waif. The free health and educational services are something of an exception, but are properly regarded as special cases, since they are not a conventional element in the network of production, distribution and exchange.

A further exception is public transport: as any tourist quickly discovers, one of the most efficient enterprises in the whole economy is the series of underground railways in the major cities. The railway system has a network of some 145,000 km., recently augmented by the prestige project of the 1970s, the Baikal–Amur Mainline (BAM), completed during 1984 and crossing Siberia to the north of the Trans-Siberian line built at the turn of the century. One of the most intensively used systems in the world, the Soviet railways carried 4,360 million passengers and 4,067 million tonnes of freight in 1987. Roads are poorly developed, in view of the vast distances and the severe climatic conditions, so that road transport carried over 6,853 million tonnes in 1987; in tonne-kilometres carried its share was less than 4 per cent of that of rail transport, about one-twentieth of the level of oil and gas pipeline transportation. Air transport, run by the state monopoly company Aeroflot, carried 119 million passengers and 3.2 million tonnes of freight in the same year.

The telephone system is less well developed, although it is improving: there were 35.3 million telephone lines installed in 1987, and automatic exchanges are being introduced to connect the major cities and to link into the international system (all figures from *Narkhoz 1987*, pp. 306–38).

Services in the regular economy, however, are severely underdeveloped, in terms of quantity and quality. This sector has been given the lowest priority, even though in the early years the Bolshevik leaders envisaged liberating the housewife by providing a whole range of public facilities for dining, laundry, cleaning and the like, and the 1961 CPSU Programme (revised in 1986) likewise spoke of further developing trade

> . . . as a necessary condition to meeeting the growing requirements of the people. Good shopping facilities will be made available throughout the country, and progressive forms of trading will be widely applied. The material and technical basis of Soviet trade—the network of shops, warehouses, refrigerators and vegetable stores—will be extended. (*KPSS v rez*., 1972, vol. 8, p. 267.)

This sector has been given greater attention in recent years, and there certainly have been some improvements; moreover, the state sector is now being augmented by the expanding private service sector. Official figures show that the number of service outlets increased from approximately 192,900 at the end of 1965 to 275,300 at the end of 1982. Repair establishments for domestic electrical appliances increased from under 21,000 to 36,000; tailoring premises increased from 33,100 to 42,000; dyers and cleaners from fewer than 1,000 (in the whole country!) to 2,300, and laundries from 2,200 to 5,000. The number of household repair and decorating firms tripled, from 4,200 to 12,200, and hairdressing salons and barbers' shops increased from 35,300 to 48,800. Furthermore, the amounts spent on services have increased markedly: from a global figure of 5,508 million in 1965 to 12,387 million roubles in 1987 (figures from *USSR in Figures*, 1983, pp. 210–11, and *Narkhoz 1987*, p. 450). How far these developments reflect the shoddy quality of consumer goods is, of course, impossible to say, although they do attest to the growing demand for such services, a reflection of increasing wealth, better supply, and more sophisticated tastes.

On top of that, it should be noted that the frequent queues are not caused simply by the inadequate supply, but also by the poor distribution system and insufficient number of consumer outlets. There just are not enough shops to cater for the needs of the Soviet population. Those that do exist are poorly and irregularly stocked, often with inferior goods. And the quality of service personnel is often very poor: the 'culture' of trade is undeveloped (as Soviet commentators express it), and the sales assistant is not responsible for either the quality of the merchandise or the physical conditions under which it is sold. Packaging is poor or non-existent (even for foodstuffs like butter), and self-service is only slowly being introduced into the larger cities. Goods commonly have to be paid for separately from where they are displayed, adding to the time spent in queues, and the cashiers deftly use the ancient form of calculator, the abacus, to total customers' bills.

Catering establishments are also of indifferent quality, with an unattractive ambience and service personnel who are too frequently indifferent to their customers' comfort and enjoyment. The printed menus are little more than an aspiration, in view of the insecure supplies of food items. Again, all these problems have long been known to the politicians, who have complained ritualistically at Central Committee plenums, yet to date have succeeded in effecting very little perceptible improvement. It is, of course, the millions of ordinary citizens who suffer—but it must also be very frustrating to be employed in the service sector, where the inadequate reward of low pay and prestige is simply compounded by a powerless inability to make radical improvements to the quality of the goods and services offered in the state sector. Bureaucratic harassment and insecurity of supplies are sources of similar frustration in the private and co-operative sector (see the articles in *Moscow News*, 20 November 1988, pp. 8–9).

Living Standards

Against this background of insufficient production and poor quality of both agricultural and industrial output, made worse by inefficient distribution and indifferent service standards, it must be said that the Soviet population as a whole is significantly better off than at almost any time in its history. Direct comparisons with other societies are difficult to make, since it is impossible to evaluate the relative contribution of the social consumption funds—health, education and social welfare provision, for example, and the heavy subsidies to food, housing, utilities, and even vacations. Yet clearly the average standard of living is significantly below that of the advanced capitalist countries, in terms of volume of goods and services consumed, and more particularly in terms of their quality: a mass-produced Soviet tape recorder, for example, cannot really be compared in quality and reliability with a Japanese or West German model. Design of clothing, furniture and virtually any other consumer product is unimaginative and 'old-fashioned' in comparison with what has come to be expected elsewhere in the world.

Nevertheless, set against the world average, the Soviet population is wealthy, the range of products wide, and the accumulated wealth (apart from current consumption) substantial—probably greater than they have ever known. On an index of 1940 = 100, per capita real income is said to have reached 298 (i.e. almost tripled) by 1965, and to have accelerated to reach 602 in 1982. Some categories, particularly the collective farmers and other lower-paid groups, have benefited rather better than the average: their real income rose over the same period by 7.3 times compared with 4.1 times for workers and white-collar employees, so that by 1982 their personal per capita income stood at some 90 per cent of that of workers and employees (*USSR in Figures*, 1983, p. 179). Average wages were said to be 178 roubles for collective farmers in 1988, and 217 roubles for factory and office workers; one worker in seven earned over 300 roubles a month, although still almost three million earned less than 80 roubles, although this was supplemented by dispensations amounting to 175,000 million roubles from the social fund of the state budget (*Pravda*, 22 January 1989). Casual observation in the Soviet Union shows that Soviet citizens are less well fed but far better dressed than twenty years ago, they live in more spacious accommodation despite a continuing housing shortage, and their apartments are better supplied with consumer durables; more and more families own a car, and co-operative apartment blocks, together with the country 'cottage' or *dacha*, are a popular form of home ownership. Backward, ignorant, primitive Russia has taken her place in the world of the relatively rich.

Research indicates, however, that the distribution of wealth is still far from equal. The average has risen to a level that many older citizens might have thought improbable a generation ago. Yet there is clear evidence that some groups are significantly better off than others. In discussing social structure above, the existence of stratification among different classes was emphasized, leading to income and status differences, and reflected also in different spending patterns and hence life-styles. In the Brezhnev years, incomes at the lower end were substantially raised, while those at the top were held steady, leading to a closing of the gap, which in the Stalin years had been substantial. Indeed, government policy represented 'a sustained attempt to alleviate poverty and to raise the standard of living of both peasants and workers' (McAuley, 1979), and it was noted in the 1970s that the average earnings of the highest-paid were only two or three times those of the lowest (Yanowitch, 1977, p. 38). However, earnings are not the only significant factor, for in addition living standards vary enormously according to whether one lives in an isolated village, a small town or a major city, reflecting not only earnings differences but, more fundamentally, the availability of goods and services, and perhaps even culturally related values that influence spending habits. Family size—which also varies regionally—also affects personal living standards. The distribution of wealth therefore follows a somewhat complex pattern that has been given considerable attention by Western researchers (see in particular A. McAuley, 1979; Yanowitch, 1977; Matthews, 1978).

In the most thorough study of this question, McAuley (1979)

dispensed with 'synthetic indicators of economic well-being' such as per capita gross national product (GNP) or national income, and calculated the incomes that accrued to families of different types (p. 302). He confirmed a significant trend towards equality of income during the late 1950s and 1960s, partly associated with repeated increases in the minimum wage. This failed, however, to eliminate pockets of urban and rural poverty, and McAuley indicates that the equalizing trend was reversed in the 1970s, and the rise in living standards slowed down (p. 308). This led Nove (1980b, p. 17) to comment that, although living standards continued to rise, they did so less rapidly than people had come to expect, and this posed the political problem of 'the increasing gap between rising expectations and slowly-changing reality'. McAuley also identified substantial regional differences in income, following 'a relatively stable hierarchy' (p. 107), probably related in part to changes in family size and similar sociological trends, and to inadequacies in the social welfare and social security systems (p. 122).

Mervyn Matthews (1978) assembled fragmentary and disparate evidence indicating significant differences in lifestyle, related less to earnings and income than to *access* to goods and services in short supply. In a deficient economy where money is available, he points out, those who enjoy privileged access to deficit goods and services can enjoy an enhanced living standard and lifestyle. There are limitations on high earnings, a prohibition on private ownership of property and control over other forms of wealth, and a veil of secrecy to hide marked discrepancies (pp. 17–21). Yet it is known that there are 'benefits, both material and moral, which are accessible only to small, restricted groups of people, and which are fixed by law or administrative practice' (p. 7). Among the 'special elite benefits' listed by Matthews (ch. 2) are extra pay packets, additional part-time jobs for beneficiaries or their families, special 'closed shops' stocking high-quality foreign goods, available only to employees of specific enterprises or departments: these include special medical facilities and similar services, better housing, private transport, special showings of Western films, trips abroad. The value of these additions is, according to Matthews's calculations (p. 54) to add 50–100 per cent of their recipients' basic income, and to do so in hidden ways that do not disturb the relatively small range of pay differentials. Matthews also adds (p. 53), that 'it may be tacitly understood [by the courts] that the maintenance of an élite life-style must entail occasional infringements of the law'. In fact, there is much evidence of the existence of a substantial 'second' or unofficial economy.

The Second Economy

Responding to the manifest shortages in the Soviet economy, and the debilitating frustrations of everyday living—particularly for the housewife, who, in the Soviet Union as elsewhere, is still expected to devote her time and energy to running the home, as well as doing a job—Soviet citizens have devised a host of ways of compensating for the inadequacy of the official economy to cope. Apart from the devious ways catalogued by Matthews for compensating 'deserving' members of the 'élite', there are indeed flourishing 'parallel' markets of varying degrees of legitimacy and legality, some of them highly specialized in terms of the products handled and the clientele (see Simes, 1975; Grossman, 1977; and, for a general account, Simis, 1982). The youngsters who would pay fabulous prices for cheap ballpoint pens in the 1960s, and who have now moved into the tourist market for Western fashions, pop records and the like, are but the most visible segment of the second economy, in which 'everyone from plumber to government minister derives illegal rewards through the theft of state goods and services' (Rumer, 1984, p. 26). These markets are supported by thousands of millions of unspent roubles in savings banks and probably in the form of cash holdings (Byrnes, 1983, p. 111).

Coloured Markets

In a fascinating and suggestive analysis, A. Katsenelinboigen (1977) defined a range of 'coloured markets' ranging from the legal red, pink and white, through the semi-legal grey, to the illegal brown and black markets: within several of these classes there were various categories. He also suggests a further form of analysis: 'immanent markets' that are 'the creation of large economic systems where the persons functioning are individuals who are endowed with the varied human passions'; 'socialist markets proper', that are 'engendered by the planned system with state ownership'; and 'rudimentary markets', the more or less spontaneous result of 'specific historical conditions' as peasant Russian society developed (pp. 62–4).

The 'red' market is the distribution system established by the regime, which controls both prices and wages (hence it is not a market proper); the 'pink' market embraces the legitimate exchange of secondhand goods in commission shops; and the 'white' market includes the sale of secondhand goods in the Soviet equivalent of 'flea markets' and the sale of farm produce through the collective farmers' markets in the cities: the Sunday morning market of badges, coins, stamps and other collectors' items on Moscow's Lenin Hills is an example.

While these activities are legal and have always been to some extent tolerated (and they are being positively encouraged under Gorbachëv), other forms of trading activity are illegal. The 'grey' market embraces goods and services for which state supply is inadequate: housing accommodation, private educational instruction, health care and legal advice outside the state-provided services; Katsenelinboigen (p. 71) particularly stresses repairs to apartments in this category, together with the satisfying of private orders for tailoring, dressmaking and shoemaking, plus street sales of privately grown flowers—another common sight in the cities, now augmented by other forms of street trade. All these transactions take place at prices that are effectively beyond state control and are not effectively taxed. The 'grey' market also includes an important figure in the legitimate economy: the 'fixer' or 'expediter' (*tolkach*) without whose efforts many more enterprises would regularly fail to fulfil their plan (see below).

Illegal markets are those in which participants when caught are normally prosecuted or otherwise disciplined (say, by dismissal) by the state. The 'brown' market covers items in short supply that are traded *nalevo* (literally, 'on the left', or under the counter) by those with access to them: shop assistants and managers with goods to supply to friends, acquaintances or others who might be able to provide a similar service in return; restaurant staff who divert oranges intended for the menu; chauffeurs who use institutional cars for private hire, and so forth. Such rackets apparently involve junior sales staff and their superiors, who commonly take a 'cut' of illegal earnings (Katsenelinboigen,

p. 76). Another segment of the 'brown' market includes foreign goods legally taken into the country by sailors or other Soviet citizens who regularly travel or live abroad, and sold at prices way above their hard-currency value. A further significant sector involves the theft of materials from state enterprises for use by, say, electrical technicians to run private repair and servicing businesses for domestic equipment. A 'brown' market also exists in producers' goods in short supply, particularly spare parts for vehicles and various types of equipment.

Finally, the 'black' market embraces strictly illegal transactions, in which the participants are deemed guilty of criminal activity and prosecuted by the state. In addition to the street purchase of highly desired foreign fashions and other modish items, this includes trade in foreign currency, gold, drugs and a range of other foreign or domestic goods (say, cars) that are normally unavailable or obtainable only with difficulty; some may have been acquired legally as a speculative venture.

The Tolkach

Mention was made above of the *tolkach*, or expediter, whose existence has been known for many years, and is in practice tolerated as an evil needed to oil the wheels of the economy, pending more sophisticated planning, more effective checking procedures, or both. The expediter is employed by many enterprises, under a fictitious title, and functions as an agent in arranging deals with other expediters or enterprise managements to supply needed resources when the planned deliveries fail to materialize. His job is to 'agitate, nag, beg, borrow, sometimes bribe, so that the necessary materials, components and equipment arrive' (Nove, 1977, p. 100). Sometimes quite complicated deals can be struck, involving several enterprises, each of which can supply another with needed output, thereby permitting them all to fulfil their plan (although perhaps causing others to fail to fulfil theirs). This type of arrangement is so well established that managements as a matter of course hold back some of their production against the need to engage in such 'private' inter-enterprise barter. Occasionally, too, local government is involved—say, giving permission for a plant to build housing in a particular district in return for the supply of transport for street cleaning or tree planting.

Whatever the reasons for these elements of economic activity that are not authorized by the plan, they are prima-facie evidence that the attempt to plan the economy has fallen down in practice. By definition, the scale of such illegal activity cannot be established with certainty, but it is evidently substantial.

Economic Reform

We have identified a number of problems and difficulties encountered by the Soviet economy and rife by the early 1980s, and the situation has not improved much, if at all, during the decade. Western specialists disagree about the seriousness of the situation. For some, the Soviet Union is in crisis, manifesting the 'failure' of its economic system (Goldman, 1983); others, however, have suggested that the use of the word 'crisis' was premature (Bialer & Gustafson, 1982, p. 87), and that 'Soviet difficulties appear only mildly disabling and chronic–not acute' (Holzman, 1982, p. 53). The contradictory assessments–shared by Soviet observers–probably reflect in part different observers' own views of the Soviet Union, and perhaps also a projection of how the same economic difficulties would appear in a Western context. They also reflect the contradictory evidence, well summed up by Campbell (in Byrnes, 1983, p. 68):

> It is an economy perpetually in crisis, wasteful and inefficient in the use of resources, bureaucratically musclebound in efforts to innovate technologically and institutionally, and scandalously callous and inept in meeting the Soviet population's consumption wants. Despite all this, its growth performance has been impressive. Lurching though its progress seems, it overcomes crises rather than allowing them to accumulate to the point of collapse, and year after year significant output increments become available, expanding the leadership's ability to achieve its goals.

Presumably the Soviet leaders and their advisers and planners, too, are confused and perplexed: Gorbachëv (1987, pp. 23–4) has referred to the country as 'verging on crisis' and 'becoming increasingly unmanageable'. Despite the politically impressive achievements of virtually full employment and–until very recently–negligible inflation (but see Kushnirsky, 1984a), the present and future difficulties are clearly apparent and solving the economic difficulties has been placed at the top of the political agenda. The objective problems include the slowdown in the expansion of the labour supply, coupled with major (and growing) regional imbalances in its distribution; the exhaustion of readily accessible resources of minerals and energy, necessitating a costly and technically difficult switch to Siberia for supplies. Indeed, there will be a number of severe demands on investment capital in the years ahead: the perpetual failure of agriculture, leading to a foreign-trade burden in basic foodstuffs; the population's rising expectations, reinforced as a political factor both by the need to compete with the capitalist West and by the experience of neighbouring countries (notably Poland and, more recently, Yugoslavia) in the face of consumer frustrations; the continuing burden of armaments following the decline of *détente* in the early 1980s, to which might be added the cost of assisting friends and allies in Eastern Europe and elsewhere. Some of these factors have already been subject to reassessment in the recent past.

These objective factors face an economy whose basic structure and administrative methods—'the economic mechanism', as Soviet economists refer to it—remained unchanged for half a century after their introduction in the 1930s. Then they were facing quite different tasks in a society that was far less complex and sophisticated than it is today, and those methods now lead to much inefficiency and waste, and failure to satisfy needs.

Not surprisingly, in view of the acknowledged deficiencies and indequacies, there has been much discussion of possible ways to overcome the difficulties, and certain approaches have been attempted. Since the range of problems is quite diverse, different measures are proposed to overcome them.

First are measures to raise the basic efficiency and productivity, particularly of industry. An exhortatory slogan common in the Brezhnev era and still heard at the end of the 1980s is 'search for reserves'—an injunction to managers and workers alike to examine the operations of their enterprise, looking for ways of saving energy, materials or time, so that more can be produced with less input. Also well developed in the Brezhnev era was the practice of 'socialist emulation' or 'socialist competition', said to symbolize a new attitude to work

(Yesipov, 1975, p. 62), in which individual workers, work teams, plants, and indeed cities, challenged one another to produce more by a certain date—the anniversary of Lenin's birthday, May Day, 7 November or 31 December. Another form of 'socialist emulation' is the drawing-up of 'counter-plans': alternative production targets, higher than those of the central plan, devised taking local 'reserves' into account (Yesipov, pp. 64–5). Party members are expected to engage in this 'voluntary' form of commitment, and the 'prizes' include both financial bonuses and non-material benefits: badges or pennants, plus local publicity. Wage incentives are also employed to encourage labour pioneers to migrate to remote or inhospitable areas.

Other specific approaches also concentrate on the individual worker: for example, the encouragement of 'inventors and rationalizers', enrolled in a nation-wide society, to examine work practices or products and suggest economies. An annual figure of nearly five million innovations and 24,000 new inventions is claimed, leading to savings by the mid-1980s of some 8,000 million roubles a year (*SSSR v tsifrakh*, 1987, p. 68). The chronic indiscipline of the work-force has been tackled: high labour turnover, drunkenness on the job, laziness and absenteeism have all been identified as contributing to the economy's failures, particularly in the last years of Brezhnev's rule. The response, initiated by Andropov in 1983 and continued under Gorbachëv, has been to underline the need for 'discipline', while mounting a vigorous campaign against drunkenness and alcohol abuse. This campaign, whatever its claimed success, cannot provide a complete solution to the problems of the Soviet economy, however.

A potentially more effective way of improving labour productivity—vital over the longer term as the growth in the labour force dwindles—is to enhance and modernize the capital stock, principally by importing foreign advanced technology. This has indeed been a favoured policy for some years: the chemical industry (including synthetic fibres and plastics) has been particularly singled out for its high dependence on foreign technology (Amann *et al.*, 1977, p. 65). However, this policy is not without its disadvantages. The first is, of course, that it has to be paid for, and in convertible currencies earned through the sale of goods or services. The government, which until recently enjoyed a total monopoly of foreign trade, has traditionally been anxious to arrange barter deals or to pay for imported technology by deliveries of the products of the installed equipment, or to seek extended credit from Western banks and governments. All these were regular features of East–West trade during the era of *détente*, coupled with the sale of basic commodities, principally oil, supplemented of late by natural gas. However, deals of this kind on the one hand make the Soviet Union vulnerable to pressure from her adversaries, and on the other require willingness on the part of those political rivals to enter such trading arrangements. For the Soviet leaders, this may require unpalatable compromises on defence and foreign policies (Rumer, 1982, p. 68). The political overtones are clear, and experience of recent years over the grain supply from the United States and over pipeline technology from Western Europe, plus the long-standing reluctance to supply the Soviet Union with computers and anything else that might conceivably be of benefit to the military, indicates that Soviet leaders might be unwise to become over-dependent on this source of economic salvation. Gorbachëv's rhetorical stress on *interdependence* is aimed largely at defusing that particular set of attitudes, for the ultimate benefit of the Soviet economy.

More interesting to outside observers is the prospect of some kind of reform. There are somewhat superficial approaches: improving the bonus schemes to encourage managements and workers to raise their productivity, or improving the planning mechanism by, say, using computers and mathematical approaches to the planning process. The difficulty with the first of these is that of breaking into the circle: unless workers see desirable goods on which to spend their extra earnings, they are unlikely to respond to incentive schemes—yet that would be the very goal of the schemes. As for the second, the economy is now too large for even the most sophisticated computers to handle. Soviet computers are not among the most advanced in the world, and the potential military application of such equipment makes Western countries reluctant to supply it. Nevertheless, the steadily expanding impact of computers in improving the quality of managerial decision-making has been judged 'a limited and unspectacular success' (Cave, 1980, p. 184), while mathematical modelling (as opposed to just using the number-crunching power of machines), in an attempt to devise an optimally functioning economy, has a respectable history in the post-

Stalin Soviet Union, even though its impact on policy has been minimal (Sutela, 1984).

More radical reform proposals have been in the air for many years, and some have been acted upon on previous occasions. They range from injecting the profit motive in one form or another, to decentralization of production decision-making and introducing a market mechanism to balance supply and demand, establishing a wholesale market, and making enterprises fully cost-accountable.

One of the best-known proposals was put forward by Professor E. G. Liberman, of Kharkov University, in 1962 (his views are summarized in Nove, 1977, pp. 308–9, although Nove, p. 309, suggests Liberman's influence has been overrated; Millar, 1981, pp. 127–8). As we saw, producing so many pairs of shoes or so many dresses says nothing about their quality or desirability; using so many tons of timber in furniture is no indication that it is elegantly designed, well made or even functional; judging machine-builders by whether they meet sales and earnings targets encourages 'goldplating', or the tendency to add costly 'extras' of little value to the user (Nancy Nimitz, in Bialer & Gustafson, 1982, pp. 144–5). So Liberman proposed establishing profit as the principal indicator of enterprises' success, on the reasonable grounds that profit reflects the efficient supply of goods and services for which there is a demand.

Aleksei Kosygin as prime minister attempted to introduce such a reform in the mid-1960s—hence it is known as the Kosygin reform. The purpose of these reforms (other measures accompanied the use of profit as a success indicator) was in fact to enhance the level of central control, by extending the area of managerial discretion and replacing the traditional success indicators by an economic measure that was amenable to straightforward central evaluation (Millar, 1981, p. 128). However, these reforms were not implemented with the necessary vigour, were resisted by those who benefited from the customary arrangements, may even have been fundamentally flawed (see Kushnirsky, 1984b, p. 34), and by the end of the decade quietly faded in a welter of disillusionment (Bialer & Gustafson, 1982, p. 143). The long-term impact has been almost negligible, and bonuses are still awarded for plan fulfilment rather than for high profitability (Millar, 1981, p. 128).

In any case, managements have been restricted in what they might do to increase profits by certain politically salient working rules of the system. Foremost among these was the guarantee and requirement of work for all. The Soviet Union has prided itself since 1930 on having 'abolished' unemployment, and it makes no provision for unemployment pay. So, while being encouraged to make efficient use of labour, the state-employed managers were not given the freedom to sack surplus workers. One well-known experiment attempted to grapple with this problem. First tried at the Shchëkino chemical combine in 1967, it permitted managers to declare workers redundant and use the wages saved to improve the remuneration of the retained workers. According to one observer, the success of the scheme 'seems to have been virtually unqualified' (Schapiro & Godson, 1984, pp. 58–64). Here, too, however, the extension of this potentially important scheme was very slow, and it did not in practice release as many workers as intended, since many were reabsorbed into the same work-force in different sectors (Nove, 1977, p. 220; Schapiro & Godson, 1984, pp. 60–1). There is an obvious fear of widespread unemployment if such a system were to be extended widely, a politically unacceptable prospect. In any case, the experiment was perhaps best seen not as another Soviet attempt to find a panacea, but rather as part of a cautious wave of reform throughout the Soviet economy under Brezhnev (Rutland, 1984).

Associated with that cautious and tentative reform is a perpetual search, not only for 'hidden reserves' but for new success indicators. A fresh attempt to introduce a new system was inaugurated in July 1979, when a decree was issued, calling for enterprise bonuses to be related to labour productivity, product quality mix (the proportion of 'state of the art' items in the plant's inventory), and the extent to which deliveries adhered to supply contracts. The reform did not envisage a radical departure from traditional methods—such as permitting enterprises to choose among suppliers as a means of improving their productivity, and even Soviet reception was reported to have been lukewarm (Bialer & Gustafson, 1982, p. 140). As a 'respectable third-best reform' (p. 141), it evoked scepticism among Western specialists. An experienced (and self-confessedly sceptical) observer commented: 'Almost nothing in the decree is new: it is a compendium of planning and incentive arrangements which have been tried out in various branches; what the decree does is to call for their general introduction, at least throughout the industrial sector' (Hanson, 1983, p. 11, n. 2). Another expert predicted that the measures might make matters worse (Gertrude E. Schroeder, in *Soviet Economy*, 1983, p. 88). Yet still Soviet commentators called for simply 'a new system of economic indicators', and yet another experiment was cautiously attempted in 1984, which aimed to replace the level of plan fulfilment by the size of the increase in net output as the basis for increases in the bonus and other incentive funds, and to give more managerial functions to the production enterprises (for an assessment, see Kushnirsky, 1984b).

What many Western and some Soviet economic experts looked for was a thorough-going reform involving serious decentralization of operational decision-making, by allowing enterprise management to take decisions regarding suppliers, product mix, employment levels, etc., within a restricted number of general guidelines, rather than operating to fulfil a highly specific plan compiled in the centre. At its most 'extreme', this would involve setting up some kind of market, with prices determined by the balance of supply and demand, and enterprises and retail outlets much freer to reject unsuitable supplies, and even choose their supplier. The very careful introduction of such a reform (the 'New Economic Mechanism') in Hungary in 1968 was suggested as a model that had produced a palpable improvement in the supply and quality of foodstuffs and manufactured goods (for a brief account see Nove, 1977, pp. 290–8).

Clearly, such a solution would deprive the centre of its detailed control over the functioning of the economy—but it is arguable how much effective control it exercised through central planning: revelations of a variety of abuses, and the known existence of 'coloured markets', lead one to scepticism on that score. More serious would be the inevitable price rises for certain goods that have traditionally been heavily subsidized (mainly food products) or are in serious deficit (household consumer goods, for example): after decades of officially non-existent inflation, the economic and political consequences could be most unwelcome—witness the experience of Poland in 1970, 1976 and 1980, when the government repeatedly tried to raise prices on heavily subsidized foods (Rumer, 1984, pp. 29–30). Equally significant is the potential for unemployment as managements take decisions to raise productivity by sacking workers. The state, ultimately, has to find alternative jobs; and while this might be an effective way of overcoming the threatened labour shortage, the social disruption involved is something neither the people nor the government have really experienced, and the institutional supports have been inadequate to cope.

Nevertheless, Western and Soviet economists argued that some kind of 'real' reform was required, as the existing system could not be adjusted to cope with the steadily increasing demands placed upon it: past reform attempts had not brought about the desired radical transformation of the economy's performance.

It fell to a new generation of leaders, younger and more dynamic, headed by Mikhail Gorbachëv, to grasp this nettle and introduce a range of reformist measures—a 'radical economic reform', Gorbachëv called it. A number of the elements have already been mentioned, including the injection of an element of competition for the indolent managements of state enterprises, in the form of individual, family and co-operative businesses. While these function principally in the area of services to the public—catering, photography, professional services of various kinds, appliance repairs, taxi and chauffeur services and so forth—some are also involved in small-scale manufacturing (often from surplus and scrap materials) to supplement the state's activity. Within the state sector itself, the status of enterprises has been changed, with all enterprises now supposedly functioning on the principle of cost-accounting (*khozraschët*), and enjoying greater freedom to choose their suppliers, decide their product mix, establish their prices, and select their customers. Moreover, the principle that the state will always subsidize its own enterprises has been abandoned: bankruptcies have been reported among Soviet firms, which have then been absorbed by successful enterprises.

In a bold attempt to open the Soviet Union to the winds of world economic pressures, the government has permitted and encouraged the investment of foreign capital in 'joint ventures', in which the Soviet side holds 51 per cent of the shares. There were 191 such enterprises registered by the end of 1988 (*Pravda*, 22 January 1989). This is seen as a means of acquiring capital investment at a time when the Soviet economy itself is incapable of generating it on the scale required, and also of gaining managerial expertise from firms that are manifestly successful elsewhere in the world. Part of that expertise will be absorbed by the new generaton of Soviet managers; but, equally significant, the experience of working with foreign management methods will help to develop a new 'culture' of the work-place among Soviet workers. The attempt to involve the Soviet economy more broadly in global economic activity goes even further. Enterprises that acquire earnings from exports are to be permitted to retain hard currency to purchase equipment on the world market. And, as a first step towards the creation of a freely convertible rouble, regular hard-currency capital auctions are being introduced to give successful exporting concerns access to the means to purchase needed technological imports.

In addition to these measures, a fundamental price reform is contemplated so as to bring economic rationality into the price structure and eliminate the budget deficit—acknowledged for the first time in 1988, and said to be of 36,000 million roubles—without, it is promised, affecting people's living standard. Certainly, basic foodstuffs, rents and utilities are likely to rise in price, while the prices of manufactured goods ought to decline.

Gorbachëv's initial expectation was that positive results would be attained within three years. The year 1988, however, was one of fairly average performance, and it was clear that the economic corner had not been turned. Wages and salaries increased by an average of 15.3 per cent (against a planned figure of 17.7 per cent); real per capita incomes rose by 3.5 per cent—higher than in earlier years, but still well below the planned 4.6 per cent; consumer goods output, at 5.1 per cent increase, was well below the planned level of 7 per cent; agricultural output, with a poor grain harvest, rose by a mere 0.7 per cent, whereas the plan reckoned on 6.3 per cent; the industrial sector just met its target of 3.9 per cent growth; only in construction, freight and passenger traffic, the wages fund and profit levels were the planned levels exceeded, suggesting a significant boost to inflationary pressure; other specific industries—notably paper manufacture—also did rather better than planned, but the majority did not meet their targets (figures from *Pravda*, 22 January 1989). The director of the Academy of

Sciences' Institute of Economics, Leonid Abalkin, told the Nineteenth Party Conference in June 1988 that there had been no serious change in the fortunes of the national economy (*Pravda*, 30 June 1988, p. 3); he was challenged, however, by another scholar, Georgii Arbatov (*Pravda*, 30 June 1988, p. 6). The resistance of bureaucrats in the ministerial apparatus is seen as one major obstacle to the successful implementation of the reforms—as it was in the 1960s. To that, however, must be added the scepticism of a demoralized work-force which still has to spend hours queueing for basic foods, and for clothing and fairly ordinary manufactured goods. As another delegate—a machine operator—told the party conference, workers in his district were asking where *perestroika* (restructuring) had got to: in the shops there was no meat, sugar was now rationed, and manufactured goods were not available at all (*Pravda*, 1 July 1988, p. 6).

It is clearly too early to assess the fate of the 'Gorbachëv reforms'. They are still in a state of evolution, and their final scope is not yet certain. Some leading economists—Abalkin, Abel Aganbegyan, Nikolai Shmelev, to name but three—would be prepared to inject a full-scale market mechanism, accompanied by a broad opening to the outside world (for a succinct summary of such views of the problems and possible solutions, see Aganbegyan & Timofeyev, 1988; also Aganbegyan 1988); yet that would have wide-ranging implications for the labour market, prices, bankruptcies, and perhaps the fluctuations of the business cycle that was one of Marx's principal targets in his critique of capitalism. Others are, of course, much more cautious, and the fear of the 'radicals' is that bold proposals will be so diluted by compromise that the economy will continue to grind along much as it has. As always, the fate of economic reform depends at least as much on political concerns as it does on economic factors.

Industrial Relations

In the light of the state ownership of the Soviet economy, relations between management and the work-force take on a form different from what is common under capitalism or in a mixed economy: the official view is that socialism '[unites] the interests of all who take part in the production process', so that workers and managers are 'equally concerned about developing production and collaborating to achieve this goal'. Labour is said to be emancipated, and this creates a new attitude towards work (Yesipov, 1975, pp. 16–17). The Soviet authorities reveal little information concerning industrial relations, particularly any that contradicts the view of near-perfect harmony, and until the policy of *glasnost'* took hold under Gorbachëv, disputes were given virtually no publicity.

Harmonious and efficient production at the work-place is the responsibility of three distinct institutions: the 'troika' of management, party organization and trade union (Ruble, 1981, p. 6). They work together in a somewhat complex relationship, although all are subordinate to policy decisions taken at the pinnacle in the party hierarchy (Lane & O'Dell, 1978, p. 22). While management is granted the prerogative of taking all operational decisions in relation to implementing the enterprise's production plan, a function of the union is to negotiate a 'collective agreement' relating to fulfilling a production plan for a stated period, and engage in its enforcement alongside management (Ruble, 1981, pp. 57–60). Unions are expected to ensure that this does not involve infringement of the law, particularly in relation to labour protection.

The effective management of shop-floor relations is no less delicate in the Soviet Union than under capitalism, however, and disputes do arise, so Soviet legislation makes provision for their resolution. Since labour relations are supposedly not conflictual, and management's hands are tied by the plan and by the ministries, disputes arise infrequently over issues of wage rates or working conditions (however, see Ruble, 1981, ch. 4). More common are disputes over management infringements of labour legislation, including such matters as illegal sackings, holiday rotas, allocation of workers to a wrong wages category or failure to pay earned bonuses, violation of rules limiting working hours, and so forth (see McAuley, 1969, pp. 160–203).

The legislative provision for handling disputes is based on a statute of 1957, slightly amended in 1974, and supplemented by a completely new law on work collectives, adopted on 17 June 1983 (text in *Pravda*, 19 June 1983). These various statutes provide for the initial resolution of disputes to be attempted at shop-floor level, through a disputes commission comprising union and management representatives;

failure results in examination by the factory trade-union committee, whose report may be challenged by the aggrieved worker or by management; if appropriate, the union may call in superior officers, or the dispute may be taken to court (Butler, 1983, pp. 215–17; Avakov & Glozman, 1971, pp. 212–25; Kaftanovskaya, 1975). However, what a Soviet union will never do is use a strike or other form of industrial action in pursuit of a dispute.

Strikes are technically not illegal; nor, however, are they legally sanctioned (Butler, 1983, p. 217); moreover, such action may be punished as a breach of the peace or as disobedience (Schapiro & Godson, 1984, p. 124). In addition, as Mary McAuley has noted (1969, p. 251), 'the unofficial strike has not formed part of the usual pattern of labour disputes' since the first decade of the regime's existence, and other forms of industrial action (the go-slow or walk-out) are 'not particularly significant'. They do occur, however, along with 'Italian strikes', 'in which workers turn up at the factory but in practice do not work'; usually the leaders are disciplined, by dismissal or by legal sanctions (Schapiro & Godson, 1984, p. 123). The changes in the authority of management as the new reforms are implemented may lead to greater indiscipline and labour unrest; the publicity now given to such actions may serve to protect future strike leaders; it is also not inconceivable that the official unions might become bolder in defending their members' position, as successive leaders have urged them to do.

In their role in regulating industrial relations, Soviet unions enjoy certain legal rights that their counterparts in market economies might envy: a virtual veto over managerial prerogatives in dismissing workers, for example. Moreover, they are closely involved in negotiating the distribution of the wages fund, the bonus fund and certain funds that managements are obliged to set aside for social or recreational purposes for their work-force.

But the very existence of such a close link with management (which means, indirectly, with the political authorities, since these ultimately appoint managers, even following 'election' by the workers) also means that if necessary Soviet trade unions can be called upon to support management even in infringing workers' rights. If, say, in order to meet the output target for a particular quarter it were necessary for a factory to extend overtime for a ten-day period, during which basic maintenance could not be done, so threatening the reliability of equipment and the safety of workers, the trade union would be under great pressure to go along with such risk-taking; this could be justified on the grounds that it was in the interests of the collective and society as a whole, and even in the financial interests of the workers, whose bonuses were thereby guaranteed. A union member who objected in such circumstances would find it very difficult to gain union support (for further examples, see McAuley, 1969; Ruble, 1981).

Such connivance by the unions in infringements of labour law was acknowledged by Brezhnev in 1981, at the height of the international publicity surrounding the independent union 'Solidarity' in Poland. The unions were 'not always sufficiently persistent in matters of fulfilling collective agreements and labour protection, and they still react feebly to cases of infringement of labour legislation . . .,' he told the Twenty-Sixth Party Congress (*Materialy*, 1981, p. 66). Gorbachëv expressed similar thoughts at the following congress, in 1986 (*XXVII s"ezd*, I, p. 80). There is undoubtedly some protection against unfair management practices, and the very fact that the unions are, as it were, incorporated gives them some authority in negotiating with management over such day-to-day matters as the holiday rota or social security arrangements (Lane & O'Dell, 1978, p. 37): hotel janitors told the author in 1975 that they had operated through the union to revert to a 24-hour work roster in place of the 12-hour shift introduced by management.

Yet quite evidently the unions are less effective than they should be in defending their members against incompetent or unscrupulous management. The words of Brezhnev, Gorbachëv and others are clear enough, and in response attempts have been made to create trade-union organizations independent of the party-sponsored ones. Two particular cases became known in the late 1970s. First, in the Ukraine a former coal-mining engineer Vladimir Klebanov was instrumental in 1977 in attempting to establish an 'Association of Free Trade Unions'; and in October 1978 there was formed a second grouping, the Free Inter-Professional Association of Workers (SMOT, from its Russian initials). The authorities responded with repression: Klebanov was interned in the Donetsk psychiatric hospital; adherents were arrested and in some cases imprisoned, although SMOT still claimed some 3,000 followers in April 1983 (Schapiro & Godson, 1984, pp. 130–1; Ruble, 1981, p. 3; for documents, see Haynes & Semyonova, 1979).

The authorities have acknowledged that workers with grievances are not simply saboteurs and 'bourgeois wreckers'; moreover, the treatment of labour discipline infringements has changed 'nearly 180 degrees' since Stalin's death (Ruble, 1981, pp. 6, 143). By and large, efforts have been made to meet genuine grievances, but attempts to establish unapproved organizations for the expression of working-class concerns have been stifled, by force if necessary (see Gidwitz, 1982, for a brief summary). This has given the government a respite from the immediate political pressures. Yet signs of worker dissatisfaction have been obvious for some years, expressed by absenteeism, poor time-keeping, drunkenness and—in a free labour market characterized by labour shortages—high turnover rates, partly related to managerial quality (Teckenburg, 1978). This compounds the inadequacies of the planning system in adversely affecting economic performance. Betsy Gidwitz (1982, p. 42) predicted the continuation and expansion of worker discontent, but expected that 'the future of Soviet labor relations will resemble their past'. Other observers are more optimistic, and the need for change has been well summed up by Blair Ruble (1981, p. 144), arguing that 'Pressure exists to narrow the gap between theory and practice in Soviet labor relations. . . . Further change in Soviet economic and social relations are in order'.

The conditions of *perestroika* and *glasnost'* make it considerably less risky for workers to express their grievances against both incompetent management and unsupportive trade unions, while also giving them, through extension of the electoral principle to managerial positions, greater opportunities to influence the appointment of those placed in authority over them. The role of the traditional trade unions remains in need of a thorough overhaul, as market principles and the demand for profitability increasingly come to dominate production relations. That is a reform that will have to be tackled in the next decade.

5 The Regime's Policies

Domestic Policies

Governing the Soviet Union must be seen as a complex task, not simply a question of manipulating more than 280 million citizens in the interests of 'building communism', although that vague phrase still represents the leaders' stated goal. Economic performance is fundamental to the attainment of other goals, and is likely to continue constraining the leaders' actions for a number of years to come (see Bialer, 1980, ch. 15; Hanson, 1980). But economic growth is not the only goal, and governing Soviet society implies the adoption of policy in a whole range of areas that also concern other governments. Four areas will be considered: education, culture, religion, and military affairs.

Education

The Soviet Union has always regarded education as a necessary prerequisite for economic development, and also a natural right for all citizens. 'He who is illiterate is blind', declared a famous poster of the 1920s, and the 1977 Constitution, like its 1936 predecessor, declares that 'Citizens of the USSR have the right to education' (article 45). Moreover, the success in educating a largely ignorant population has been rightly seen as 'one of the most positive facets of Soviet reality' (Matthews, 1982, p. 200).

A literacy drive soon after the revolution was very successful. Despite doubts about its effectiveness, particularly among the older population, official statistics claim that a rural illiteracy rate of 76.2 per cent in 1897 was reduced to 49.4 per cent by 1926 and a mere 16 per cent at the end of the 1930s; by the 1970 Census, almost universal literacy was claimed (see *Naselenie SSR*, 1980, p. 18).

The Soviet Union has a complex set of education facilities, including crèches and kindergartens, elementary and general secondary schools, special secondary schools for intensively training linguists, artists, mathematicians, etc., vocational schools, polytechnics and universities, teacher training colleges, agricultural institutes and other special, industry-focused establishments. In 1987–8, there were some 135,000 general educational schools, employing 3.2 million teachers educating some 43.8 million pupils; over 4.3 million pupils were in professional or trade schools, and more than 4.4 million pupils in the 4,508 special secondary schools. In higher education there were over 1 million new enrolments, bringing the total of tertiary students to a little over 5 million (all figures from *Narkhoz 1987*, pp. 476–511). Numbers graduating with higher diplomas and degrees rise steadily, standing at 855,000 in 1984 (*SSSR v tsifrakh*, 1985, p. 251). In addition, the party has set up training schemes to give its officers, and those of the higher state administration, the required skills and ethos.

Many institutions offer part-time, evening and correspondence courses alongside the standard educational facilities. Thus, in 1986–7 among the 4.5 million pursuing courses in the special secondary schools, 384,000 were attending evening courses and 1.2 million acquiring education by correspondence; at the higher level, 620,000 students were taking evening lectures and almost 1.8 million training for diplomas by correspondence, as against a little under 2.7 million day students (figures from *SSSR v tsifrakh*, 1987, pp. 229–31). The total number of students in most categories has fallen in line with demographic trends.

Extra-curricular activities for children and young people are arranged by the Little Octobrists, the Young Pioneers and the Komsomol, which have a prime role in imparting attitudes of patriotism, hard work, honesty, etc., while also channelling young people's energy and enthusiasm in approved directions; that includes giving the rising generation the desired political values (see Avis, 1987, esp. ch. 6).

The whole system of formal education is state-run; religious bodies are constitutionally barred from such activity, and private schools are prohibited. An exception, within the second economy, is private coaching, which, although quite expensive, takes place widely in cities and in practice places 'middle-class' youth (i.e. the children of those able and willing to pay for it) at an advantage at university entrance. Elementary and secondary education is compulsory, and it is free of direct charge at all levels, including advanced research degrees. Schools are coeducational, with no streaming by ability; however, the special schools provide an element of selection. The system is centrally directed, although local traditions such as language may be catered for in the republics. Indeed, in non-Russian areas pupils usually have a choice of language of instruction—Russian or the local language—which has the practical effect of spreading the use of Russian. A school reform adopted in 1984 extends primary education by beginning schooling at the age of six; in the higher classes of secondary schools, pupils are able to specialize in physics, mathematics, chemistry, biology, social sciences or the humanities, according to choice, while the senior class curriculum incorporates a measure of vocational training. In explaining this reform, the Soviet Union's minister of education stressed the needs of the economy, with the additional thought that 'No matter what career a school graduate may choose, work training will help him in every field of human endeavour' (*Soviet News*, 11 January 1984, p. 11; also Avis, 1987, ch. 2).

Such are the bare facts of the Soviet educational system's organization. Its successes are to be seen in the numbers of graduates, and to some extent in the intense competition for admission into the more prestigious higher institutions, such as Moscow and Leningrad universities. Its failures concern the uneven quality: the best institutions are in the major European cities; the worst facilities are in rural schools, where quite commonly reluctant village teachers work in cramped and poorly equipped classrooms on two shifts.

These facilities exist to promote several aims. First, they provide society with the skills needed by the rapidly developing economy, and to this end the training programmes are co-ordinated with Gosplan's predictions of future skill needs. In the 1980s this means emphasis on technical skills, as the proponents of the 1984 school reform argued, to raise labour productivity in an era of demographic slow-down.

A second aim is to regulate society's development by facilitating advancement for the disadvantaged, through imparting the skills needed in a largely meritocratic society. For this purpose there exist special courses for workers and peasants on completing their military service, so they may reach the required literacy and general education standards and embark on third-level courses. Yet social background affects access to higher education, with children of educated parents doing significantly better than workers' children (Matthews, 1981, pp. 158–61; Pankhurst & Sacks, 1980, ch. 5). It seems, too, that the tendency to see a higher diploma as a passport to a white-collar job hampers the recruitment of engineers into industry, and distorts the development of Soviet society (see Lane & O'Dell, 1978, pp. 87–91).

A further aim is to socialize the rising generation in the ideology's collective and communal values, as part of the goal of 'bringing up communist man'. Pupils are encouraged to show commitment by wearing their Young Pioneers' red neckerchief, and to model themselves on Pavlik Morozov, a Pioneer 'hero' who earned notoriety by denouncing his father in the farm collectivization drive (the boy was murdered—'martyred'—by villagers); they are also involved in disciplining their own classmates, and the general ethos is one of not letting down the class or school (see Bronfenbrenner, 1974, ch. 2; Grant, 1979, ch. 3). The same desire to inculcate appropriate values is reflected in the compulsory courses in Marxism–Leninism, 'scientific atheism' and similar subjects in higher education, coupled with constant denigration of capitalism and the West. The effectiveness of this has been seriously doubted (see Matthews, 1982, pp. 202–5; Avis, 1987, ch. 9), and the existence of crime, delinquency and other forms of anti-social activity on a significant scale—including various illegal, anti-state economic activities—testifies to the inadequacy of Soviet education in imbuing citizens with a sound community and civic spirit (see Connor, 1972; Juviler, 1976; Pankhurst & Sacks, 1980, ch. 9; Sacks & Pankhurst, 1988, ch. 9).

Culture

In the cultural realm, however, the Soviet regime has long been attacked by liberals. Cultural policy applies on two levels: high culture (the arts and letters), and popular culture, including ethnic cultures.

Bolshevik leaders take the view that the artist must serve in ways defined by the party leadership. This idea was well established among the Russian radical intelligentsia three-quarters of a century before the Bolsheviks came to power—art for art's sake has long been rejected in Russia. So the creative segment of the society has always been required to submit to a censorship that under Stalin rigidly defended 'socialist realism'. The depiction of 'muscle-bound defenders of the faith' (Irwin

Weil, in Cracraft, 1983, p. 247) striving to build communism under the party's benevolent leadership has typified Soviet artistic production, leading to a sterility and banality transcended by only a minority of great artists, who even then sometimes suffered at the hands of the regime: the composer Dmitri Shostakovich is a prime example.

Significant change came only in the late 1950s and 1960s, and that mood, too, proved transient. Whereas Solzhenitsyn was permitted to publish *One Day in the Life of Ivan Denisovich* under Khrushchev's patronage in November 1962, Brezhnev's leadership was early marked by the trial of Sinyavskii and Daniel, accompanied by the refusal to publish Solzhenitsyn's later work, his expulsion from the Writers' Union and exile from the country in 1974. Others suffered a similar fate (including not only writers but musicians of the stature of the cellist Mstislav Rostropovich), while leading dancers and others fled on tours to the West. Under the crude artistic values of the period of 'building socialism' and later, experimentation was frowned upon, as was the favourable depiction of traditional values, such as the rural way of life, religious faith or local patriotism.

The Soviet Union never returned to the *zhdanovshchina*—the period from 1946 to 1953, when A. A. Zhdanov (related by marriage to Stalin) contrived to make 'socialist realism' the all-pervading orthodoxy, and created a 'wilderness' in literature (*Cambridge Encyclopedia*, 1982, p. 217). After Brezhnev's death, in June 1983 Chernenko chastised writers and artists who portrayed 'only failures, life's disorders, and such discontented, bellyaching characters', and urged them to present instead 'a hero who embodies the nobleness of life's goals, ideological conviction, diligence and courage' (*Pravda*, 15 June 1983). On another occasion, as General Secretary, he defined socialist realism as 'the basic artistic method of our literature and art' (*Pravda*, 26 September 1984). Past experience suggests that in practice only a rare individual can combine the required political commitment with artistic genius to create plausible characters and present them in a lively and attractive way.

Nevertheless, Soviet artistic life was never dead. For example, Irwin Weil (in Cracraft, 1983, p. 248) saw a 'vibrancy and joyous energy' that 'often produce admirable artistic and cultural results', while Katerina

Clark (also in Cracraft, ch. 21) saw with optimism several artistic trends vying with one another, noting especially a flourishing school of 'village prose' that has developed since the mid-1950s, in part reflecting the rebirth of Russian nationalist sentiment (Dunlop, 1984, ch. 5), but also revealing a yearning for a rural past, in reaction to this century's rapid industrialization (see Hosking, 1980, ch. 3). Even under Brezhnev, much literature was provocative and revealing about Soviet reality, including some of its hidden and negative sides, and (quite apart from renowned writers like Pasternak and Solzhenitsyn) even examining some aspects of the Stalinist experience (see Hosking, in Cracraft, 1983, ch. 22; Crouch & Porter, 1984, especially ch. 2; Seton-Watson, 1986). This also includes the emergence of significant non-Russian writers, one of the most distinguished being the Kirgiz, Chingiz Aitmatov, producing successful works within the principle of 'national in form, socialist in content'.

Under Gorbachëv, however, the winds of *glasnost'* have blown through the world of culture, and artistic freedom has been extended to a degree not encountered since before the Stalin era. Films such as *Pokoyanie* ('Repentance', by Chingiz Abuladze, released in 1987) and 'It's Not Easy to Be Young' (by Juris Podnieks, 1987), novels such as Aitmatov's *Plakha* ('The Executioner's Block') and Anatolii Rybakov's *Deti Arbata* ('Children of the Arbat'), or plays such as Mikhail Shatrov's 'The Treaty of Brest' (with its distinctive portrayals of Lenin, Stalin and Trotsky) and Vladimir Gubarev's 'Sarcophagus' (about the Chernobyl nuclear accident) have transformed cultural life unrecognizably in the second half of the 1980s. The literary renaissance includes publishing for the first time such formerly banned works as Pasternak's *Doctor Zhivago* and Anna Akhmatova's poem cycle *Requiem*, works by *émigrés* such as Nabokov, and even anti-totalitarian (long seen as anti-Soviet) works such as Orwell's *Nineteen Eighty-Four*. Cultural liberalization is thus a part of Gorbachëv's quest for a moral regeneration of Soviet society, and it also extends to the mass media, particularly the press and television, which now debate controversial questions that had long been banned from public discussion (see O'Meara, in Hill & Dellenbrant, 1989, ch. 7).

This is a new policy, which can be seen in the context of other aspects of Gorbachëv's return to the values of the early 1920s, when the search to establish new principles for a free socialist society was on in earnest. Conversations with Soviet citizens indicate that the policy has captured the imagination of broad sections of society. It has been seen by some as a means of distracting attention from the acute material shortages, or of winning over the intelligentsia to Gorbachëv's cause (see, for example, Yury Yarym-Agayev in *Glasnost–How Open?*, 1987, p. 16; Hough, 1987). In any case, it has also raised the wrath of conservatives, including leading politicians such as Ligachëv, and even the more traditionally minded writers and artists themselves, shocked at the portrayal of crime, drug abuse and other social ills in *belles lettres*. It is therefore not yet certain that the policy will be permanent.

The liberalization has also had its effect on the position of popular cultures, including the legitimation of the former counter-culture of rock, punk and similar imports from Western youth culture, and demands for greater scope for self-expression by the non-Russian peoples. Some Russians take a rather patronizing attitude towards these, expressed in the officially approved notion of the Russians as the 'leading' nation in the 'family'. But equally, while bringing the benefit of Russian—a major world language that provides opportunities for advancement within the Soviet Union and opens up access to much of world culture—the authorities have sponsored the literary development of some four dozen unwritten languages, in which works appear where none could be published previously. The larger nationalities complain of Russian cultural domination, and of reduced opportunities for self-expression in their native tongue (see, for example, Dzyuba, 1968, ch. 10; also, the reports of street demonstrations in Georgia in 1978, and more recently in the Baltic republics, demanding greater cultural autonomy); however, several smaller national groups have benefited from a policy that has enhanced their national culture and status.

Yet this policy must produce ambiguous results. It may reduce criticism that the official policy entails imposing Russian language and culture, against the interests and wishes of the minor nations; yet it also reinforces the nationalities' sense of separateness (see Karklins, 1986).

There may be no solution to the policy-makers' dilemma. The government must demonstrate success by creating a society in which all nationalities live harmoniously together. It must also counteract the ever-present charge of 'Russification', by fostering separate national cultures; it may do this by facilitating education through native languages, thereby possibly attracting charges of denying chances of social and economic advance that a thorough familiarity with Russian offers. The Soviet regime has an impressive and enviable record in creating jobs and wealth in peripheral regions. But Russians feel no obligation to learn other nationalities' languages, even when they live outside Russia proper, so Russian remains the lingua franca throughout the Soviet Union. Bilingualism, a favoured policy for bringing nationalities together (Marinesku, 1975), is essentially for the non-Russians: the language in the new cities peopled by migrants from many corners is Russian, which is also the medium through which different Soviet nations gain familiarity with one another's literary culture. In bringing economic development, the government is steadily eroding and ultimately destroying the traditional cultures of colourful peoples—yet not to do so could attract the accusation of committing them to a primitive lifestyle and perhaps exploitation for the Russians' benefit. This is a version of the dilemma facing governments in all modernizing countries, where an educated élite must impose its values on an uncomprehending populace: the national overtones in the Soviet case are simply a further complication.

Finally, there is a Russian nationalist 'backlash' that takes many forms, demanding a variety of measures to protect the Russian cultural heritage, and in some chauvinistic cases to buttress that nation's dominating position within the Soviet Union (see Dunlop, 1984). This, too, influences the regime's continuing concern to play down nationality as a factor in relations in Soviet society, while maintaining the existence of distinct nationalities, at least until the eventual 'merging' (*sliyanie*) that it is intended will take place over the very long term, after the world-wide victory of socialism when all national cultural distinctions should disappear (see Suzhikov, 1978, pp. 226–30).

Whatever the medium- and long-term trends—whether towards the genuine integration into a single, culturally and linguistically homogeneous nation, or even towards the disintegration of what some see as the Russian Empire in a new form—the national question has not been 'solved': indeed, what would constitute a 'solution'? Clearly, the Soviet Union, in common with other Marxist-ruled states, is still faced with 'the unwithering national question' (Walker Connor, 1984, pp. 581–5).

Religion

Religion is fundamentally incompatible with Marxism–Leninism, and Soviet leaders find it difficult to understand, and therefore to cope with. It is seen as a vestige of the past, a harmful superstition, characterized by Marx as 'the opium of the people' and by Lenin as 'a spiritual gin', through which the exploited classes obliterate their misery. It rejects materialism, so is seen as a major obstacle to the exercise of the party's 'scientific' ideology and as a challenge to party rule.

Successive constitutions have decreed the separation of church from state and of the school from the church, while simultaneously guaranteeing freedom of conscience, defined as 'the right to profess or not to profess any religion, and to conduct religious worship or atheistic propaganda' (1977 Constitution, article 52); the same Constitution also states that 'incitement of hostility or hatred on religious grounds is prohibited'. However, the enforcement of this law concerns many observers, for whom 'The record of infringement of the rights of religious groups and individuals by Soviet authorities is simply too voluminous, glaring, and consistent to be ignored' (David M. Abshire, writing in Boiter, 1980, p. 6).

Despite the 'separation of church and state', laws and regulations—some of them secret—have repeatedly been passed that controlled directly the activities of organized religion. Beginning with a law of 1929, significantly amended in 1975, individual congregations were made the basis of legal religious activity, subject to authorization by the local soviet, as agent of the USSR Council of Ministers' Council on Religious Affairs. Local laws proscribe as 'criminal' many religious activities, and the observation of such a key Christian occasion as Easter has been severely hampered (even by such crude stratagems as late-night showings of Western films). The printing of the Koran, Bibles, prayer books and other religious publications is heavily restricted (although both the Orthodox and the official Baptists publish a periodical), while Jews find difficulty in preparing Kosher foods.

Acts of worship by believers are generally not interfered with, and administrative action against religious organizations or believers is normally strictly within the (fairly flexible) law; nor does the state interfere in theological controversy (Boiter, 1980, p. 40). But the state, enacting the party's policy of eventually eradicating religious observance—particularly its transmittance from one generation to the next—has sometimes taken extremely firm measures against both institutional churches and individual believers (particularly those, such as Jehovah's Witnesses, who refuse to recognize the flag or to perform military service). An anti-religious drive by Stalin in the 1930s closed some 95 per cent of all places of worship, many of them converted into museums or warehouses; seminaries were shut down, and priests were exiled or imprisoned by the thousand; other measures were taken to eliminate the influence of religion on a people building socialism. During the Second World War, the Orthodox Church in particular was harnessed to the patriotic war effort, and rewarded by recognition of the Patriarchate in 1943. Churches were reopened and membership grew. But in 1960–1, Khrushchev launched a massive church-closing campaign, in which congregations were forcibly amalgamated and disused buildings were destroyed or taken over for profane use.

Nevertheless, religion has not been eradicated, and the evidence on policy since 1964 is contradictory. It is impossible to estimate accurately the number of worshippers, let alone of 'believers', but it must run into scores of millions, taking all denominations into account. Boiter (1980, p. 63) reports an official assertion of 1977 that there were over 20,000 functioning churches, mosques, etc., including 180 synagogues: yet Jewish agencies in the West have identified only one-third of that number of synagogues, and Western specialists reckon there are only half that total number of places of worship. A more recent Soviet source puts the number of believers at 8–10 per cent of the adult population (i.e., some 12–15 million, undoubtedly a gross underestimate: the authors identified 97–8 per cent of those under 20 and 92–4 per cent of those in their twenties as atheists (P. Kurichkin & V. Timofeev, in *Pravda*, 30 March 1979); Western sources estimate that perhaps even 45 per cent of the population profess religious belief (Sacks & Pankhurst, 1988, p. 167). Important religious feasts are heavily supported by worshippers, and many millions, including known communists or Komsomol members, go through religious rites of passage: funerals, baptisms, and with decreasing frequency weddings (C. Lane, 1979, pp. 60–1). Rural populations regularly observe saints' days, to the dismay of the authorities who have renamed some of them as 'socialist' holidays (C. Lane, 1981, ch. 8).

More alarming, from the authorities' point of view, is the marked religious revival among intellectuals, dating from about the late 1950s (Lawrence, 1969, pp. 124–5; see also Anderson, 1983, p. 27). Since religion is perceived as a superstition to be eradicated by education in a scientific world view, this renewed interest is inexplicable. The standard response is to step up anti-religious education and propaganda, hoping for greater effectiveness. Boiter's comment (1980, p. 20) is that 'Today Soviet atheist propaganda is somewhat less shrill [than Lenin's], but it is still unbelievably crude, one-dimensional, and aimed at the emotions. The basic emphasis is still to ridicule religious belief'. This effort, which receives considerable time and energy, includes atheistic instruction in schools and universities and a broad onslaught in the press and other communications media, while religious dissent (as opposed to religious worship) has been attacked with the rising or falling pressure on dissent in general, itself associated with the East–West political climate. At the same time, state control over organized religion, including supervision over the appointment of clerics and scrutiny of the curriculum of seminaries, has been tightened up (Anderson, 1983, p. 27).

The authorities may have begun to recognize that attempts to stamp out religious observance and belief may backfire, if only by lending the excitement of a forbidden activity to a phenomenon with a centuries-old history and tradition of persecution strengthening faith. Anderson (1983, p. 25) quotes a Soviet source to the effect that 'closing a parish church does not turn believers into atheists', while repeatedly over the years those engaged in the anti-religious drive have been urged not to use administrative means against believers, since 'attempts by forcible measures to make the believer renounce his convictions are not only worthless but even harmful' (*Pravda*, 30 March 1979). Yet the regime has certainly not renounced the need to eliminate religion from the entire population, identifying it still as 'anti-materialist, anti-scientific' (Gorbachëv, speaking to Nineteenth Party Conference, *Materialy*, 1988, p. 42).

Meanwhile, it uses religion for its own purposes. Stalin harnessed the patriotism of Russian Orthodox believers in the Second World War, and that church's participation in the World Council of Churches has been used to promote the government's line on peace. Astonishingly, on 6 April 1983, the government newspaper *Izvestiya* carried an 'open letter' to President Reagan from Patriarch Pimen, complete with quotations from the Bible, reminding the American leader of the first commandment to Christians, 'Thou shalt not kill', followed by a further article (*Izvestiya*, 6 May 1983) containing statements from leaders of other religious organizations. The weekly magazine *Moscow News* (published in Russian and several foreign languages) now devotes much reportage to religious matters; a new yearbook contains an 11-page chapter on various religions (*USSR '88*, ch. 14); and Gorbachëv himself congratulated the Orthodox Church on its millennium in 1988. The impact of these public utterances on citizens is hard to guess, but some may have been encouraged to take a different line on both the content of Christian teaching and the status of the Orthodox Church as a result of this governmental *imprimatur*. Likewise, the widespread refurbishing of old church buildings, complete with the re-gilding of long-tarnished domes, and the return of monasteries and cathedrals to the churches, effectively presents afresh solid symbols of an alternative view of the world: this may have results the officially atheistic regime might not find entirely palatable.

Gorbachëv appears to have adopted a much more open-minded approach to religious observance than his predecessors. Religious believers are still in prison, and unofficial publications contain many reports of alleged persecution (for example, various issues of the unofficial periodical *Glasnost*). Yet Gorbachëv has insisted that believers have an honourable place as citizens in Soviet society, and announced the preparation of a law on freedom of conscience (*Materialy*, 1988, p. 42). Time will tell whether this represents a new accommodation with the more prominent denominations, and whether it will be extended to evangelizing sects and all individual believers: for the moment, the politicians still firmly set the guidelines within which religion operates (see Dunlop, 1988). Many outside observers, and many believers inside the Soviet Union, would probably still concur with Boiter's judgement (1980, p. 18) about recent religious policy:

> Since 1965 they have refined it, made it more sophisticated—and thus better camouflaged from foreign eyes—and at the same time more effective. . . . CPSU policy toward church and religion over the years has become steadily less rather than more realistic, flexible and liberal.

Military Policy

An essential element in Soviet economic development has been the determination to create the means of self-defence, in what was seen as a hostile world. With this in mind, the country has invested massively in developing a modern arms industry, capable of producing all the military hardware its statesmen deem necessary. Indeed, the Constitution (article 32) declares that the state 'ensures the security and defence capability of the country, and supplies the Armed Forces with everything necessary for that purpose'. Wholly accurate knowledge of the scale of investment, in rouble terms or as a proportion of the country's economic output, is unavailable. Estimates vary, depending on the assumptions underlying the measurements, although intelligence information gives an additional basis for assessment (see Becker, 1983). Soviet statements about military investment and capability cannot be taken at face value, so the question must be approached by a process of more or less reliable guesswork.

Even then, interpretation is not necessarily clear. Defence expenditures rose from the mid-1970s, while those of the USA fell. Yet, as pointed out by Democratic Congressman Les Aspin, the reduction in US expenditures following the Vietnam War primarily explains that decline, whereas Soviet expenditure remained relatively stable as a percentage of GNP; also, one convention employed in making the estimates assumes the Soviet soldier's pay to be comparable with that of the professional American soldier. 'The absurdity of this calculation', Aspin observes, 'becomes evident when one considers that if we returned to the draft and the old pay scales, the US defense budget would fall, but the Soviet "dollar" budget would plummet even further because they have more people' (in Neal, 1979, pp. 87–108).

Furthermore, experts differ on the potential effectiveness of this capacity, some pointing to the known inefficiency of conscript armies, particularly when handling ultra-sophisticated weaponry (see, for example, David R. Jones and Mikhail Tsypkin, both writing in Cracraft, 1983). Even reasonably accurate estimates of expenditure and hardware do not guarantee reliable deduction of the Soviet Union's war-fighting capacity, since assessment requires assumptions about accuracy of weapons, leadership quality and troop morale (see, for example, Holloway, 1983, p. 50).

A further area of doubt concerns Soviet intentions. What is the purpose of the military build-up? Does it reflect a genuine concern for the country's safety? Is it a nationalistic desire to match the United States, with everything a superpower role demands? Does it, more sinisterly, indicate a continuing belief in war as an instrument of policy? Does the Soviet Union, in other words, really believe it can fight and win a nuclear war, as suggested by Pipes (1977): is it a way of attaining global dominance? In fact, it may be all of these—plus even a crude and dangerous means of compensating for political and economic weakness (Bialer, 1980, p. 419). Whatever the speculation, one thing is not in doubt: following a fundamental decision taken in the early 1960s, the Soviet Union had within a decade acquired global power status, for the first time possessing both the capacity and the willingness to 'use her military power to decide the outcome of distant crises' (Legvold, in Bertram, 1980, p. 11); indeed, this is perhaps the country's most impressive achievement under Brezhnev (Bialer, 1980, p. 411).

In view of the Soviet Union's proximate and global concerns, the military establishment is powerful, flexible and impressive. One of the more reliable and careful assessments is the annual, *The Military Balance*. The latest volume to hand (1988, pp. 30–44) gives the following estimates; they differ somewhat from the official figures, first published in January 1989, giving details of the Warsaw Pact's military strength (for example, in *The Independent*, 31 January 1989).

Total armed forces numbered 5,096,000, excluding border guards and other special categories. Of these, 1,900,000 were in the army, the majority (1.3 million) conscripts; 458,000 served in the navy (nearly three-quarters conscripts); the air force accounted for 315,000; air defence embraced over half a million, the strategic rocket forces almost

300,000; the naval air force 70,000 and the aviation armies 95,000. Other identified categories included strategic rocket forces reserves (almost 300,000), and marines (17,000). All males are required to serve for at least two years as conscripts, while males up to age 50 are liable to recruitment, bringing the possible total reserve to some 55,000,000.

These forces were well supported by hardware which is being modernized even as it is being reduced in quantity. This includes intercontinental ballistic missiles (ICBMs) equipped with nuclear warheads, to be launched by about 100 launchers, backed up by ship-launched missiles and strategic nuclear bombers. These are the subject of active negotiations between the Soviet Union and the United States. The 405 deployed intermediate-range missiles and their warheads (including the SS-20, the object of much consternation in the West), and the 245 missiles that had not been deployed, together with their launchers constitute a category which is scheduled to be destroyed under the terms of the Intermediate-Range Arms Reduction Treaty, signed in Washington in December 1987 and ratified in May 1988: their destruction at sites capable of satellite surveillance began in the second half of 1988.

The navy, deployed in the last fifteen years in waters far from Soviet shores (in particular, the Indian Ocean, but including fleets in the North Atlantic, the Pacific and the Mediterranean), had 372 submarines (including 75 carrying strategic weapons) and 268 surface fighting ships: these included 4 aircraft carriers, 36 cruisers, 62 destroyers and 166 frigates, plus patrol and coastal craft. The army was organized in 52 tank divisions, equipped with 53,300 battle tanks, and 150 motor rifle divisions, 10 air assault brigades and 18 artillery divisions. The air force possessed over 1,000 bombers, including 175 with long-range capability and 570 medium-range, plus some 2,500 fighter aircraft and 8,600 surface-to-air missile-launchers and their weapons; the air force also possesses a substantial military transport capacity. Also, for the first time, the Soviet Union acknowledged at the end of 1987 that it possessed chemical weapons.

The Soviet Union also has a serious and comprehensive programme of civil defence (although doubts as to its reliability have occasionally been raised, inside the Soviet Union and outside), backed up by a part-time organization, DOSAAF, with a membership of some 110 million who engage in military-relevant sports and hobbies such as rifle-shooting, flight-training, parachuting, orienteering, radio-operating and the like.

In the 1980s, apart from Soviet territory, Soviet troops were deployed in Central and Eastern Europe, including East Germany, Poland, Czechoslovakia and Hungary (plans for the withdrawal of some of these troops were announced at the end of 1988), and in Mongolia and Afghanistan (the withdrawal of Soviet forces following military failure after almost a decade of war in Afghanistan was completed in mid-February 1989). Small contingents, including advisers, were stationed in various countries of Africa, the Middle East, South-East Asia, India, Cuba and Nicaragua.

Whatever the Soviet government's military intentions, the rest of the world must be aware of the *political* influence that the possession of such armed might gives the Soviet Union. This policy has had clear repercussions on Soviet domestic policy, to the extent that some Western observers have spoken of the 'militarization' of Soviet society (Odom, 1976). Not only, and most obviously, does the massive military investment deprive Soviet citizens of the benefit of a higher standard of living, and has involved large numbers of them in military and military-related employment; it also engages students and secondary school pupils in military education, and involves almost all citizens by 'entangling' them in national civil defence arrangements (Odom, p. 34); there is, in short, according to this view, a pervasive 'military-educational complex' (p. 36), with military officers holding posts in even some of the least military establishments, including the Moscow Conservatoire (p. 49). Partly for these reasons, some Western commentators have held the view that the Soviet Union is actively preparing for war.

The picture is enhanced by the evident development of a military-industrial complex, in which those charged with producing increasingly costly defence hardware—their work co-ordinated by a Central Committee Secretary, currently Oleg Baklanov—necessarily have significant impact on the basic resource allocation decisions within the economy (Spielmann, 1976). It is clear, too, that military-related industrial plant also produces civilian goods—trucks, for example, or consumer durables such as television sets, radios and refrigerators—so that production could very quickly revert to direct military purposes. Moreover, military production is likely to be positively affected by any general improvement in economic performance resulting from the current reforms (see Bova, 1988).

In other areas, too, military influences are in evidence. For example, the ubiquitous uniforms on the streets are a striking feature of Soviet cities; construction brigades from the Soviet army can be seen on building projects in urban centres; others help with the harvest; the compulsory military service for young males performs an important socializing function, integrating the various nationalities into the multinational 'Soviet people', giving them technical and political training, and perfecting their command of the Russian language (see Cracraft, ch. 9; Holloway, 1983, pp. 160–3). Moreover, a long-established ceremony in Soviet society is that of sending off the newly recruited conscripts at the railway station, by friends, family and Komsomol. National holidays, such as 23 February (Army Day) and 9 May (Victory Day), celebrate military themes; children in Pioneers' uniform mount guards of honour at war memorials as part of their civic training, and classes of six-year-olds may be made to march in step on a school museum outing; objects such as the Eternal Flame to the fallen in war symbolize 'the sacrifices of the Soviet people, the eventual triumph which arose from the sacrifices and the love of, and pride in, the Motherland in whose name they were endured' (C. Lane, 1981, p. 197). In short, awareness of military objects and other phenomena is a natural part of everyday Soviet life.

The impact of all this is not entirely clear, particularly since it is masked by vociferous propaganda in support of 'peace': ordinary Soviet citizens in casual conversation spontaneously express an earnest desire for peace coupled with evidently sincere fears for the future; at the same time they applaud a particularly well-drilled company of soldiers in a May Day procession. Perhaps all this reflects genuine concerns about external threats. But it has been interpreted otherwise, and the fear expressed in the West that it betokens a willingness to contemplate the use of military means in pursuit of policy has been flatly denied by Gorbachëv, who announced to the United Nations on 7 December 1988 an intention to reduce Soviet troop levels by half a million men, withdraw military contingents from East European countries, and redeploy Soviet forces in a manifestly defensive posture. What remains true is that Soviet citizens are more aware than their counterparts in other nations of the significance of the military factor in human relations.

Foreign Policy

In the Soviet Union, as in other countries, foreign policy-making is a complex process involving many variables. Some of these are within the Politburo's power to control: for instance, the allocation of resources to build up and re-deploy the Soviet navy. Others, however, are beyond Soviet influence: other states' actions, or technical discoveries that give rivals an advantage. Moreover, the various factors are not in complete harmony: the insistence on loyalty among neighbouring allies may lead to action that conflicts with the carefully nurtured image of peace and responsibility, or that provokes a hostile response, such as sanctions affecting Soviet economic needs. Here, some salient features will be examined.

There are, first, the *objective conditions* that would face any government of that territory at any time, regardless of its ideological complexion.

The sheer size of the territory presents long borders to be protected, plus a crucial problem of communication and control. At its simplest, the issue is whether such a vast land can be effectively ruled from a single centre, and to what extent decentralization of decision-making is desirable and possible.

Secondly, the country's place on the globe renders it exceptionally vulnerable to invasion, as past experience shows. Clearly, the Soviet Union's defence needs are quite different from those of, say, the United States. It has common borders with NATO member states, and outlets to the oceans can be controlled by NATO members.

Thirdly, a harsh and unreliable climate, combined with variable soil conditions, places certain restraints on the country's economic possibilities, with implications for foreign relations. Self-sufficiency is possible only at a relatively low level of development and sophistication: raising living standards impels trade with the rest of the world.

A fourth factor, potentially crucial, is the national diversity of the population, varying widely in their cultural heritage, language, racial type and other features. Some have their 'own' national state outside the Soviet Union: this immediately makes them of concern in foreign relations; others have a linguistic or religious affinity with peoples outside the Soviet Union, which likewise incorporates a foreign-policy dimension.

The country's tremendous industrial potential in Siberia and elsewhere needs protection from foreign powers, while also giving the country virtually unrivalled long-term potential for economic might, which appropriate policies could convert into military might (as has indeed been happening). But the technical difficulties of exploiting these resources may demand collaboration with foreign powers that possess the necessary expertise.

The country has the potential to be a 'Great Power', so this is a logical and realistic aspiration, as it has been for centuries. In the twentieth century the Soviet Union has achieved that status, influenced by the dominant *values of the age*. The Soviet Union is a modern state, with all that implies in terms of its role and interests. It has an obligation to protect the territory and the citizens, most obviously from military attack, but also perhaps from nuclear fallout caused by explosions set off by other countries, or from atmospheric and water pollution (in the Baltic, for example); it may also feel obliged to protect them from 'subversion'. All states attempt to perform such functions, independently of their professed ideology: to this extent the Soviet Union has been socialized to the values of the international system in this century (see Waltz, 1979, pp. 127–8).

The modern state also reflects the values of industrial society and technical progress, since industrial power is the basis of political influence. The effectiveness of Soviet economic development has been an important element in a great shake-up among the countries of the world, as the country rose to acceptance as an equal by the Great Powers of the day. Europe has subsequently declined in global importance, and the Soviet Union measures its achievement against that of the other superpower, the USA, with which it claims equality in a process of competitive imitation or emulation (see Bertram, 1980, p. 36).

Both are big countries, possessing an industrial economy and sophisticated technology (witness the success in space exploration and the military hardware), and supported by defence treaties that bind other countries to them, and treaties of friendship that establish clients in the Third World. The dominant ethos in both is of a desire to be superlative—to produce the biggest, the most, the highest, the best.

As a superpower the Soviet Union has certain interests. The United States is a natural rival for Russia or the Soviet Union, as is China, a great nation and civilization with which she shares a continent. Equally naturally, relations with smaller countries on the border—Finland, Poland, Afghanistan—must be affected by the Soviet Union's sheer size and power: relations could not be 'equal' in the sense that relations between, say, Norway and Sweden are. Nor can other countries ignore the mighty and powerful Soviet Union. That would be the case even if there were still a tsar on the throne. But there is not: the Soviet Union is ruled by communists, and *ideology-related factors* also affect the country's place in the world.

Marxism–Leninism does not so much define policy as make its adherents see the world in a particular way. It allows them to identify their friends and enemies, even though for tactical reasons they may adopt apparently contradictory policies—such as the non-aggression pact with Hitler in 1939. Hostile to capitalism, they oppose governments (although, they argue, not people) that promote it, and support movements and governments struggling against imperialism. So, rivalry with the United States as a superpower is compounded by antagonism towards it as the unashamed leading exponent of capitalism. However, intensity of the antagonism is moderated by short- and medium-term calculation of advantage.

The Soviet view of relations between the West and the Third World is coloured by Lenin's definition of imperialism as 'the highest stage of capitalism'. The Soviet Union is favourably disposed towards movements engaged in a 'freedom struggle', whether or not it actually engages in fomenting such movements. The Bolsheviks, after all, were 'a national liberation front *avant la lettre*' (Waller, 1982, p. 41). In addition, 'proletarian internationalism' obliges the Soviet Union to render 'fraternal assistance' to these movements, even if only by giving propaganda support. Often, of course, it has meant much more, particularly in terms of military assistance (as in Vietnam during the

1960s and early 1970s, in Ethiopia and Angola in the mid-1970s, in Afghanistan for most of the 1980s, and perhaps also in Nicaragua). Hence, countries of the Third World become a theatre for superpower rivalry, presented in ideological terms.

The ideological dimension also operates in the reverse direction: the Soviet adherence to Marxism–Leninism and communism affects the stance adopted by other states. Furthermore, Russia's place as the first country to experience the socialist revolution endows it with a sense of mission and responsibility for the world-wide fortunes of the ideology. As Robert Legvold has expressed it, 'From the start . . . the Bolsheviks arrogated to their country the role of history's vanguard, a pose requiring a permanent concern for the character of change virtually everywhere' (in Bertram, 1980, p. 5). It became clear very early that the Bolsheviks identified Soviet state interests with those of socialism, a plausible argument in the early 1920s. The socio-economic transformation successfully undertaken almost simultaneously with capitalism's greatest crisis (the Great Crash of 1929 and the subsequent Depression) boosted Moscow's self-confidence, and the Soviet 'model' was later presented as the appropriate way of building socialism, a pioneering venture in creating a new society. By establishing and controlling international organizations, the Soviet Union imposed such a view on foreign communist parties, and on attaining power they became tributary states or 'satellites'.

The rift with China, however, from the late 1950s onwards brought an unexpected dimension to Soviet ideological claims. Mao directly challenged the post-Stalin interpretation of Marxism–Leninism, and split the communist movement. Although most ruling parties have remained loyal to Moscow, Maoist parties appeared in the late 1960s, and other communist parties, traditionally pro-Moscow, have modified their ideological posture. 'Polycentrism', the notion that each communist party could best judge the appropriate road to communism for its own country, rather than slavishly applying the Soviet model, became the dominant feature of inter-party relations in the 1960s. It resulted in the 'Eurocommunist' strain of Marxism, developed by the Italian, Spanish and French parties, and led to the virtual excommunication of the Italian party in January 1982 (Soviet statement, *Pravda*, 24 January 1982), followed in Spain by the establishment of a new pro-Moscow communist party in January 1984 (see Bell, 1984).

These developments greatly complicated Soviet foreign relations, already made complex by the fact that CPSU contacts with foreign communist parties paralleled state-to-state relations pursued through standard diplomatic channels.

Also not to be ignored in understanding foreign policy are *psychological factors*, which relate to political culture, and are extremely difficult to identify systematically, but are possibly very significant.

The first point is a feeling of vulnerability, associated with the knowledge that living standards, technical levels and economic performance are far below their rivals'. In the Soviet mind, military power is not seen as a substitute for economic and other forms of power (Bertram, 1980, p. 9): so military capacity not backed up by a strong economy and political support cannot guarantee security. Indeed, 'the dialectics of weakness' have been seen as the framework for the Soviet role in the 1980s (Philip Windsor, in Bertram, p. 21).

One result is a national inferiority complex, a 'perennial feeling of inferiority vis-à-vis "Europe"' (Adam Ulam, in Bialer, 1980, p. 3): a defensive sense of being the underdog. The West is 'worshipped', according to Solzhenitsyn, for its wealth and its technical achievements: hence the references in the 1961 CPSU Programme to catching up with and surpassing the United States on a range of indicators. But Soviet backwardness and dependency (for grain and technology) on the main adversary enhances the lack of self-esteem.

Fear of encirclement accompanies the envy. Education teaches about the anti-Bolshevik foreign intervention during the Civil War; and the direct experience of forty years ago, perpetuated in the memory by a stream of sentimental films, reminds citizens of the suffering that war can bring.

More specifically, there is a hatred and fear of the Germans, and a profound fear of the Chinese, seen by many as cruel oppressors, in their teeming millions, who might flood over the long border at any moment. Ordinary Soviet citizens (and, one assumes, Moscow's military planners) fear most the establishment of a grand alliance embracing North America, Western Europe, Japan and China, with, in addition, a ring of missile bases surrounding the Soviet Union's southern borders (see Holloway, 1983, p. 78). One response to these fears and the sense of vulnerability is an 'overriding, possibly pathological concern about national security' (Hammer, 1974, p. 387).

But the Soviet people are proud of their own achievements. They bore the brunt of the Nazi onslaught and had the honour of capturing Berlin. As a people they are materially richer than ever, despite current difficulties. They are impressed by their sputniks, by their Olympic medals, by the standard of their opera and ballet and folk dance troupes, and by the military hardware trundled across Red Square on 7 November. There is a widespread feeling that they have achieved this despite the odds, starting from nothing, in the face of world-wide hostility. Even if they are frustrated by some aspects of the system, they share a sense of pride in achievement: in the 1980s there was even a nostalgia for Stalin, in response to both the 'visible drift and inertia' (Bialer, 1980, p. 224) of the Brezhnev years and what some see as the chaos caused by Gorbachëv's twin policies of *glasnost'* and *perestroika*.

Equally significant is the national pride of a superpower, as depicted by the superior West. One thing learnt from the other superpower is a need for enough strength to avoid being pushed around, militarily or politically. The Soviet government's attitude here echoes the popular sentiment, which says: 'If American fleets can cruise the oceans thousands of miles from America, have military bases around the world, encourage its bankers and industrialists to penetrate other national economies, and even intervene directly in the internal affairs of other sovereign states such as the Dominican Republic in 1965 and Grenada in 1983, then the Soviet Union, as another superpower, has the same right.' There is no *rational* answer to such a claim of parity. When under pressure, the ordinary masses tend to rally round the flag, now the Red flag, and the communist government, the only government they have.

That may not apply to the non-Slavic peoples, a point so far untested. Amalrik (1970, pp. 59–62) suggested that in a severe crisis (say, war with China) the pressure on central government would cause disintegration, as the non-European nations rebelled. In addition, Moscow must be aware that by the year 2000 approaching half of all army conscripts will come from the non-Slavic southern republics. The crucial political question is whether these can be relied upon to defend a people whom they may regard as white colonists, and to that there is no reliable answer. Even their basic military efficiency may be in doubt, given their perhaps inadequate command of Russian, and the known tensions among ethnic groups (Feshbach, 1982, pp. 29–30). The same may also apply to the Soviet Union's allies.

International Organizations

The Soviet-led bloc's mutual security is guaranteed by the Warsaw Treaty Organization, formed in 1955 under Soviet sponsorship in response to the creation of NATO six years earlier. Strategically it is an extension of Soviet military might. Joint manoeuvres are held regularly on member states' territory (the Soviet Union, Bulgaria, Hungary, the German Democratic Republic, Czechoslovakia, Poland and Romania; formerly also Albania). The national armies are not integrated, and co-ordination is achieved through a Political Consultative Committee and a committee of treaty countries' defence ministers. These issue lengthy statements, usually reiterating the theme of peace and condemning the 'warmongering' actions and rhetoric of NATO. Among the member countries, the Soviet Union alone possesses and controls nuclear weapons, although some of these are deployed on the territory of allies.

Although the Soviet Union's leadership of the Warsaw Treaty Organization is an important factor in her world posture, other organizations also serve as vehicles for the pursuit of foreign policy. The principal one is the United Nations, of which the Soviet Union under Stalin was a founder member, and a permanent member of the Security Council, and to which it contributes some 11–12 per cent of the budget; two Soviet republics, Belorussia and the Ukraine, are separate members, and in 1983 the latter was for the second time elected to the Security Council; their policies totally reflect the Soviet government's stance.

In the 1950s the UN was seen as a tool of the Western powers, and its Secretary-General Dag Hammarskjold depicted as a NATO puppet (so Khrushchev campaigned unsuccessfully for his replacement by a three-man '*troika*'—one each from the West, the Soviet bloc and the Third World). Now this forum is used to present Soviet views and ideological perspectives to a large audience of Third World states, including many adherents of the non-aligned movement, which receives broad Soviet encouragement. In the early years, the Soviet delegation gained a reputation for its profligate use of the veto; it still does so, although far less frequently. The opening sessions of the General Assembly, held annually in September, are regularly addressed by the Soviet foreign minister or the party general secretary who often uses the occasion to reveal foreign policy initiatives. In July 1982, at a UN session, foreign minister Andrei Gromyko solemnly announced a Soviet pledge not to be the first to resort to nuclear arms.

In using military force in Hungary (1956), Czechoslovakia (1968) and Afghanistan (1979), the Soviet Union invoked the principle of *proletarian internationalism*, whereby the socialist countries are pledged to mutual assistance if their individual security is threatened: as interpreted, 'security' includes that of the socialist system, not simply external security. Indeed, in justification of the intervention in Czechoslovakia, the so-called 'Brezhnev doctrine' was enunciated in November 1968 in the following terms:

> . . . when internal and external forces that are hostile to socialism try to turn the development of some socialist country towards the restoration of a capitalist regime . . . it becomes not only a problem of the people of the country concerned, but a common problem and concern of all socialist countries. [Quoted in James, 1969, p. 157.]

A third international organization, through which the Soviet Union pursues her foreign economic relations, is the Council for Mutual Economic Assistance (CMEA, or Comecon). Formed in 1949 in Soviet response to the Marshall Aid programme for post-war economic recovery, it is the main instrument for channelling intra-bloc trade and co-ordinating economic development among the member states (principally, Warsaw Pact countries, plus Cuba and Vietnam as observers). Long-term plans well under way include the establishment of a power grid and an oil and gas pipeline network, linking Eastern Europe with the Soviet sources of these energy supplies, and the creation (begun in the late 1970s) of a motorway network. This development aims to cement the CMEA countries in firm substructure links. Since the early 1970s, Comecon has attempted to supervise the harmonization of the various member states' economic plans, although the idea of an international labour division in which the various countries would develop very specialized economies was abandoned, following Romanian refusal to remain an agricultural producer for the industrialized Soviet Union (see Ionescu, 1965). Soviet foreign trade is conducted largely through this organization, her main trading partners being the GDR, Poland, Bulgaria, Hungary and Czechoslovakia.

In the past, there existed organizations to co-ordinate communist parties' activities and policies, under CPSU leadership: the Communist International (Comintern) and the Communist Information Bureau (Cominform). Comintern was established in 1919 as a successor to the Second International which effectively collapsed in the First World War. Comintern itself was disbanded during the Second World War, and replaced in 1947 by Cominform to serve similar purposes, in a world now containing several ruling communist parties. In 1948 Yugoslavia was expelled from the Bureau, which was disbanded in 1956 during de-Stalinization.

These ostensibly international organizations of communist parties were instruments for imposing ideological orthodoxy; moreover, they made use of all the facilities of embassies and other resources of the Soviet state, despite protestations to the effect that 'The Soviet Government cannot accept and has not accepted any responsibility for the Comintern' (Sivachev & Yakovlev, 1979, p. 131). Comintern pursued the Soviet state's foreign policy: indeed, '. . . it would be difficult at any stage to point to a single case where the policy of the Comintern ran counter to the interests of the Soviet state or for that matter to the age-long aspirations of old Russia' (Adam Ulam, in Bialer, 1980, p. 6).

Recently, less institutional forums have performed such consultative and co-ordinating functions: for example, international conferences of communists and workers' parties, such as that held in East Berlin in June 1976. CPSU Congresses are attended by communist party leaders, who confer with one another and with Soviet leaders, and address the congress with fraternal greetings. In the 1970s it became customary for the leaders of the ruling parties within the bloc to join the CPSU General Secretary on vacation at a Crimean resort for conversations on matters of mutual concern.

Other Soviet organizations and institutions participate in international bodies, and may also further foreign policy. Professional associations are affiliated to world bodies—such as the International Political Science Association (the Soviet Association of the Political Sciences) and the International Sociological Association (the Soviet Sociological Association)—to which delegations are sent, and which occasionally elect Soviet members to office and hold meetings and conferences in the Soviet Union. The Supreme Soviet has since 1955 belonged to the Inter-Parliamentary Union, and sends deputies on tours abroad and welcomes delegations of foreign public representatives: Politburo member Mikhail Gorbachëv led a delegation to Britain in December 1984 under those auspices. The Orthodox Church, with the permission of the Soviet government, attends the World Council of Churches. There are also Soviet branches of the Red Cross and Red Crescent Societies. In all these forums, Soviet spokesmen promote the general lines of Soviet foreign policy, particularly its stress on peace, disarmament, *détente* and peaceful coexistence.

On 7 December 1988, as USSR President and CPSU General Secretary, Mikhail Gorbachëv presented from the United Nations' General Assembly rostrum a broad-ranging vision of a world characterized by interdependence (see, for example, *The Independent*, 8 December 1988). It was an example of Gorbachëv's 'new thinking' (a major theme of his policy of *perestroika*: see Gorbachëv, 1987, Part 2), which displayed a breadth of interest and concern rarely manifested in the utterances of statesmen. This speech was initially overshadowed by the almost simultaneous earthquake in Armenia. Nevertheless, so visionary was its content, and so new and unexpected some of its ideas, coming from a Soviet source, that its impact is likely to take some time to take effect, either on the rest of the world or even on the Soviet Union's own approach to international affairs. For the moment, that country pursues its foreign relations and policy through various, more or less traditional, channels and forums, using a range of means and modes of operation. It pursues trade and other bilateral and multilateral inter-state transactions; it uses an array of means to present its policies and viewpoints (including its foreign-language broadcasting, embracing a World Service in English); and simultaneously it uses an increasingly sophisticated—and, according to the best estimates, still growing—array of military weaponry as an underlying guarantee in projecting a global role.

Conclusion: the USSR under Gorbachëv

This study has surveyed the Soviet Union's development out of the tsarist Russian Empire, through the world's first communist-led revolution, via a process of forced socio-economic growth and change into a superpower. The profound modifications to the social and economic structure amount to a complete transformation, effected through the use of political institutions and practices that, however distasteful and unacceptable at other times and in other places, proved their worth in achieving the goal set by the Bolshevik Party under Stalin's leadership: to modernize the country in the shortest possible time.

Russia entered the twentieth century as a backward, weak and primitive colossus, poised uneasily on two continents, envious of Europe yet aware that she was no real part of it; disdaining Asia yet aware of the long history of contact with that continent, into which she had expanded her influence in the nineteenth century. As the twentieth century approaches its final decade, the Soviet Union vies with the United States of America for military supremacy, and serves as a model for emulation by a ring of tributary states sponsored by itself and for other countries around the world that have followed its example of revolution and social, political and economic transformation.

Internally, it has developed a powerful economy that now makes the Soviet people one of the world's wealthiest (however far it may lag behind the advanced capitalist countries), and certainly allows it to gain universal prestige in scientific endeavour, space exploration and military power. A society of peasants engaging in the most basic agriculture by the most primitive methods now possesses a complex and diverse social structure, characterized by high levels of employment, a sophisticated system of role differentiation and occupational stratification, a steadily expanding fund of skills, educational attainment and experience, and a population with heightened demands for material wealth, welfare and cultural developments scarcely dreamt of by the masses only two or three generations ago.

In those terms—and that is more or less how the official interpretation of Soviet history presents the story—Soviet development has proved enormously successful. It has been achieved, moreover, on the basis of the efforts of the Soviet people themselves: their blood was spilled, both metaphorically and in reality, as the country pulled itself up by its own bootstraps in the face of a world broadly inimical to the regime.

The system devised by Stalin in the late 1920s and the 1930s, when the process of socio-economic development got under way in earnest, remained in existence in its broad features until this decade. These features together were deemed to be 'socialism' and were adopted by or imposed on other states that fell within Moscow's orbit: the party's leading role, and the concomitant emasculation of other institutions, including those of the state; the organizing principle of democratic centralism and the insistence on strict discipline; the use of censorship as a means of restricting the generation and circulation of competing ideas. These are features of the Soviet system as it was fashioned in the second quarter of the century, and by and large they have not been abandoned, although the widespread and capricious use of terror as a basic form of rule was largely dispensed with in the mid-1950s, and the application of other features has been substantially relaxed.

A question that has long exercised the minds of many thinking persons in the modern Soviet Union is how to break away from such a system once it has become entrenched and seen, if not approved, as the normal and even natural way of running a society. Many Western commentators argued with vigour that the traditional way was no longer adequate. The Stalinist system could not cope with the demands placed on it. Economic growth rates slumped, while evidence mounted of social malaise that in part reflected dissatisfaction with the system's performance or its values, or both.

The accession of Mikhail Gorbachëv to the CPSU general secretaryship on 10 March 1985 opened a new chapter in Soviet history, marking the political arrival of a new generation of Kremlin leaders. Born in the late 1920s and afterwards, their formative political experiences have been in the Khrushchev and Brezhnev periods; their knowledge of the Stalin era has been learnt rather than gained at first hand. They are better educated and more sophisticated in their approach to government than perhaps any previous generation of Soviet leaders, with the possible exception of those who made the revolution in 1917 (Hough, 1980). Displaying physical vigour and political astuteness coupled with imagination and vision, Gorbachëv adopted policies aimed at transforming the system, doing so under the slogan of *perestroika*, or restructuring, a Russian word that now enjoys international currency. His approach is not to denigrate the sacrifices of the past, but, in essence, to argue that times have changed, and old methods will no longer serve the cause adequately. The chapters above have chronicled some of the changes that have already been implemented or are contemplated for the future, including modifications to the traditional forms of economic ownership and management, moves to democratize the political system while retaining a leading and guiding role for the communist party, opening up the press and other media to broad discussion of ideas, encouraging the cathartic reassessment of closed pages of Soviet history, and making bold moves on the international stage. The underlying assumption is that 'socialism' is not cognate with 'Stalinism': that it is possible to induce the evolution of Soviet society to a democratic form of socialism, under the benevolent guidance of a reformed communist party.

In approaching this task, which he himself sees as revolutionary, Gorbachëv has met with the opposition of bureaucrats anxious to preserve their position in an administered society, with scepticism on the part of the Soviet masses who have heard reformist talk before and are more interested in literally bread-and-butter issues, with suspicion on the part of the West and of some of the country's allies, and with downright hostility from neo-Stalinists who still occupy significant positions in society. But through *glasnost'*—openness, publicity—he has also unleashed a wave of creativity and excitement that could scarcely have been imagined when he came to office, including aspirations for greater cultural and political autonomy among nations that have long suppressed their resentment at their subordinate status. The stagnant society of the late Brezhnev years clearly harboured seeds that lay dormant but could be encouraged to sprout and develop into the lush vegetation of passionate argument that is now characteristic of Soviet public life. The men and women of 1956—those who optimistically joined the party at the time of Khrushchev's denunciation of Stalin—are now coming into their own, and are being placed in positions from which they can influence the development of the Soviet system along more rational, humane, civilized and democratic lines. The outcome of the intense political struggle is by no means certain, even following the Nineteenth Party Conference, in June–July 1988, which was intended to guarantee the irreversibility of *perestroika*.

Gorbachëv and his colleagues have demonstrated their willingness to introduce bold and imaginative changes, presenting their own disagreements and their willingness to admit past mistakes as signs of strength, not (as was formerly the case) of weakness. Yet there are still vast problems looming that require political decisions of the first order, including perhaps even a decision to shift the country's economic and social centre of gravity away from the depleted heartlands of old Russia to the more dynamic regions of Siberia and Central Asia. The scale of the tasks involved in pursuing this course is daunting, but so is the problem of trying to revitalize a stagnant economy.

The rest of the world's security very much depends on decisions taken in the Kremlin in the next few years, yet their opportunities for influencing those decisions are small (see Colton, 1984, p. 98). So far, the West has been cautiously supportive of Gorbachëv, who has had a far greater positive impact on Western opinion than perhaps any of his predecessors. At most the West can attempt to create international conditions in which decisions can be taken calmly and rationally, and continue to encourage the Kremlin leaders to support the further evolution of a system that in many areas has already come a long way from its tsarist origins.

Bibliography

Aganbegyan, Abel 1988. *The Challenge: Economics of Perestroika*. London, Hutchinson.

— & Timofeyev, Timor 1988. *The New Stage of Perestroika*. New York, Institute for East–West Security Studies.

Amalrik, Andrei 1970. *Will the USSR Survive until 1984?* London, Allen Lane.

Amann, Ronald, Cooper, Julian & Davies, R. W. (eds) 1977. *The Technological Level of Soviet Industry*. New Haven, Conn., Yale University Press.

Amvrosov, A. 1978. *The Social Structure of Soviet Society*. Moscow, Progress.

Anderson, John 1983. Soviet religious policy under Brezhnev and after. *Religion in Communist Lands*, vol. 11, no. 1, pp. 25–30.

Andreeva, Nina 1988. Ne mogu postupat'sya printsipami. *Sovetskaya Rossiya*, 13 March.

Armstrong, John A. 1973. *Ideology, Politics, and Government in the Soviet Union: An Introduction*. 3rd edn, London, Nelson.

Avakov, M. M. & Glozman, V. A. 1971. *Trudovoe zaknondatel'stvo: Spravochnaya kniga v voprosakh i otvetakh*. Minsk, Izd. BGU im. V. I. Lenina.

Avis, George (ed.) 1987. *The Making of the Soviet Citizen: Character Formation and Civic Training in Soviet Education*. London, Croom Helm.

Avtorkhanov, Abdurakhman 1966. *The Communist Party Apparatus*. Chicago, Henry Regnery.

— 1973. *Proiskhozhdenie partokratii*. Frankfurt-am-Main, Possev.

Barabashev, G. V. & Sheremet, K. F. 1967. 'KPSS i Sovety'. *Sovetskoe gosudarstvo i pravo*, no. 11, pp. 31–41.

Baron, Samuel H. 1963. *Plekhanov: The Father of Russian Marxism*. London, Routledge & Kegan Paul.

Barghoorn, Frederick C. 1976. *Détente and the Democratic Movement in the USSR*. New York, The Free Press.

Bater, James H. 1980. *The Soviet City: Ideal and Reality*. London, Edward Arnold.

Becker, Abraham S. 1983. Sitting on bayonets?: the Soviet defense burden and Moscow's economic dilemma. *Soviet Union/Union Soviétique*, vol. 10, pts 2–3, pp. 287–309.

Bell, Daniel 1962. *The End of Ideology: On the Exhaustion of Political Ideas in the Fifties*. New York, The Free Press.

Bell, David S. 1984. Formation of a new pro-Russian communist party, Madrid, 13–15 January 1984. *Communist Affairs*, vol. 3, no. 4, p. 491.

Bergson, Abram 1981. Soviet economic slowdown and the 1981–85 Plan. *Problems of Communism*, vol. XXX, no. 3, pp. 24–36.

Bertram, Christoph (ed.) 1980. *Prospects of Soviet Power in the 1980s.* London, Macmillan.

Bialer, Seweryn 1980. *Stalin's Successors: Leadership, Stability, and Change in the Soviet Union.* Cambridge, Cambridge University Press.

— & Gustafson, Thane (eds) 1982. *Russia at the Crossroads: The 26th Congress of the CPSU.* London, Allen & Unwin.

Biddulph, Howard 1979. Religious participation of youth in the USSR. *Soviet Studies*, vol. XXXI, no. 3, pp. 417–33.

Birman, Igor 1978. From the achieved level. *Soviet Studies*, vol. XXX, no. 2, pp. 153–72.

Bloch, Sidney & Reddaway, Peter 1977. *Russia's Political Hospitals: The Abuse of Psychiatry in the Soviet Union.* London, Gollancz.

Boiter, Albert 1980. *Religion in the Soviet Union*, Washington Papers, no. 78. Beverly Hills and London, Sage.

Bondarskaya, G. A. 1977. *Rozhdaemost' v SSSR (etnodemograficheskii aspekt).* Moscow, Statistika.

Bor, Mikhail 1967. *Aims and Methods of Soviet Planning.* London, Lawrence & Wishart.

Bornstein, Morris 1985. Improving the Soviet economic mechanism. *Soviet Studies*, vol. XXXVII, no. 1, pp. 1–30.

Bourdeaux, Michael 1965. *Opium of the People: The Christian Religion in the U.S.S.R.* London, Faber.

— 1971. *Faith on Trial in Russia.* London, Hodder & Stoughton.

— 1975. *Patriarchs and Prophets: Persecution of the Russian Orthodox Church Today.* London, Mowbray.

Bova, Russell 1988. The Soviet military and economic reform. *Soviet Studies*, vol. XL, no. 3, pp. 385–405.

Bronfenbrenner, Urie 1974. *Two Worlds of Childhood: US and USSR.* Harmondsworth, Penguin.

Brown, Archie 1984. The Soviet succession: from Andropov to Chernenko. *The World Today*, vol. 40, no. 4, pp. 134–41.

— & Kaser, Michael (eds) 1978. *The Soviet Union Since the Fall of Khrushchev*, 2nd edn. London, Macmillan.

— &— (eds) 1982. *Soviet Policy for the 1980s.* London, Macmillan.

Brzezinski, Zbigniew 1966. The Soviet political system: transformation or degeneration? *Problems of Communism*, vol. XV, no. 1, pp. 1–15.

Butler, W. E. 1983. *Soviet Law*. London, Butterworth.

Byrnes, Robert F. (ed.) 1983. *After Brezhnev: Sources of Soviet Conduct in the 1980s.* London, Frances Pinter.

Cambridge Encyclopedia 1982. *The Cambridge Encyclopedia of Russia and the Soviet Union.* Cambridge, Cambridge University Press.

Carr, E. H. 1966. *The Bolshevik Revolution, 1917–1933*, vol. 1. Harmondsworth, Penguin, First published in 1950.

Carrère d'Encausse, Hélène 1979. *Decline of an Empire: The Soviet Socialist Republics in Revolt.* New York, Newsweek Books, translation of *L'Empire Éclaté*. Paris, Flammarion, 1978.

Casals, Felipe García, pseud. 1980. *The Syncretic Society*. White Plains, NY, M. E. Sharpe.

Cattell, David T. 1964. Local government and the Sovnarkhoz in the USSR, 1957–1962. *Soviet Studies*, vol. XV, no. 4, pp. 430–42.

Cave, Martin 1980. *Computers and Economic Planning: The Soviet Experience.* Cambridge, Cambridge University Press.

Chernenko, Konstantin U. 1981. *Human Rights in Soviet Society.* New York, International Publishers.

Chislennost' i sostav 1984. *Chislennost' i sostav naseleniya SSSR. Po dannym Vsesoyuznoi perepisi naseleniya 1979 goda.* Moscow, Finansy i statistika.

Chornovil, Vyacheslav 1968. *The Chornovil Papers.* New York, McGraw-Hill.

Christman, Henry M. (ed.) 1969. *Communism in Action: A Documentary History.* New York, Bantam Books.

Churchward, L. G. 1973. *The Soviet Intelligentsia: An Essay on the Social Structure and Roles of the Soviet Intellectuals during the 1960s.* London, Routledge & Kegan Paul.

— 1975. *Contemporary Soviet Government*, 2nd edn. London, Routledge & Kegan Paul.

Clark, Alan 1966. *Barbarossa: The Russo-German Conflict 1941–45.* Harmondsworth, Penguin.

Clarke, Roger A. 1967. The Composition of the USSR Supreme Soviet, 1958–66. *Soviet Studies*, vol. XIX, no. 1, pp. 53–65.

Cocks, Paul, Daniels, Robert V. & Heer, Nancy Whittier (eds) 1976. *The Dynamics of Soviet Politics.* Cambridge Mass., Harvard University Press.

Colton, Timothy J. 1984. *The Dilemma of Reform in the Soviet Union.* New York, Council on Foreign Relations.

Communist Manifesto 1973. Karl Marx & Friedrich Engels, *Manifesto of the Communist Party*, in Karl Marx, *The Revolutions of 1848: Political Writings, Volume 1*, edited and introduced by David Fernbach. Harmondsworth, Penguin, pp. 62–98.

Connor, Walker, 1984. *The National Question in Marxist-Leninist Theory and Strategy*. Princeton, NJ, Princeton University Press.

Connor, Walter D. 1972. *Deviance in Soviet Society: Crime, Delinquency, and Alcoholism.* New York, Columbia University Press.

Cornell, Richard (ed.) 1970. *The Soviet Political System: A Book of Readings.* Englewood Cliffs, NJ, Prentice-Hall.

Cracraft, James (ed.) 1983. *The Soviet Union Today: An Interpretive Guide.* Chicago, Bulletin of the Atomic Scientists.

Crouch, Martin & Porter, Robert (eds) 1984. *Understanding Soviet Politics through Literaure: A Book of Readings.* London, Allen & Unwin.

Debo, Richard K. 1979. *Revolution and Survival: The Foreign Policy of Soviet Russia, 1917-1918.* Liverpool, Liverpool University Press.

Deutscher, Isaac 1967. *The Unfinished Revolution.* Oxford, Oxford University Press.

Dienes, Leslie 1975. Pasturalism in Turkestan: its decline and its persistence. *Soviet Studies*, vol. XXVII, no. 3, pp. 343–65.

Downs, Anthony 1967. *Inside Bureaucracy.* Boston, Mass., Little, Brown.

Dunlop, John B. 1984. *The Faces of Contemporary Russian Nationalism.* Princeton, NJ, Princeton University Press.

— 1988. The Russian Orthodox Church in the millennium year: what it needs from the Soviet state. *Religion in Communist Lands*, vol. 16, no. 2, pp. 100–16.

Dzyuba, Ivan 1968. *Internationalism or Russification?* London, Weidenfeld & Nicolson.

Edmonds, Robin 1983. *Soviet Foreign Policy: The Brezhnev Years.* Oxford, Oxford University Press.

Elliot, Iain F. 1974. *The Soviet Energy Balance: Natural Gas, Other Fossil Fuels, and Other Power Sources.* New York, Praeger.

Fainsod, Merle 1959. *Smolensk Under Soviet Rule.* London, Macmillan.

Farukshin, M.Kh. 1973. *Partiya v politicheskoi sisteme Sovetskogo obshchestva (protiv kontseptsii sovremennogo antikommunizma).* Kazan, Izdatel'stvo Kazan'skogo Universiteta.

Feshbach, Murray 1982. *The Soviet Union: Population Trends and Dilemmas. Population Bulletin*, vol. 37, no. 3. Washington, DC, Population Reference Bureau.

Foteeva, Ye. V. 1984. *Kachestvennye kharakteristiki naseleniya SSSR.* Moscow, Finansy i statistika.

Friedgut, Theodore H. 1978. Citizens and soviets: can Ivan Ivanovich fight City Hall? *Comparative Politics*, vol. 10, pp. 461–77.

— 1979. *Political Participation in the USSR.* Princeton, NJ, Princeton University Press.

Gehlen, Michael P. & McBride, Michael 1968. The Soviet Central

Committee: an élite analysis. *American Political Science Review*, vol. LXII, no. 4, pp. 1232–41.

Gerhart, Genevra 1974. *The Russian's World: Life and Language.* New York, Harcourt, Brace, Jovanovich.

Gidwitz, Betsy 1982. Labor unrest in the Soviet Union. *Problems of Communism*, vol. XXXI, no. 6, pp. 25–52.

Gilison, Jerome M. 1968. Soviet elections as a measure of dissent: the missing one percent. *American Political Science Review*, vol. LXII, no. 3, pp. 814–26.

Glasnost–How Open?, 1987. New York, Freedom House (Perspectives on Freedom No. 8).

Goldman, Marshall I. 1983. *USSR in Crisis: the Failure of an Economic System.* New York, Norton.

Golod, S. I. 1984. *Stabil'nost' sem'i: sotsiologicheskii i demograficheskii aspekty.* Leningrad, Nauka.

Gorbachëv, Mikhail 1987. *Perestroika: New Thinking for Our Country and the World*. London, Collins.

Grant, Nigel 1979. *Soviet Education*, 4th edn. Harmondsworth, Penguin.

Groshev, I. 1967. *A Fraternal Family of Nations: A Review of Soviet Experience in Solving the National Question.* Moscow, Progress.

Grossman, Gregory 1977. The 'Second Economy' of the USSR. *Problems of Communism*, vol. XXVI, no. 5, pp. 25–40.

Gustafson, Thane 1981. *Reform in Soviet Politics: Lessons of Recent Policies on Land and Water.* Cambridge, Cambridge University Press.

— & Mann, Dawn 1986. Gorbachëv's first year. *Problems of Communism*, vol. XXXV, no. 3, pp. 1–19.

— & — 1987. Gorbachëv's next gamble. *Problems of Communism*, vol. XXXVI, no. 4, pp. 1–20.

Hahn, Jeffrey W. 1988a. *Soviet Grassroots: Citizen Participation in Local Soviet Government*. Princeton, NJ, Princeton University Press.

— 1988b. An experiment in competition: the 1987 elections to the local soviets. *Slavic Review*, vol. 47, no. 3, pp. 434–47.

Hammer, Darrell L. 1974. *USSR: The Politics of Oligarchy.* Hinsdale, Ill., Dryden Press.

Hanson, Philip 1980. Economic constraints on Soviet politics in the 1980s. *International Affairs*, vol. 57, no. 1, pp. 21–42.

— 1982. The Soviet eleventh Five-Year Plan, 1981–85. *Communist Affairs*, vol. 1, no. 1, pp. 202–5.

— 1983. Success indicators revisited: the July 1979 Soviet decree on planning and management. *Soviet Studies*, vol. XXXV, no. 1, pp. 1–13.

Harasymiw, Bohdan 1969. *Nomenklatura:* The Soviet Communist Party's leadership recruitment system. *Canadian Journal of Political Science*, vol. 2, no. 3, pp. 493–512.

— 1984. *Political Élite Recruitment in the Soviet Union.* London, Macmillan.

Harding, Neil (ed.) 1984. *The State in Socialist Society*. London, Macmillan.

Haynes, Viktor & Semyonova, Olga (eds) 1979. *Workers Against the Gulag: The New Opposition in the Soviet Union.* London, Pluto Press.

Hill, Ian H. 1975. The end of the Russian peasantry? *Soviet Studies*, vol. XXVII, no. 1, pp. 109–27.

Hill, Ronald J. 1972. Continuity and change in USSR Supreme Soviet elections. *British Journal of Political Science*, vol. 2, no. 1, pp. 47–67.

— 1973. Patterns of deputy selection to local soviets. *Soviet Studies*, vol. XXV, no. 2, pp. 196–212.

— 1976. The CPSU in a Soviet election campaign. *Soviet Studies*, vol. XXVIII, no. 4, pp. 590–8.

— 1977. *Soviet Political Élites: The Case of Tiraspol.* London, Martin Robertson.

— 1980a. *Soviet Politics, Political Science and Reform.* Oxford, Martin Robertson.

— 1980b. Party-state relations and Soviet political development. *British Journal of Political Science*, vol. 10, no. 2, pp. 149–65.

— 1988. Gorbachëv and the CPSU. *Journal of Communist Studies*, vol. 4, no. 4, pp. 18–34.

— & Dellenbrant, Jan Ake 1989. *Gorbachëv and Perestroika: Towards a New Socialism?* London, Edward Elgar.

— & Frank, Peter, 1986a. *The Soviet Communist Party*, 3rd edn. Boston, Unwin Hyman. First edn, 1980.

— &— 1986b. Gorbachëv's cabinet-building. *Journal of Communist Studies*, vol. 2, no. 2, pp. 168–81.

Hirszowicz, Maria 1976. Is there a ruling class in the USSR?: a comment. *Soviet Studies*, vol. XXVIII, no. 2, pp. 262–73.

Hoffmann, Erik P. & Fleron, Frederic J., Jr (eds) 1980. *The Conduct of Soviet Foreign Policy*, 2nd edn. New York, Aldine.

Holloway, David 1983. *The Soviet Union and the Arms Race.* New Haven and London, Yale University Press.

Holzman, Franklyn D. 1982. *The Soviet Economy: Past, Present and Future*, Headline Series no. 260. New York, The Foreign Policy Association.

Hosking, Geoffrey 1973. *The Russian Constitutional Experiment: Government and Duma 1907-14.* Cambridge, Cambridge University Press.

— 1980. *Beyond Socialist Realism: Soviet Fiction Since 'Ivan Denisovich'*. London, Elek.

— 1985. *A History of the Soviet Union*. London, Fontana.

— 1988a. Informal associations in the USSR. *Slovo: A Journal of Contemporary Soviet & East European Affairs*, no. 1, pp. 7–10.

— 1988b. A civil society in embryo. *The Listener*, 24 November 1988, pp. 14–17.

Hough, Jerry F. 1977. *The Soviet Union and Social Science Theory*. Cambridge, Mass., Harvard University Press.

— 1980. *Soviet Leadership in Transition*. Washington, DC, The Brookings Institution.

— 1983. Andropov's first year. *Problems of Communism*, vol. XXXII no. 6, pp. 49–64.

— 1987. Gorbachëv consolidating power, *Problems of Communism*, vol. XXXVI, no. 4, pp. 21–43.

— & Fainsod, Merle 1979. *How the Soviet Union is Governed*. Cambridge, Mass., Harvard University Press.

Ionescu, Ghita 1965. *The Break-up of the Soviet Empire in Eastern Europe*. Harmondsworth, Penguin.

Jackson, W. Douglas 1974. Urban expansion. *Problems of Communism*, vol. XXIII, no. 6, pp. 14–24.

Jacobs, Everett M. 1970. Soviet local elections: what they are, and what they are not. *Soviet Studies*, vol. XXII, no. 1, pp. 61–76.

— 1972. The composition of local soviets, 1959–1969. *Government and Opposition*, vol. 7, no. 4, pp. 503–19.

— (ed.) 1983. *Soviet Local Politics and Government*. London, Allen & Unwin.

James, Robert Rhodes (ed.) 1969. *The Czechoslovak Crisis 1968*. London, Weidenfeld & Nicolson.

Juviler, Peter 1976. *Revolutionary Law and Order: Politics and Social Change in the USSR*. New York, The Free Press.

Kadeikin, V. A. *et al.* (eds) 1974. *Voprosy vnutripartiinoi zhizni i rukovodyashchei deyatel'nosti KPSS na sovremennom etape*. Moscow, Mysl'.

Kaftanovskaya, A. M. 1975. *Poryadok rassmotreniya trudovykh sporov*. Moscow, Profizdat.

Kahan, Arcadius & Ruble, Blair 1979. *Industrial Labor in the U.S.S.R.* New York and Oxford, Pergamon.

Karklins, Rasma 1986. *Ethnic Relations in the USSR: The Perspective from Below*. Boston, Allen & Unwin.

Katsenelinboigen, A. 1977. Coloured markets in the Soviet Union. *Soviet Studies*, vol. XXIX, no. 1, pp. 62–85.

Kelley, Donald R. (ed.) 1980. *Soviet Politics in the Brezhnev Era*. New York, Praeger.

Kerblay, Basile 1983. *Modern Soviet Society*. London, Methuen.

Kerimov, D. A. 1980. *Demokratiya razvitogo sotsializma*. Moscow, Politizdat.

— *et al.* (eds) 1979. *Politicheskie otnosheniya: prognozirovanie i planirovanie*. Moscow, Nauka.

Kharchev, A. G. *et al.* (eds) 1976. *Moral' razvitogo sotsializma (Aktual'nye problemy teorii)*. Moscow, Mysl'.

Khrushchev, Nikita 1971. *Khrushchev Remembers*. London, André Deutsch.

Kosolapov, Richard 1972. On the way to a classless society. *Social Sciences*, Moscow, no. 1, pp. 59–70.

KPSS v rez. 1971–8. *KPSS v rezolyutsiyakh i resheniyakh s"ezdov, konferentsii i Plenumov TsK*, 12 vols. Moscow, Politizdat, vol. 8 (1972).

Krawchenko, Bohdan (ed.) 1983. *Ukraine after Shelest*. Edmonton, Canadian Institute of Ukrainian Studies.

Kushnirsky, Fyodor I. 1984a. Inflation Soviet style. *Problems of Communism*, vol. XXXIII, no. 1, pp. 48–53.

— 1984b. The limits of Soviet economic reform. *Problems of Communism*, vol. XXXIII, no. 4, pp. 33–43.

Labedz, Leopold & Hayward, Max 1967. *On Trial: The case of Sinyavsky (Tertz) and Daniel (Arzhak)*. London, Collins and Harvill Press.

Lane, Christel 1974. Some explanations for the persistence of Christian religion in Soviet society. *Sociology*, vol. 8, no. 4, pp. 233–43.

— 1979. *Christian Religion in the Soviet Union: A Sociological Study*. London, Allen & Unwin.

— 1981. *The Rites of Rulers: Ritual in Industrial Society–the Soviet Case*. Cambridge, Cambridge University Press.

Lane, David 1971. *The End of Inequality?: Stratification Under State Socialism*. Harmondsworth, Penguin.

— 1978. *Politics and Society in the USSR*, 2nd edn. Oxford, Martin Robertson.

— 1982. *The End of Social Inequality? Class, Status and Power under State Socialism*. London, Allen & Unwin.

— & O'Dell, Felicity 1978. *The Soviet Industrial Worker: Social Class, Education and Control*. Oxford, Martin Robertson.

Lawrence, Sir John 1969. *Russians Observed*. London, Hodder & Stoughton.

Lebedev, P. N. (ed.) 1980. *Sistema organov gosudarstvennogo upravleniya (Opyt sotsiologicheskogo issledovaniya)*. Leningrad, Izd. Leningradskogo Universiteta.

Lewin, M. 1968. *Russian Peasants and Soviet Power: A Study of Collectivization*. London, Allen & Unwin.

Little, D. Richard 1972. Soviet parliamentary committees after Khrushchev: obstacles and opportunities. *Soviet Studies*, vol. XXIV, no. 1, pp. 41–60.

Löwenhardt, John 1982. *The Soviet Politburo*. Edinburgh, Canongate, revised translation of *Het Russische Politburo.* Assen, The Netherlands, Van Corcum, 1978.

McAuley, Alistair 1979. *Economic Welfare in the Soviet Union: Poverty, Living Standards, and Inequality.* London, Allen & Unwin.

McAuley, Mary 1969. *Labour Disputes in Soviet Russia.* Oxford, Oxford University Press.

— 1977. *Politics and the Soviet Union.* Harmondsworth, Penguin.

McCauley, Martin 1976. *Khrushchev and the Development of Soviet Agriculture: The Virgin Lands Programme, 1953–64.* London, Macmillan.

— 1981. *The Soviet Union Since 1917.* London, Longman.

McLellan, David 1971. *The Thought of Karl Marx: An Introduction.* London, Macmillan.

Malia, Martin 1961. *Alexander Herzen and the Birth of Russian Socialism, 1812–1855.* Cambridge, Mass., Harvard University Press.

Marinesku, D. I. 1975. *Dvuyazychie–faktor sblizheniya sotsialisticheskikh natsii i narodnostei.* Kishinev, Kartya Moldovenyaske.

Materialy 1981. *Materialy XXVI s"ezda KPSS.* Moscow, Politizdat.

Materialy, 1988. *Materialy XIX Vsesoyuznoi konferentsii Kommunisticheskoi partii Sovetskogo Soyuza*. Moscow, Politizdat.

Matthews, Mervyn 1972. *Class and Society in Soviet Russia.* London, Allen Lane.

— 1978. *Privilege in the Soviet Union: A Study of Elite Life-Styles under Communism.* London, Allen & Unwin.

— 1982. *Education in the Soviet Union: Policies and Institutions Since Stalin.* London, Allen & Unwin.

Mawdsley, Evan 1987. *The Russian Civil War*. Boston, Allen & Unwin.

Maynard, Sir John 1962. *The Russian Peasant and Other Studies.* New York, Collier Books, first published in 1942.

Mellor, Roy E. H. 1982. *The Soviet Union and its Geographical Problems.* London, Macmillan.

The Military Balance, 1988. *The Military Balance, 1988–1989*. London, International Institute for Strategic Studies.

Millar, James R. 1981. *The ABCs of Soviet Socialism.* Urbana, Ill., University of Illinois Press.

— (ed.) 1987. *Politics, Work, and Daily Life in the USSR: A Survey of Former Soviet Citizens*. Cambridge, Cambridge University Press.

Miller, John H. 1977. Cadres policy in nationality areas: recruitment of first and second secretaries in non-Russian republics of the USSR. *Soviet Studies*, vol. XXIX, no. 1, pp. 3–36.

Miller, R. F., Miller, J. H. & Rigby, T. H. (eds) 1987. *Gorbachëv at the Helm: A*

Minagawa, Shugo 1975. The functions of the Supreme Soviet organs, and problems of their institutional development. *Soviet Studies*, vol. XXVII, no. 1, pp. 46–70.

Moses, Joel C. 1974. *Regional Party Leadership and Policy-Making in the USSR.* New York, Praeger.

Mote, Max E. 1965. *Soviet Local and Republic Elections.* Stanford, Calif., The Hoover Institution.

Narkhoz 1977 1978. *Narodnoe khozyaistvo SSSR v 1977 godu.* Moscow, Statistika.

Narkhoz 1987 1988. *Narodnoe khozyaistvo SSSR v 1987g.* Moscow, Finansy i statistika.

Narkhoz za 60 let 1977. *Narodnoe khozyaistvo SSSR za 60 let: Yubileinyi statisticheskii yezhegodnik.* Moscow, Statistika.

Naselenie SSSR 1980. *Naselenie SSSR: po dannym Vsesoyuznoi perepsi naseleniya 1979 goda.* Moscow, Politizdat.

Naselenie SSSR 1987 1988. *Naselenie SSSR 1987: Statisticheskii sbornik.* Moscow, Finansy i statistika.

Neal, Fred Warner (ed.) 1979. *Détente or Debacle: Common Sense in U.S.–Soviet Relations.* New York, Norton.

Nikolov, P. Ye. 1981. *Otdely i upravleniya ispolkomov mestnykh Sovetov.* Moscow, Yuridicheskaya literatura.

Nogee, Joseph L. & Donaldson, Robert H. 1981. *Soviet Foreign Policy Since World War II.* New York, Pergamon.

Nove, Alec 1964. *Was Stalin Really Necessary?: Some Problems of Soviet Political Economy.* London, Allen & Unwin.

— 1972. *An Economic History of the USSR.* Harmondsworth, Penguin.

— 1975. Is there a ruling class in the USSR? *Soviet Studies*, vol. XXVII, no. 4, pp. 615–38.

— 1977. *The Soviet Economic System.* London, Allen & Unwin.

— 1980a. Does the Soviet Union have a planned economy?: a comment. *Soviet Studies*, vol. XXXII, no. 1, pp. 135–7.

— 1980b. Problems and prospects of the Soviet economy. *New Left Review*, no. 119, pp. 3–19.

— 1982. Soviet agriculture: new data. *Soviet Studies*, vol. XXXIV, no. 1, pp. 118–22.

Odom, William E. 1976. The militarization of Soviet society. *Problems of Communism*, vol. XXV, no. 5, pp. 34–51.

Pankhurst, Jerry G. & Sacks, Michael Paul (eds) 1980. *Contemporary Soviet Society: Sociological Perspectives.* New York, Praeger.

Party Rules 1961. Ustav Kommunisticheskoi partii Sovetskogo Soyuza. Reprinted in *KPSS v rez.*, vol. 8, pp. 306–25.

Paskar', P. N. 1974. *Sovety deputatov trudyashchikhsya v sisteme politicheskoi organizatsii obshchestva (na materialakh Moldavskoi SSR).* Kishinev, Shtiintsa.

Perry, Jack 1973. The USSR and the environment. *Problems of Communism*, vol. XXII, no. 3, pp. 52–4.

Pipes, Richard 1977. Why the Soviet Union thinks it can fight and win a nuclear war. *Commentary* (July), pp. 19–32.

Potichnyj, Peter H. (ed.) 1988. *The Soviet Union: Party and Society*. Cambridge, Cambridge University Press.

Pravda, Alex 1982. Is there a Soviet working class? *Problems of Communism*, vol. XXXI, no. 6, pp. 1–24.

Razvitoi sotsializm 1978. Moscow, Politizdat.

Reddaway, Peter 1972. *Uncensored Russia: The Human Rights Movement in the Soviet Union.* London, Cape.

— 1988. Soviet psychiatry: an end to political abuse? *Survey*, vol. 30, no. 3, pp. 25–38.

Reed, John 1966. *Ten Days that Shook the World.* Harmondsworth, Penguin, first published in 1926.

Rigby, T. H. 1964. Party elections in the CPSU. *Political Quarterly*, vol. 35, no. 4, pp. 420–43.

— 1968. *Communist Party Membership in the USSR, 1917–1967.* Princeton, NJ, Princeton University Press.

— 1976. Soviet Communist Party membership under Brezhnev. *Soviet Studies*, vol. XXVIII, no. 3, pp. 317–37.

— 1977. Soviet Communist Party membership under Brezhnev: a rejoinder. *Soviet Studies*, vol. XXIX, no. 3, pp. 452–3.

—, Brown, Archie & Reddaway, Peter (eds) 1980. *Authority, Power and Policy in the USSR: Essays dedicated to Leonard Schapiro.* London, Macmillan.

— & Harasymiw, Bohdan (eds) 1983. *Leadership Selection and Patron–Client Relations in the USSR and Yugoslavia.* London, Allen & Unwin.

Riordan, Jim 1986. Growing pains of Soviet youth. *Journal of Communist Studies*, vol. 2, no. 2, pp. 145–67.

Rogovin, V. Z. 1984. *Obshchestvo zrelogo sotsializma: sotsial'nye problemy.* Moscow, Mysl'.

Ross, Cameron 1987. *Local Government in the Soviet Union: Problems of Implementation and Control*. London, Croom Helm.

Ruble, Blair A. 1981. *Soviet Trade Unions: Their Development in the 1970s.* Cambridge, Cambridge University Press.

Rumer, Boris 1982. Soviet investment policy: unresolved problems. *Problems of Communism*, vol. XXXI, no. 5, pp. 53–68.

— 1984. Structural imbalance in the Soviet economy. *Problems of Communism*, vol. XXXIII, no. 4, pp. 24–32.

Rutland, Peter 1984. The Shchekino Method and the struggle to raise labour productivity in Soviet industry. *Soviet Studies*, vol. XXXVI, no. 3, pp. 345–65.

Ryavec, Karl W. 1975. *Implementation of Soviet Economic Reforms: Political, Organizational, and Social Processes.* New York, Praeger.

— (ed.) 1978. *Soviet Society and the Communist Party.* Amherst, University of Massachusetts Press.

Sacks, Michael Paul & Pankhurst, Jerry 1988. *Understanding Soviet Society*. Boston, Unwin Hyman.

Safarov, R. A. 1975. *Obshchestvennoe mnenie i gosudarstvennoe upravlenie.* Moscow, Yuridicheskaya literatura.

Schapiro, Leonard 1961. The party and the state. *Survey*, no. 38, pp. 111–16.

— & Godson, Joseph (eds) 1984. *The Soviet Worker: From Lenin to Andropov*, 2nd edn. London, Macmillan.

Scott, D. J. R. 1969, *Russian Political Institutions*, 4th edn. London, Allen & Unwin.

Senyavskii, S. L. 1982. *Sotsial'naya struktura sovetskogo obshchestva v usloviyakh razvitogo sotsializma (1961–1980 gg.).* Moscow, Mysl'.

Seton-Watson, Mary 1986. *Scenes from Soviet Life*. London, BBC/Ariel.

Shakhnazarov, Georgi 1974. *The Role of the Communist Party in Socialist Society.* Moscow, Novosti.

Shanin, Teodor (ed.) 1971. *Peasants and Peasant Societies: Selected Readings.* Harmondsworth, Penguin.

Shchekochikhin, Yurii 1988. Ekstremal'naya model'. *Literaturnaya gazeta*, 12 October 1988, p. 13.

Shtromas, Alexander 1981. *Political Change and Social Development: The Case of the Soviet Union.* Frankfurt-am-Main and Bern, Peter Lang.

Shvets, I. A. & Yudin, I. N. 1980. *Kak stroitsya, zhivët i deistvuyet KPSS.* Moscow, Politizdat.

Simes, Dimitri 1975. The Soviet parallel market. *Survey*, vol. 21, no. 3, pp. 42–55.

Simis, Konstantin 1982. *USSR: Secrets of a Corrupt Society.* London, Dent.

Sivachev, Nikolai V. & Yakovlev, Nikolai N. 1979. *Russia and the United States.* Chicago, University of Chicago Press.

Solov'ëv, N. Ya. 1981. *Sem'ya v sotsialisticheskom obshchestve.* Moscow, Politizdat.

'Sotsialisticheskii plyuralizm' 1988. Sotsialisticheskii plyuralizm (obsuzhdenie za 'kruglym stolom' APN i redaktsii 'Sotsiologicheskikh issledovanii'). *Sotsiologicheskie issledovaniya*, no. 5, pp. 6–24.

Soviet Economy 1983. *Soviet Economy in the 1980's: Problems and Prospects, Part 1. Selected Papers submitted to the Joint Economic Committee, Congress of the United States.* Washington, DC, US Government Printing Office.

Spielmann, Karl F. 1976. Defense industrialists in the USSR. *Problems of Communism*, vol. XXV, no. 5, pp. 52–69.

SSSR v tsifrakh 1985. *SSSR v tsifrakh v 1984 godu*. Moscow, Finansy i statistika.

SSSR v tsifrakh 1987. *SSSR v tsifrakh v 1986 godu*. Moscow, Finansy i statistika.

Stewart, Philip D. 1968. *Political Power in the Soviet Union: A Study of Decision-Making in Stalingrad.* Indianapolis and New York, Bobbs-Merrill.

Sutela, Pekka 1984. *Socialism, Planning and Optimality: A Study in Soviet Economic Thought.* Helsinki, Finnish Society of Sciences and Letters.

Suzhikov, M. M. (ed.) 1978. *Razvitie i sblizhenie Sovetskikh natsii: Problemy upravleniya.* Alma-Ata, Nauka.

Szajkowski, Bogdan 1982. *The Establishment of Marxist Regimes.* London, Butterworth.

Taagepera, Rein 1969. National differences within Soviet demographic trends. *Soviet Studies*, vol. XX, no. 4, pp. 478–89.

Taubman, William 1973. *Governing Soviet Cities: Bureaucratic Politics and Urban Development in the USSR.* New York, Praeger.

Teckenberg, Wolfgang 1978. Labour turnover and job satisfaction: indicators of industrial conflict in the USSR? *Soviet Studies*, vol. XXX, no. 2, pp. 193–211.

Tikhomirov, Yu. A. (ed.) 1975. *Demokratiya razvitogo sotsialisticheskogo obshchestva.* Moscow, Nauka.

Tökés, Rudolf L. (ed.) 1975. *Dissent in the USSR: Politics, Ideology, and People.* Baltimore, Johns Hopkins.

Trotsky, Leon 1932–3. *History of the Russian Revolution*, 3 vols. London, Gollancz.

— 1960. *My Life.* New York, Grosset & Dunlap, first published in 1930.

Ukrainets, P. P. 1976. *Partiinoe rukovodstvo i gosudarstvennoe upravlenie.* Minsk, Belarus'.

Unger, Aryeh L. 1977. Soviet Communist Party membership under Brezhnev: a comment. *Soviet Studies*, vol. XXIX, no. 2, pp. 306–16.

The USSR in Figures for 1982: Brief statistical handbook. 1983. Moscow, Finansy i statistika.

USSR '88. *USSR Yearbook '88*. Moscow, Novosti.

Valentei, D. I. (ed.) 1979. *Sem'ya segodnya.* Moscow, Statistika.

Vanneman, Peter 1977. *The Supreme Soviet.* Durham, N. Carolina, Duke University Press.

Vasil'ev, V. I. 1973. *Demokraticheskii tsentralizm v sisteme Sovetov.* Moscow, Yuridisheskaya literatura.

Vernadsky, George 1961. *A History of Russia*, 5th edn. New Haven, Conn., Yale University Press.

Vinogradov, N. N. 1980. *Partiinoe rukovodstvo Sovetami v usloviyakh razvitogo sotsializma.* Moscow, Mysl'.

von Laue, Theodore H. 1966. *Why Lenin? Why Stalin?* London, Weidenfeld & Nicolson.

Voslensky, Michael 1984. *Nomenklatura: Anatomy of the Soviet Ruling Class.* London, Bodley Head.

Waller, Michael 1982. Review of Hill and Frank, 1980. *International Affairs*, vol. 58, no. 2, pp. 371–2.

— 1982. A movement is a movement is a movement. *Communist Affairs*, vol. 1, no. 1, pp. 40–4.

Waltz, Kenneth N. 1979. *Theory of International Politics.* Reading, Mass., Addison-Wesley.

Webb, Sidney & Webb, Beatrice 1944, *Soviet Communism: A New Civilization.* London, Longman, Green, first published in 1935.

Wheeler-Bennett, John W. 1966. *Brest-Litovsk: The Forgotten Peace, March 1918.* London, Macmillan, first published in 1938.

White, Stephen 1979. *Political Culture and Soviet Politics.* London, Macmillan.

Wilhelm, John H. 1979. Does the Soviet Union have a planned economy? *Soviet Studies*, vol. XXXI, no. 2, pp. 268–74.

— 1985. The Soviet Union has an administered, not a planned, economy. *Soviet Studies*, vol. XXXVII, no. 1, pp. 118–30.

XXIV s"ezd 1971. *XXIV s"ezd Kommunisticheskoi partii Sovetskogo Soyuza: Stenograficheskii otchët*, 2 vols. Moscow, Politizdat.

XXVII s"ezd, 1986. *XXVII s"ezd Kommunisticheskoi partii Sovetskogo Soyuza: Stenograficheskii otchet*, 3 vols. Moscow, Politizdat.

Yampolskaya, Ts. 1975, *Social Organizations in the Soviet Union: Political and Legal Organisational Aspects.* Moscow, Progress.

Yanowitch, Murray 1977. *Social and Economic Inequality in the Soviet Union: Six Studies.* White Plains, NY, M. E. Sharpe.

— & Fisher, Wesley A. 1973. *Social Stratification and Mobility in the USSR.* White Plains, NY, International Arts & Sciences Press.

Yesipov, A. 1975. *How the Soviet Economy is Managed.* Moscow, Novosti.

Yezhegodnik (various years). *Yezhegodnik Bol'shoi sovetskoi entsiklopedii.* Moscow, Sovetskaya entsiklopediya.

Zaslavsky, Victor & Brym, Robert J. 1978. The functions of elections in the USSR. *Soviet Studies*, vol. XXX, no. 3, pp. 362–71.

1970 Census, Itogi Vsesoyuznoi perepisi naseleniya 1970 goda, 7 vols. Moscow, Statistika, 1972–4.

Newspapers and Journals Cited

Glasnost. Information bulletin edited in Moscow, circulated in Samizdat, and published in English translation by the Center for Democracy, New York.

Izvestiya: Izvestiya narodnykh deputatov trudyashchikhsya. Moscow, Izvestiya Publishing House, daily.

Izvestiya TsK KPSS. Moscow, Pravda Publishing House, monthly from January 1989.

Kommunist, Moscow, Pravda Publishing House, 18 issues per year.

Moscow News. Moscow, Novosti, weekly.

Partiinaya zhizn'. Moscow, Pravda Publishing House, twice monthly.

Pravda. Moscow, CPSU Central Committee/Pravda Publishing House, daily.

Religion in Communist Lands. Keston, Kent, Keston College, quarterly.

Sovety: Sovety narodnykh deputatov. Moscow, Izvestiya, monthly.

Soviet News. London, Soviet Embassy Press Department, twice monthly.

Vestnik statistiki. Moscow, Tsentral'noe statisticheskoe upravlenie, monthly.

Index